Mental Health and Crime

Does mental disorder cause crime? Does crime cause mental disorder? And if either of these could be proved to be true what consequences should stem for those who find themselves deemed mentally disordered offenders? *Mental Health and Crime* examines the nature of the relationship between mental disorder and crime. It concludes that the broad definition of what is an all too common human condition – mental disorder – and the widespread occurrence of an equally all too common human behaviour – that of offending – would make unlikely any definitive or easy answer to such questions.

For those who offend in the context of mental disorder many aspects of the criminal justice process, and of the disposals that follow, are adapted to take account of a relationship between mental disorder and crime. But if the very relationship is questionable, is the way in which we deal with such offenders discriminatory? Or is it perhaps to their benefit to be thought of as less responsible for their offending than fully culpable offenders? The book thus explores not only the nature of the relationship, but also the human rights and legal issues arising. It also looks at some of the permutations in the therapeutic process that can ensue when those with mental health problems are treated in the context of their offending behaviour.

Jill Peay is a Professor of Law at the London School of Economics and Political Science.

Contemporary Issues in Public Policy
Series editors: David Downes and Paul Rock
London School of Economics

This series of books is intended to offer accessible, informed and well-evidenced analyses of topical policy issues – from the national health through women's work to central issues of crime and criminal justice – as a counterweight to the manner in which they tend to be presented in political and public debates. The mass media can be sensationalising and overly-simple. Many observers and commentators are too engaged politically or professionally to take a dispassionate stand. By contrast, what is offered here is considered expert commentary laid out in a literate and helpful manner. Moreover, in the wake of globalisation, the revolution in information technology and new forms of regulation and audit, an immense proliferation of data has occurred which can swamp all but the most experienced and duly sceptical analyst. Providing an excellent core for teaching in social policy, criminology, politics and the sociology of contemporary Britain, the series is also intended for politicians, policy-makers, journalists and other concerned people who wish to know more about the world they live in today.

Mental Health and Crime

Jill Peay

Routledge
Taylor & Francis Group
a GlassHouse book

First published 2011
by Routledge
2 Park Square, Milton Park, Abingdon, Oxon, OX14 4RN

Simultaneously published in the USA and Canada
by Routledge
711 Third Avenue, New York, NY 10017

A GlassHouse book

Routledge is an imprint of the Taylor & Francis Group, an informa
business

First issued in paperback 2011

Typeset in Sabon by RefineCatch Limited, Bungay, Suffolk

British Library Cataloguing in Publication Data
A catalogue record for this book is available from the British Library

Library of Congress Cataloging in Publication Data
Peay, Jill.
  Mental health and crime / Jill Peay.
    p. cm.
  ISBN 978–1–904385–60–8
  1. Offenders with mental disabilities. 2. People with mental disabilities and
  crime. 3. Crime–Psychological aspects. 4. Criminal psychology. I. Title.
    HV6133.P39 2010
    364.3–dc22   2010012336

ISBN: 978-1-904385-60-8 (hbk)
ISBN: 978-0-415-52116-1 (pbk)

Contents

Foreword

Analysing the links between mental disorder and crime must be one of the most daunting tasks confronting any scholar. It demands at least an adequate working knowledge of the substance and relations of very different and complex fields: criminology, law, sociology, politics, psychology and psychiatry; and it demands that those fields are properly mined, assessed, summarised and synthesised each time their arguments and methods are turned on diverse problems. Almost all the pivotal terms and definitions commonly in use have been or are actively contested, not only because they refer to such elusive and ambiguous phenomena, but also because they have very major consequences both for the administration of criminal justice and psychiatry, and for the lives of individual victims and offenders. Yet the problems they throw up require urgent, daily resolution. There are few who have the skills, learning and judgment to furnish answers, and it is no surprise that the field that has not been well-populated in the past.

A Professor of Law at the London School of Economics, Jill Peay is one of those very few. Her professional history includes a training in psychology at the University of Birmingham; reading for the Bar; employment as a research criminologist at the University of Oxford; and expertise as a socio-legal scholar. She has written copiously on mental health and crime, concentrating on issues raised by ideas of risk, dangerousness and compulsion; the office of the Director of Public Prosecutions; the application of human rights legislation; the working of mental health tribunals and of inquiries after homicide; and law reform, and the reform of the 1983 Mental Health Act, in particular. *Mental Health and Crime* draws on all that extraordinary range, and it amounts to what almost no one else could have accomplished: a virtually encyclopedic review of a massive theme, written judiciously in clear and intelligible language, and with great flair and authority. It treads step by step and with confidence to elucidate a chain of seemingly intractable problems. It has no rivals, and must be read by practitioners, students and scholars in all the disciplines that bear on its theme.

David Downes and Paul Rock

Acknowledgements

This book, like most academic books, was a long time in the writing. As a result, the list of people to whom I am indebted is extensive. Rather than try to recall them all, at the risk of inappropriately excluding some, I would simply acknowledge that their contributions are many and varied. Indeed, some people will not realise that I have taken something away from reading their work, listening to them lecture or even just having a snatched conversation, and that I have gone on shamelessly to exploit and probably to misrepresent these nuggets. I know that I have behaved like a gannet, scooping up your gems and germs. I am grateful to you all.

In addition to all those who have given me wonderful support, wittingly and unwittingly, three people have gone way beyond what anyone could reasonably have expected. David Downes and Paul Rock read a draft text over the Christmas of 2009. I can't imagine what they sacrificed to do this; I just know that the scope of what I have written was immeasurably improved by their efforts. Andy Ward, who makes no claims of subject expertise, generously then read a further version and provided me with the kind of detailed corrections on my writing style that should and did make me squirm. He also has an aversion to academic writing. Subsequently I have tried to remove as many semi-colons, convoluted sentences and fog-infused paragraphs as possible; for which I hope you will all be grateful. None of these three are in any way responsible for anything with which you may disagree or dislike. I am.

But I also need to thank Al. He has nurtured me, my computer and our obvious incompatibilities. His technical expertise has rescued me on numerous occasions. But he has also taken me, by kayak, to places I would otherwise not have gone. And been there to photograph ideas I could not capture. His is the cover photograph.

Thank you.

Jill Peay
February 2010

Acronyms

AIDS	Acquired Immune Deficiency Syndrome
CNVs	Copy Number Variations
DoH	Department of Health
DPP	Director of Public Prosecutions
DSM	Diagnostic and Statistical Manual
DSPD	Dangerous and Severe Personality Disorder
DVCVA	Domestic Violence, Crime and Victims Act
ECHR	European Convention on Human Rights
ECtHR	European Court of Human Rights
HMI	Her Majesty's Inspectorate
HIV	Human Immunodeficiency Virus
ICD	International Classification of Diseases
IPP	Indeterminate Sentence for Public Protection
MHA	Mental Health Act
MHRT	Mental Health Review Tribunal
NICE	National Institute for Health and Clinical Excellence
PET	Positron Emission Tomography
UKHL	United Kingdom House of Lords
WHO	World Health Organization
WMD	Weapons of Mass Destruction

Table of cases

Introduction

This book is about mental health and crime; or rather, about mental disorder and crime since to some it seems almost a *sine qua non* that the commission of a crime signifies a state of disorder or disarray in the perpetrator. Significantly mental disorder is a term with sufficient expansionary capacity readily to embrace many forms of deviant or disconcerting behaviour, so its role in explaining crime has considerable and arguably growing prominence. This book questions that prominence by posing some ordinary questions that perhaps do not have conventional or comfortable answers; but the questions themselves are commonplace. Indeed, the contexts in which they are posed, those of the phenomena of mental disorder and crime, are so widespread as to be almost ubiquitous. This book is about the relationship, if any, between mental disorder and crime; and of the consequences that do or should stem from the establishment or refutation of any such relationship.

Amongst the ordinary questions that will be addressed are: does mental disorder cause crime? Are mentally disordered offenders as culpable for their offending as normal offenders? To what extent, if any, are their mental disorders treatable? How can we fully protect the human rights of those deemed mentally disordered offenders, when they have caused damage to others, and perhaps damage of an irreparable nature? And what consequences do the answers to these questions have in respect of how we should deal with those who have offended and who co-incidentally have mental disorders? This last question is posed in such a long-handed way since it is almost certainly inappropriate and misleading to refer to such people as 'mentally disordered offenders'. Indeed, do the answers to any of these questions differ if one poses them the other way around? For example, does crime cause mental disorder? Or do those with mental disorders who have coincidentally offended have any different expectations with respect to how they should be treated by the criminal justice and health systems? One illustration of just how complex these issues are will suffice at this point: if serious mental disorder reduces one's culpability for offending, does it make more likely an early return to society following some period of incarceration because the mental disorder can be treated; or does it make such a return less likely, leading to a form of preventive detention, because if the disorder cannot be treated the individual poses more of a threat of future offending than his or her comparator ordered offender? This is one of a number of conundrums that this book will address.

It is not hard to bring to mind images of those about whom the book might be concerned: Peter Sutcliffe, the 'Yorkshire Ripper', who was convicted of murdering thirteen women; Christopher Clunis, who killed Jonathan Zito in a sudden and unprovoked attack at Finsbury Park tube station; and Dennis Nilsen, who killed and dismembered the bodies of young men lured to his flat. But should we add the likes of Joseh Fritzel from Austria, Dr Harold Shipman, or Fred and Rosemary West? Or Ian Huntley, who killed Holly Wells and Jessica Chapman, girls aged only ten years at the time? It might be expected that a book with the title *Mental Health and Crime* would focus on this range of the mad and bad; many do. But that is not the intention here. Indeed, all of these individuals were held criminally culpable, albeit that that culpability was reduced in the case of Christopher Clunis. These offenders largely did not benefit from any allowance that might have been made with respect to their mental state, even though a number of them did ultimately find themselves confined in psychiatric rather than penal institutions. Rather the book will examine some of the issues thrown up by the many thousands of sad and difficult individuals who find themselves in conflict with the criminal law, incidents that occur on a daily basis. It will also venture briefly into territory that is much less accessible: the offending sleepwalker, where reason is not present in any meaningful form, or those living under what Terry Pratchett has coined 'the fog of Alzheimer's'. The issues concerning those who have offended in the most serious way invariably inform the book, in part because they comprehensively infiltrate the popular understanding of this field, and in part because it tends to be only in the most serious cases where psychiatric evidence is tendered and examined. But my intention is that these most serious cases should not unduly skew the book's content. Rather the focus will be on understanding some of these difficult issues, and trying to understand them across the range of offenders and the spectrum of disorders. In so doing, the archetypal case should be one of criminal damage or theft by someone whose mental inadequacies may never feature, as they perhaps should, in the assessment of culpability. It is a superficially less enticing prospect for the reader, but I hope keeping it in mind will make the book ultimately more enriching.

The first half of the book examines the knotty problem of the links between mental disorder and crime; and by way of introduction to this material the book starts with a very basic description of some of the key concepts; some readers might wish to move quickly through this introductory material. Then the book looks at some of the human rights related issues, since these are likely to be fruitful in thinking about the borderlines between deviance and disorder, and thus the justifiable distinctions between those deemed fit to punish and those for whom mental health professionals have a legitimate role; and in the final chapters the book examines some of the difficult terrain of culpability and treatability, through the problematic extremes of disorder and offending, and the consequent issues of process. In so doing, it looks at offending behaviour whilst in a state of automatism, which may indeed not constitute 'crime' as such; and the problem of 'dangerous and severe personality disorder', which may not constitute a 'disorder' as such. Both of these extremes pose their own problems for the criminal justice process.

Mental disorder and crime, the matters that form the core of the book, evoke largely negative images, and their co-occurrence in the term 'mentally disordered offender' is likely to be doubly unattractive; each term reinforcing the other's negative attributes, rather than moderating them by providing a mitigating context. For as Bolton (2008:xv) has observed, although the medical model of mental disorder provides some saving graces where disorder is couched as illness or damage, should that model be rejected the likely perception is one of 'sin, corruption, immorality, inadequacy and irrationality, these signifying in each case the opposite of what is regarded as the highest good'. These are not things that happen to one, but rather something for which one is assumed to be morally responsible. Whether one might be responsible for poor mental health looks, at first blush, unlikely. But since in the current climate responsibility for one's physical health seems ever more prevalent, with increasingly urgent calls to moderate one's drinking, consume the requisite portions of fruit and vegetables and take regular exercise, it is not inconceivable that responsibility for good mental health may similarly emerge as a social expectation. In stark contrast, criminal behaviour is, and largely has always been, regarded as being primarily in this mould; not as something that happens to one, but rather as a species of event for which one is responsible. Inflicting damage on others, whether maliciously, recklessly, or merely thoughtlessly, is something for which one should be held culpable and liable. These two conflicting rationales are unlikely easily to be reconciled when they compete for explanatory dominance within any one individual.

One caveat is necessary: the term 'mentally disordered offender' is itself contentious. It is used throughout this book as shorthand for a number of different potential manifestations; for someone with a mental disorder who may have offended, for someone who has offended who may have a mental disorder, and for those where certainty about the presence of both mental disorder and offending can be established. But it also includes those where, because of the peculiarities of the processes of establishing criminality and mental disorder, neither is, in fact, either present or still present. And these confusing multiple presentations mean that one can never be certain whether one should conceive of the mentally disordered offender as an offender with a right to a proportionate measure of punishment or as a mentally disordered person with a need for a health intervention; or both in some ineffable mix, challenging us all to re-examine our preconceptions.

Chapter 1

Mental health and crime

The link between mental illness and crime is well known.
(General Synod, 13 Feb 2008)

The first chapters of this book examine the complicated relationship between mental disorder and crime. Teasing out the various strands makes considerable demands. By way of introduction it is important to bear in mind the broad range of the manifestations of mental disorder: personality disorder, learning disability, and psychotic disorders such as schizophrenia, have at one time or another all been deemed to be mental disorders. But equally, some of these manifestations have, at other times, been contested as properly falling within a definition of mental disorder. At present, the legal definition of mental disorder under s 1 of the Mental Health Act 1983 (MHA 1983), as amended by the Mental Health Act 2007, is 'any disorder or disability of the mind'; a definition seemingly so broad as to include the world at large. Indeed, it includes many who might consider themselves, and who might be considered by others, to be mentally healthy. For example, whilst learning disability needs to be associated with 'abnormally aggressive or seriously irresponsible conduct' in order to invoke a number of the Act's other sections, it is not wholly excluded (see s 1(2A) and (2B) of the MHA 1983). Similarly, whilst 'dependence on alcohol or drugs' alone is not considered to be a mental disorder (s 1(3)), the Code of Practice 2008 under the MHA 1983 (Department of Health 2008: para 3.8–3.12) sets out the situations in which such dependence might bring one within the scope of the definition of mental disorder.

The scope of offending behaviour is similarly wide, embracing property and commercial crimes, offences of personal violence (from the petty to the most heinous) and a host of other activities which do not immediately come to mind as offences, but which range from the terrifying and bizarre to the merely ridiculous. The likelihood therefore of there being any straightforward relationship between the constructs of mental disorder and crime is small. And whilst a number of texts (eg Stone, 2003; Littlechild and Fearns,

2005) have sought to describe the process whereby the criminal justice system in England and Wales deals with mentally disordered offenders, there is less available in an accessible form that reflects on the fundamental nature of the relationship. Indeed, even those texts that engage admirably with the difficulties (for example, Blumenthal and Lavender, 2000) tend to take mental disorder and violence as their focus, and then trail in its wake issues of risk prediction and management, without really grappling with crime per se.

So what fundamental questions dog the field? Does mental disorder cause or contribute to offending behaviour; does engagement with the criminal justice process through offending lead or contribute to mental disorder; does the occurrence of mental disorder make offending less likely; does engagement with the criminal justice process reduce the incidence of further offending and/or lead to the successful treatment of mental disorder; are crime and mental disorder generally unrelated, but the relevant populations of those with mental disorder and those who have offended overlap by reason of other factors (discrimination, exclusion, poverty etc)? Are offenders who have mental health problems coterminous with people who have mental health problems who offend (James et al, 2002)? Indeed, whatever the complex nature of the relationship between crime and mental disorder, that relationship has implications for the relevant procedures utilised in both the criminal justice and mental health systems. Do those procedures and systems deal fairly and equitably with either or both mentally disordered people who have offended, or offenders with mental disorders?

Whilst the latter parts of this book focus on questions of how mentally disordered offenders are processed by the criminal justice and health systems, and whether those dealings are indeed fair and equitable, the first chapters examine the fundamental nature of the relationship between mental disorder and crime, and the evidence relied upon to support the various assertions made. This is difficult terrain and it will be necessary to proceed slowly, charting a path through definitions of crime and mental disorder, and of concepts of causation. There will be a slow descent through levels of detail, both in respect of particular types of crime, and particular types of disorder. And paradoxically, as one digs into the detail, the evidence becomes more persuasive in respect of the logic of limited associations, but at the same time the empirical strength of those associations is undermined because of the progressively smaller number of people involved. Moreover, it simultaneously becomes evident that the associations are not between particular disorders and particular crimes, but between the specific symptoms people can experience at given times, the context in which they experience them and the likelihood of the occurrence of particular kinds of behaviour.

Preliminary difficulties

Crimes and criminals are not coterminous. People who commit crime are not necessarily deemed criminals by the law. The most obvious example of this concerns under-age 'offenders'. In England and Wales the legal age of criminal responsibility is 10; before the abolition of the presumption of *doli incapax* by s 34 of the Crime and Disorder Act 1998 it used to be, for all intents and purposes, 14 years old.[1] The age limit is also culturally determined; in Scotland it is eight, in Germany and Italy 14, and Belgium 18. What it means is that no matter how heinous an act committed in England by a nine year old, he or she cannot be convicted of a crime or deemed a criminal. Yet it is well known that under-age 'offending' is commonplace: figures released under the Freedom of Information Act 2000 noted that, in 2006, children were the chief suspects in no fewer than 2,840 crimes. Although over half of these were offences of criminal damage or arson, 66 sexual offences were noted, together with offences of burglary and wounding (Glendinning, 2007).

Similarly, people who fall within the terms of the 1843 M'Naghten Rules, that is those who are found not guilty by reason of insanity, may well have committed the act deemed an offence by society, but they will not be held criminally responsible (and hence do not become convicted criminals) because at the time the act was committed the individual concerned did not have the requisite *mens rea* or guilty mind. Where a person labours under a 'defect of reason, from disease of the mind, as not to know the nature and quality of the act he was doing, or, if he did know it, that he did not know that he was doing wrong' then that person will receive a therapeutic disposal determined on health grounds rather than a punitive disposal in response to criminal offending (Loughnan, 2007; Mackay, 2006, 2009).

Thus, superficially what looks like a good starting point – to examine what causes crime – becomes complicated by the meaning of 'crime' per se. Indeed, if one were to ask the question 'what causes crime?' the answer would, I suspect, depend on who is answering the question, and when. The man in the street, in the pub or on the Clapham omnibus may answer, 'people commit crime'. This answer is, in many respects, not ill-informed. Alternatively a feminist in any of those locations might respond, somewhat more accurately, 'men commit crime'. But both would be indicating an explanation based in normal individual behaviour, whether motivated by opportunity, greed, lust, wickedness, testosterone or any other of a legion of explanations that may, or may not, verge at their extremes into individual pathology. Ask the question of a criminologist and the answer may come back in a different form or forms, depending on whether the criminologist

---

1 *R v JTB (Appellant)(on appeal from the Court of Appeal (Criminal Division))* [2009] UKHL 20.

has more of a sociological or psychological bent. For the sociologist perhaps the emphasis would be on inequalities in social structure; for the psychologist, some variant of social learning theory may be at the forefront or an emphasis on neurobiological factors beyond an individual's seeming control. Moreover, whatever the professional explanation or explanations offered, when the question is asked will also be critical, for academic opinion is fluid; causal explanations are like hemlines, they go up and down, and are in and out of fashion. There is perhaps, one positive glimmer here. For, as both psychological and sociological criminologists have gone through periods where they have been variously disenchanted with one another's explanations, a consensus seems to be emerging, albeit one that is so broad as to be all-embracing; namely, that crime is caused by a multiplicity of factors, some individually based, some in the individual's environment and some the interaction between the two, whether historical or contemporaneous. And, whilst it may seem self-evident that the causes of crime are complex, it is important to remember that this basic insight can sometimes be lost when thinking about crimes committed by people who are mentally disordered.

Accepting some level of individual responsibility for crime merely raises the further question of why people commit crime. When posed to one 12 year old, this question was answered with 'because they are greedy or not right in the head'. These admittedly instant responses were subsequently supplemented by the more generalised suggestion that people who commit crime do so 'to benefit themselves' and then by the much more specific 'because voices in their head tell them what to do'. Ironically, the former displays considerable insight as a generalised explanation; Cornish and Clarke (1986) for example, argue that personal benefit is the prime motivation for crime and that social factors play only a background role: whether a crime is committed at any particular point by the 'reasoning criminal' will depend upon the prevailing circumstances at the point of potential commission. In this sense they are not interested in dispositional accounts, although it is fair to observe that in drawing on the economic notion of bounded rationality there is an acknowledgement that such rationality is governed by the information available, the time in which the decision has to be made and the cognitive abilities of the decision-maker. In this context, mental disorder is a relevant, albeit neglected, factor.

The latter explanation, that the person is 'not right in the head', arguably illustrates the influence that the media have had in forging common understandings of the link between mental illness and crime (Shift, 2008, Thornicroft, 2006). And that these understandings are present even in the comparatively young. For not only does this youngster's explanation reflect that of many adults, but it also illustrates a reversal of the received wisdom with respect to normal offending: thus, pathology is dominant in explaining the behaviour of those with mental disorder, but environment, heredity and choice dominate the explanation of normal criminal behaviour. Somehow, if people have a mental disorder, this becomes the primary explanatory factor. Yet the research does not bear this out. When meta-analyses (statistical procedures designed to combine the results of a number of studies with related hypotheses) are performed of our predictive abilities with respect to recidivism amongst those with mental disorder, it seems that the routine criminological factors outperform those relating to mental disorder (Bonta et al, 1998). Indeed, John Monahan, perhaps the most influential thinker in the field of violence risk assessment, has asserted in his recent review of the violence-related literature that:

> Compared to the magnitude of risk associated with the combination of male gender, young age, and lower socio-economic status, for example, the risk of violence presented by mental disorder is modest. Compared to the magnitude of risk associated with alcoholism and other drug use, the risk associated with 'major' mental disorders such as schizophrenia and affective disorder is modest indeed.
>
> (Monahan, 2007:144)

Thus, the critical question that the early parts of this book will address becomes why should mental disorder make any difference to the incidence of criminal behaviour? Like many simple questions this is deceptive. And to answer the question it will be necessary to unpack, albeit briefly, our understanding of what we mean by crime, by mental disorder and by what causes crime. And of course, the causes of crime are notably elusive, as New Labour discovered with its ambitions to be 'tough on crime, tough on the causes of crime'. In practice, being tough on crime was both seductive and pursuable. Being tough on the causes of crime proved arguably too problematic to address and certainly too tough to solve within the policy constraints, for example, in relation to tackling inequality, that New Labour adopted.

Problems of definition

There is thus one inherent difficulty in thinking about the relationship between mental disorder and crime: namely, both are ill-defined concepts. We recognise them when we see them in their most frank forms: the person suffering from paranoid schizophrenia, who believes that thoughts are being broadcast into their head by aliens, is by most yardsticks mentally ill; the man convicted of raping a stranger deserves punishment as an offender. But most mental disorder and much of what is deemed crime are not so self-evident, so determining the relationship between them is problematic. In many respects, it would be like trying to think of the relationship between happiness and wealth: both are culturally and individually defined; people can rightly think of themselves as wealthy when they have little money or happy in the face of adversity. Similarly, when I ask my criminal law students to assert with a show of hands that they have never committed a crime, it is clear that many, if not most of the class, consider themselves to be law abiding. But as I ask them further questions about driving, copying videos or, more recently, downloading music, buying alcohol, travelling beyond their stop on public transport, failing to return excess change to shops and many other of the day-to-day infractions of the criminal law which they will have committed, but for which they will most certainly not have been caught or convicted, hands quickly go down. Indeed in a recent survey of 3,118 teenagers aged 17–18, seven per cent admitted to driving under the influence of drugs, 20 per cent to drinking and driving and 32 per cent to being a passenger in a car with a driver under the influence of drink or drugs (*The Guardian*, 30 August 2007). It is a common misunderstanding to assume that crime is only committed by criminals, namely, those who have been publicly caught, convicted and censured for their actions. Committing crime is almost a hazard of living.

My students' experiences are replicated and amplified by the research. The Home Office Offenders Index (Home Office, 1995) relates to offenders convicted in a criminal court of standard list offences (that is, all indictable offences and some of the more serious summary offences). On the basis of this the Home Office have calculated that, of males born in 1953, 34 per cent of them will have a conviction for a standard list offence by their 40th birthday (and that figure excludes motoring offences): seven per cent had four or more convictions. The pattern for women is different, showing overall much lower rates of conviction (nine per cent by age 46). Similarly, self-report data, including the Cambridge Study in Delinquency Development (Farrington, 1995), document the prevalence of offending (with a peak age of 17), the influence of early onset (associated with persistent offending), and that offending frequency is the strongest predictor of someone being a violent offender. The study also notes that offenders are heterogenous in their offence patterns (but see also MacDonald et al, 2009, Vizard et al, 2007), that is they don't specialise in violent offending; and that a small group of offenders are disproportionately responsible for offending. Being the victim of crime is, logically, also commonplace.[2] Thus, crime really is all around us, and very few are untainted by some history of legal infractions, even if comparatively trivial and even if undetected. A criminally blameless life is the aberration. Similar problems relate to the definition of mental disorder, but for the moment the focus will be on crime.

---

2 Again, this applies equally to children: 95 per cent of surveyed 10–15 year olds had experienced crime at least once, the majority of it perpetrated by other children. Hitting, kicking, being robbed of money or a mobile phone, often at school or between home and school were frequently cited (*The Guardian*, 10 October 2007).

Chapter 2

Crime

What do we mean by crime?

Agreeing that offences of violence, theft and burglary are crimes is not problematic. Getting agreement that various financial and environmental activities are crimes may take more elucidation. And whilst crimes committed by the state may elicit an agreement that technically they may be crimes, this can be accompanied by a desire to justify them by making reference to the particular political context in which they occur. Nor do regulatory offences and offences of strict liability come readily to mind when defining what is meant by crime; drug taking may be recognised as an offence, but not considered wrong; and the advent of a criminal penalty for the breach of a civil order, as happens with the anti-social behaviour order (ASBO), begins to confound people's notions of what committing a crime entails. For where the mere presence of a named individual in a particular street, a street that is otherwise open to all others without penalty, attracts the possibility of a five year prison sentence for that individual, as is the case with ASBOs, then the common boundaries of 'what is crime' are challenged. The fact that the criminal law itself is not a static thing is evident; it has been argued that over 3,000 new criminal offences were introduced during the first nine years of the Blair government (Cooper, 2008; Solomon et al, 2007). It is hard to work out how robust this figure is – whether it is an underestimate or an overestimate will depend upon what is counted as a discrete criminal offence – but what is clear is that any shared understanding of what crime might be is susceptible to political revision. And whilst the boundaries of what constitute crime are frequently subject to extension, rarely are 'crimes' abolished.[1] It is, moreover, a common problem when considering the relationship between mental disorder and crime to slip into thinking only about crimes of interpersonal violence, even though these are exceptional rather than routine. Crime is simply diverse in its nature (see Amos et al, 2010 for a discussion of 'normal' offending by those with mental diosrder).

---

1 Reform of aspects of the law on homosexuality would be one example.

What causes crime?

Since the manifestations of crime are both so varied and so numerous, the likelihood of there being any single 'cause of crime' is remote (see generally Reiner, 2007 for an analysis of contemporary trends in crime). A cursory glance at two chapters in the *Oxford Handbook of Criminology* (Maguire et al, 2007) Paul Rock's, on 'Sociological Theories of Crime', and Clive Hollin's, on 'Criminological Psychology', quickly confirms that the causes of crime are complex, multi-factorial, contingent and contentious. A brief synopsis of some of the common ground follows, although its interaction with mental disorder is dealt with more extensively below. Moreover, whilst this brief synopsis should be read in the light of Garland's aspirational notion that criminology is the 'science of the causes of crime', the assertion by David Downes that criminology is a 'rendez-vous discipline' more properly emphasises, as Rock notes, the degree of pragmatism and blurring of disciplines entailed. Theoretical purity is neither the goal, nor the grail; understanding 'mere parts and fragments of larger totalities' is the stuff of criminologists' concerns (Rock, 2007:35).

To argue that criminal behaviour is a consequence of an interaction between an individual and his [intentionally his] social and cultural environment, and the legal variables that define and locate crime, is a starting place. But all of those terms require further analysis. Individuals are constituted by their unique genetic endowment, their upbringing, their personality, their emotional and social resources, their cognitive processes, their education, and their life experiences. Each of these can be unpacked further into such applicable factors as age and gender. Concepts like 'hegemonic masculinity', namely the way power, wealth and physical strength, which are all arguably encouraged in men and in turn underpin risk-taking and aggression, are also relevant (Connell, 1987). Given the male bias in offending such analyses, albeit vague, cannot be ignored. Whether the make-up of our personality interacts with our ability to learn control over our impulses and actions is another potentially crucial issue (Eysenck, 1977, 1996); can our identities and behaviour change over time in a dynamic relationship with the society in which we find ourselves and the society we keep? Social learning theory, social information processing and operant conditioning will all have a part to play in why we are who we are (see generally Hollin, 2007).

Then there are those factors that relate to an individual's adherence to social norms. Explanations of crime that instrumentally combine opportunities for crime with intermittent lack of controls have an inherent appeal. That crime occurs in 'hot-spots' might favour some kind of environmental or opportunity based explanation, but attractive as an explanation based in routine activities might seem, hot-spots are hot because of the interaction between people and these locations. Not everyone who routinely passes through them invariably indulges in criminal activity. So what motivates some people to break the law, and others to restrain themselves? Is it that society promises too much and then frustrates our abilities equally to achieve those goals, a position that would crudely reflect a Durkheimian analysis (Durkheim, 1964; see also, on 'Anomie', Merton, 1995)? This is not to argue that poverty causes crime, for the relief of deficit is relative: the rich can equally experience relative deprivation and resort to illegal means to relieve it (Hagan, 1977). Is it more that given free rein, people will break the law if it is to their advantage, which in turn raises the question of whether some people are inherently less able to control themselves; or is it that others have the necessary skills successfully to commit crime? Or is it that people's desires get shaped by their environment, including their peers, and a heady cocktail of leisure time, alcohol and drugs supersedes any inherent moral order to which people might otherwise claim allegiance? Certainly it would be wrong to think of all crime as being mundane or calculated and rational; as Jock Young asserts, much crime is, rather, expressive, relying on an adrenaline rush and the pleasure to be derived from the illicit risk-taking; joy-riding, vandalism and even a significant proportion of crimes with instrumental value, for example, shoplifting, would fall into this net (Young, 2007:19, drawing on the work of Presdee, 2000 and Hayward, 2004). What role then does emotion and emotional arousal play? What cognitive factors are at play; are some of us more reflective than others, more able to see things from another's perspective and thus to moderate our behaviour? The further one unpacks and defines the possibilities, the more compelling the answer becomes that crime is contingent. It is not abnormal or confined to a pathological few; it is all around us.

Similarly, is the separation between violent crime and the petty temptations to which we all occasionally succumb a false separation? What does violent behaviour signify? An inability to operate otherwise; a belief that violence is acceptable; or what? Is it perhaps as Jock Young (2007:35) argues essentially attributable to a process of mutual dehumanisation: largely brought about by a sense of economic injustice (for which read relative deprivation) combined with ontological insecurity (the notion that people's sense of identity and social worth is under threat)? Together these vulnerabilities allow us both to construct others as essentially different – perhaps inherently evil, but as likely just different, lacking our qualities and virtues whilst possessing negative attributes – and permit us temporarily to act in an inhumane (violent) manner because we are dealing with those who are also acting inhumanely. Techniques of neutralisation are further used to justify the transgression of prohibitions against violence. As Young asserts (2007:39) 'if unfairness provides a rationalisation for violence, dehumanisation permits it.' And it perhaps goes without saying, that if this analysis is persuasive, it is as persuasive for the mentally disordered as for the mentally ordered. And arguably, it is even more persuasive when thinking about violence against the mentally disordered (see below) where pre-existing stigma can facilitate the process of dehumanisation.

The temptation is, of course, to resort to particular theories that fit with our preconceived notions. Thus, as Siegal advocates:

> Psychological theories are useful as explanations of the behaviour of deeply disturbed, impulsive, or destructive people. However, they are limited as general explanations of criminality. For one thing, the phenomenon of crime and delinquency is so widespread that to claim that all criminals are psychologically disturbed is to make that claim against a vast majority of people.
>
> (Siegal, 1986:175–6)

The implication seems to be that psychological theories are good to explain abnormal behaviour, and that the mentally disordered (note the linkage of disturbance, impulsivity and destruction) are associated with the more extreme forms of criminality. But where is the evidence for that? As Hollin (2007:70) tellingly concludes 'it is time to put to rest the question of pathology, that psychological theories are only fit for explanations of abnormal states'. I would similarly argue that if we are properly to understand criminal behaviour by those with mental disorders, we need first to understand behaviour, then to understand criminal behaviour and finally to assess what contribution, if any, is made by the presence of mental disorder.

There is, of course, a wealth of analysis that has attempted to look at, prove, and disprove the various theoretical approaches. Much of it is flawed and much floored by the impossibility of disentangling the many and various contributing factors. Much of the work *is* a product of the study of normal behaviour, but that which focuses more directly on aberrant behaviour has tended to use selected samples, and often the subjects of those samples are convicted offenders. This, in turn, makes separating factors that predict offending from factors that predict conviction (unsuccessful offending) problematic.

At this point it might be helpful to step back from this morass and address some basics. When thinking about the causation of crime, the common starting place for texts on criminology is the philosophical divide between classicism and positivism (see, most recently, Newburn, 2007). Classicism takes the offence as its focus, assumes that offenders are free-willed, rational, calculating and ordered, and promotes punishment which is proportionate to the offences as the appropriate response to offending. Positivism focuses on the offender, and stresses offending behaviour as determined, driven by, amongst others, psychological and biological factors, and sees the offender's behaviour as pathological. Its response to offending is thus treatment oriented, indeterminate and based around individual differences. The immediate temptation is to argue that mentally disordered offenders fit neatly within positivism, whilst classicism is the explanatory mode of choice for the majority of ordered offenders. This, of course, falls into the trap of seeing mentally ordered and mentally disordered offenders as distinct groups, an analysis I have criticised elsewhere (Peay, 2007); but it is a useful device for thinking about how helpful it might be to assume that criminal behaviour is determined, and hence subject to accurate prediction and controlled intervention.

Whilst issues of treatment are dealt with more extensively below, two preliminary points will be made. First, if the causes of crime are multi-factorial, treatment interventions need to be similarly broad. Intervening merely at an individual level is unlikely to be efficacious without tackling the prevailing economic and social conditions. Programmes relating to educa-tion, training, jobs and housing, as Crow (2001:78–9) has noted, all need to be established alongside programmes for individual offenders, otherwise their 'impact may be no greater than that of Sisyphus rolling a rock uphill'.

Second, people are self-evidently a mixture of static and dynamic factors, albeit that the number of truly static factors is limited. Age is an obvious example; whilst one might not act one's age, or even look it, biologically one's date of birth is a fixed event. However, one's age does change sponta-neously with time, so it is a curious static factor. Height, once fully grown, is perhaps a better static factor, since it is a physical characteristic that is problematic to alter; similarly, ethnicity. Yet, the static factors, including one's previous offending, are amongst the strongest predictors both of crim-inal activity and of desistance. There can therefore only be a limited role for treatment and care (albeit that those limits are far from fixed) in altering the predicted likelihood of future offending (and all the consequences that go with predictions of a high probability of future offending) since treatment can only address dynamic factors.

Cause, effect and correlation

Before shifting the focus of discussion on to mental disorder it is necessary to undertake a preliminary exploration of the problematic notion of cause and effect in the light of the distinction between static and dynamic factors. One of the static factors not mentioned above is that of genetic endowment. Despite remarkable technological advances, this remains as good as fixed. And if our genetic inheritance is amongst the best of the static factors can it be used as a basis for exploring the difficulties that will be faced when trying to establish any link between one's genes and, for example, the ability to choose to engage in or refrain from any particular behaviour: in short, the ability to exercise free will? And if this proves problematic, what does it say about our abilities to establish causal mechanisms underlying behaviour based in pathological explanations? Before embarking on this exploration, it should be stressed that some authors (eg Kraemer et al, 1997) adopt the position that since genes per se are fixed markers, static factors in the termi-nology above, they cannot in any event be causal factors, because they are not capable of manipulation. For in order to demonstrate that something is a causal factor, you have to be able to show that changes in it precede an outcome and influence it. However, since it is possible that some of the products of genes may be causal factors, the discussion below will proceed on the basis that genes can influence behaviour.

One starting point is the work of Alper (1998:1607), who sets out four fundamental difficulties faced by statistical theories that attempt to predict and quantify behaviour, in this case criminal behaviour. First, problems relating to defining behavioural traits make comparisons between studies, and even between researchers in the same study, problematic. Second, the quantification of the trait is problematic; how can a criminal act be reduced to a number? Third, causal mechanisms are necessarily oversimplified; why should an increase in factor A lead to a proportionate increase in behaviour B? And finally, since statistical models cannot include all the causal factors for explaining an individual's behaviour, any model will only assist in predicting those factors that account for a large proportion of the variation within the majority of individuals in a study, and in that sense statistical models are problematic when thinking about causality at the level of individual behaviour. This last problem will bedevil much of the analysis of the relationship between mental disorder and crime. This is because, as will become clear, the literature which asserts a positive relationship is based on analyses relating to large numbers of individuals, whereas clinicians and the law are primarily interested in what relationship, if any, can be established within any one individual (see generally Szmukler, 2003).

It is, moreover, important to remember these limitations when thinking about the role of genetic factors. To the uninitiated these would appear to be amongst the factors most likely to have a clear deterministic link with behaviour. Yet this is not the case. Alper (1998:1599), who as an academic geneticist is amongst the initiated, argues that 'as a general rule, behaviour influenced by genes is no more deterministic than is behaviour influenced by the environment'; thus he asserts 'genetics has little to add to the analysis of free will, determinism and criminal responsibility'. Alper's argument, that even if behaviour were genetically determined it does not mean that free will cannot exist, has interesting parallels with the argument about thought/ control-override theories discussed below: just because you have an intrusive voice telling you to do something, it does not mean it cannot be resisted, any more than an external voice could, or, for that matter, a memory of someone telling you to do something. Or as Monahan and Steadman (1983) asked, why should those with paranoid delusions be any more or less likely to attack their tormentors than those who are in fact being tormented?

Complex systems, like humans, are subject to chaotic or unpredictable deterministic behaviour. The analogy Alper draws is with billiard balls: even if the initial position and velocity are accurately known, after the first few collisions with the walls and with other balls, their motion becomes unpredictable. Moreover, Alper argues, there is a categorical difference between an emergent property, like consciousness or temperature, and the more fundamental properties like the velocities of individual molecules in a gas, or the activities of neurons or neurotransmitters. And people are more complex than billiard balls. Thus, whilst it may become possible to explain how the system operates when someone undergoes pain, that won't necessarily explain the feeling of pain. Similarly, Dennett's (1967) use of two explanatory strategies, the physical stance, entailing neurobiological constructs for explaining autonomic behaviour, and the intentional stance, for purposeful behaviour, helps us to understand why complicated human behaviour can only be explained from an intentional stance: thoughts, feelings, rationality and free will are necessary to explain normal purposeful behaviour. Again the parallels are clear: once irrational behaviour enters the equation, there is a tendency to revert to physical stance explanations, relying on biological factors. But is irrational behaviour necessarily pathological?

I am not an expert in behavioural genetics, but it might be helpful to counterpoise any sense of scientific certainty that may derive from our very impressive ability to identify individuals through their DNA (the material basis of genes and the fixed inherited genetic markers or genotype) and the expression of those genes in both the manifest physical properties of individuals, their physiology and, ultimately, their behaviour – the phynotypic descriptors. The causal pathways of one's heredity and subsequent development, as demonstrated by Mendel's Laws, are separate; acquired characteristics cannot not be inherited. Thus, whilst the genome is a cause of the phenotype, the phenome cannot influence the genotype.

There is however an argument about the comparison between genetic markers and biological ones. When thinking about the relationship with criminality, it is possible that biological markers might be a product of, for example, aggressive criminal behaviour, rather than a cause of it. Genetic markers will at least have the advantage of pre-dating any criminal behaviour. Thus, if a strong association appears between a genotype and a form of criminal behaviour, and that association holds constant for all individuals in all environments, then one might conclude that the behaviour was a product of the genotype and not the individual's free will. But since it is widely agreed by behavioural geneticists that if criminal behaviour is genetic, a number of genes will be involved, this makes interactions both between the genes and the environment extremely complex. The likelihood therefore of identifying the influence of any individual genetic factors, or the interaction of a limited number of such factors, and then being able to separate this out from the environmental factors that have significance for the individual and their behaviour looks implausible. Setting aside Jones's (2010) telling example of the gene for male gender, offending behaviour is not, cannot, and will not be proven to be a simple product of one's genetic endowment.

Moreover, whilst convincing either a scientific or lay audience of this might be considered challenging, constructing a sufficiently persuasive account in order to satisfy a court when determining criminal responsibility looks nigh impossible. To date attempts by defence lawyers to use genetic factors to explain criminal behaviour have failed (see, for example the case of Stephen Mobley, discussed in Eastman and Campbell 2006), albeit that an Italian Appeal Court in Trieste is reported to have reduced the sentence imposed on a murderer by one year on evidence from cognitive and molecular neuroscientists to the effect that his genetic endowment would have made him particularly aggressive in stressful situations.[2] In short, as Alper implies (1998:1606) looking for a genetically based deterministic cause or causes of criminal behaviour looks like a hopeless aspiration. Paradoxically, this in no way seems to have undermined the influence of such genotype determinism in common thinking. And as Nelkin and Tancredi (1994) have illustrated, considerable dangers lie in such thinking.

To take a specific example, the relationship between the genetic basis of schizophrenia, and schizophrenia and violence is pertinent. Controversy has raged about whether a genetic basis of schizophrenia is ever likely to be established. Amongst the latest research studies, a trio cited in *New Scientist* (30 July 2008:18) report several common genetic variations that 'slightly' increase the risk of developing schizophrenia; and rare ones which raise the risk 'significantly'.[3] Differences in copy number variations (CNVs) – sections of genetic material that were either repeated or missing from the genome altogether – were compared between 3,391 people suffering from schizophrenia and 3,181 'healthy' people. Those with schizophrenia had, on average, 15 per cent more CNVs. And one in 1,000 people suffering from schizophrenia were missing several CNVs that were associated with a much higher risk of developing the disease, perhaps making it as much as 15 times as likely. And a third study identified three convincing associations in specific genes. But as one of the researchers commented 'Together, the new studies show that many of us carry some risk genes for schizophrenia, but the people who have the illness simply carry more of them'. Equally, the rarity of some of the genetic variations means that they account for less than 0.5 per cent of the cases of schizophrenia. It is possible that there are many thousands of genetic variations that account for schizophrenia; certainly, there is not some kind of magic gene. Indeed, it has recently been observed that

2 See the case of *Abdelmalek Bayout*, *The Times*, 17 November 2009.
3 The papers emerge from an International Scientific Consortium with some 30 collaborators: lead authors include O'Donovan, M. (*Nature Genetics*, 2008: 40, 1053) and Stefansson, H. (*Nature* 2008: 455, 11 September 2008).

... all but the most dogged of genetic determinists have revised their view of the primacy of genetic factors so as to encompass a central role for the environment in the development of mental disorder.

(Sonuga-Barke, 2010:113)

Social factors, and in particular the family, are being re-recognised as the crucial organising vector which can mediate the effects of environmental influences on mental health outcomes. As Sonuga-Barke (2010:113) observes, the stand-off over nature versus nurture can now be bypassed: whole genome association studies have highlighted 'the complexity and heterogeneity of the causal architecture of common mental disorders and the way that genes and environments work together to shape development'.

And even for those who doggedly believe that the basis of schizophrenia may lie in a complex interaction of gene sequences, and missing sequences and specific genes regulating the activity of other genes, that brings one no closer to determining that the disorder schizophrenia is related in any meaningful way to criminal or specifically violent behaviour. As Bentall trenchantly observes about what the heritability statistic tell us:

... genes play some role at some point in increasing the risk of mental illness, but nothing else ... By relying on it, geneticists have assumed that they can estimate environmental factors by exclusion, that these effects are what is left over when genetic influences have been accounted for. In reality, however, the only way of discovering whether environmental influences are important is by looking for them.

(Bentall, 2009:127)

Another perspective on this is offered by Arboleda-Florez et al (1998: S39–40). Drawing on David Hume's famous positivist analysis of cause, first published in 1740, they note that 'cause cannot be directly demonstrated, but can be invoked when high correlations are involved, and inferred if three conditions are present'. The three conditions are contact or proximity between cause and effect (given the episodic nature of some mental disorders this can be problematic where offending is necessarily invariably assessed retrospectively); temporal precedence, that is, the mental disorder precedes the offending behaviour (as will be discussed below, this can also be problematic, especially in the context where offending can contribute to the occurrence of mental disorder); and thirdly, constant conjunction, that is the cause is always present whenever the effect is obtained. Since much, if not most, offending takes place in the absence of frank mental disorder this latter condition is also problematic. Indeed, since most of those with mental disorder are not perpetually deviant, and since even those people with disorders which are thought to be chronic, like schizophrenia, tend to offend primarily during their younger years, when most 'normal' offenders offend, establishing a causal link begins to look precarious. But this is, in itself, revealing. For the life course of schizophrenia can follow a particular pattern, with acute episodes with positive symptomatology occurring earlier in someone's life and the negative symptoms appearing later: flat affect is rarely a precursor to offending. Indeed, negative symptomatology may be a protective factor (Swanson et al, 2006). Again, perhaps we need to think in a more detailed way about those elements of schizophrenia that may have some relevance to offending, rather than seeking correlations between the diagnosis as a whole and the perpetration of particular crimes.

Of course, the difficulty here is that we are not dealing with simple cause and effect. As the causes of crime are multifarious, whatever effect mental disorder might be having, other factors will always be at play at the same time. Similarly, in the absence of crime, mental disorder can always be present, although it bears stressing that the crime may be the event that causes the mental disorder to be diagnosed. But since neither of Hume's present-present and absent-absent conditions is likely to be satisfied, interpretations other than causality of the co-variation will be necessary. Thus, conclusions about causality are merely judgments about likelihood; how willing one is to accept them depends upon one's threshold for being convinced. A low threshold will draw more examples into the net, with all of the consequences that may follow for the individuals involved, and a high threshold will exclude more cases, leaving offenders to be dealt with, perhaps in error, as if they were mentally ordered.

Indeed, different disciplines are apparently satisfied with different levels of probable cause. Clinicians may be prepared to accept proof of a relationship between two factors, perhaps schizophrenia and violence, on the strength of evidence that would not satisfy a court. Such clinicians may be motivated by the expectation that making the assumption and intervening with treatment will be to the individual's benefit, whereas in court, considerably stronger evidence might be required before concluding that causation could be established or absolving an individual of criminal responsibility.[4] Scientific evidence on all sorts of issues can, of course, be highly persuasive in court. But whether the leap from such evidence of an individual's make-up, perhaps in relation to their genetic endowment, their physiology or neuroscientific evidence about the state of their brains, translates in court to a finding that someone is neither legally guilty nor morally responsible for their actions would stretch scientific evidence into a domain to which it is ill-suited (Eastman and Campbell, 2006). And ironically the one environmental factor that has been found to have a possible causal association with criminal activity, namely lead poisoning (Denno, 1993, Needleman et al,

---

4 In whole or in part via either the rarely used M'Naghten defence, or the defence of diminished responsibility to a charge of murder.

1996), has been rejected by the courts when put forward as a basis for a criminal defence (Alper, 1998). Free will is apparently thought to have a sufficient potential to override any deterministic influence the environment might have. Criminal responsibility is not so easy to evade.

In this context it is important to be clear about what is meant by claiming a causal relationship. One helpful analysis is provided by Kraemer et al (1997). Some preliminary terms need to be understood. First, prevalence.[5] Prevalence measures the probability that subjects in a particular population have the outcome being measured at a defined point in time; the examples given are that of autism and Alzheimer's. For the former, which is present from birth, the prevalence will not alter over time. For the latter, a disorder with a late onset but unremitting nature, the prevalence will increase, albeit slowly at first, as a function of time. With an episodic disorder, like schizophrenia or depression, the prevalence fluctuates over time. To illustrate, looking at the prevalence of probable psychotic disorder in a general household survey in 2000 (Singleton et al, 2001) the finding ranged in the previous year from a low of one per 1000 (for the age group 25–29) to a high of 10 per 1000 (for the age group 40–44). Notably, the age group 30–34 had a prevalence of nine per 1000. Some prevalence studies ignore time and ask whether the subject has ever had the disorder (see for example, Appleby, et al (2006) which produces a measure of life-time prevalence). As Kraemer et al observe (1997:339) 'If all the respondents are at the same point in time when the question is asked, what results is the incidence (not prevalence). If the respondents are not at the same time, what results is an uninterpretable mixture of incidences.' Of course, if the age distribution varies, then what is produced is not comparable with other studies unless they also have similar age distributions. Thus, in any risk assessment study, the notion of examining the extent to which factor (a) is related to factor (b) is critically dependent on issues of time.

The implications of this are problematic. It is well established that the statistics of criminal activity are themselves artefacts (Maguire, 2007). Statistics, as Harper (1991) has tellingly observed, are not about numbers, but an approach to understanding what is a very complex world, and one that is not easily understood: 'If everything appears simple and crystal clear probably you have misunderstood the issue you are considering' (cited in Maguire, 2007:241). Yet much of the literature discussed below does not take account of prevalence rates over time, and nor is it always clear about denominator issues, in effect, what is being compared with what: for example, Goldacre (2007) powerfully illustrates the differences that emerge in the statistics of survival rates of babies born under 24 weeks of gestation

---

5 Incidence, another common term, but of less relevance here, is the number of new cases occurring in a given population over a specific time period.

if one uses a denominator of 'all live births' or 'all births admitted to a neonatal unit'. Since the latter is much smaller than the former, survival rates increase dramatically if the latter is used as the denominator. (For an excellent examination of the problematic statistics of risk, see Gigerenzer, 2002.)

When thinking about cause Kraemer et al (1997) argue that a causal risk factor is a risk factor that changes either spontaneously within a subject, like age or weight, or is manipulable, for example in response to medication or other therapy, and that when such a factor changes, it can be shown to change the risk of an outcome. Terminological confusion also arises because there is a difference between a causal risk factor and a cause. The illustration helpfully given by Kraemer et al relates to HIV. The cause of AIDS is the human immunodeficiency virus. A causal risk factor would be having unprotected sex. But having unprotected sex in the absence of the virus will have no influence on the risk of acquiring AIDS. However, as they note, empirical evidence about the incidence of AIDS in various populations engaging in various activities has provided clues as to where to look for the cause.

Almost all studies will have some retrospective element to them. A retrospective approach brings difficulties: recall is imperfect and sometimes misleading. Moreover, the point at which one is required to recall something can also be critical: for example, recalling childhood sexual abuse before the onset of depression may indicate that it is a risk factor; recalling it after the onset of depression may 'reflect the subject's perception of the happenings reported as sexual abuse modified by the experience of the disorder, a consequence, not a risk factor' (Kraemer et al, 1997:342). And the most fundamental difficulty which occurs repeatedly below is that neither cross-sectional studies nor retrospective studies can claim that risk factors are causal, since they cannot know that they precede the outcome in time.

Finally, there is Monahan's cautionary footnote:

> To say that a variable is a 'risk factor' for violence means two things and only two things: (1) the variable correlates with the outcome (in this case violence), and (2) the variable precedes the outcome. To call a variable a risk factor does not imply that its relationship to the outcome is 'causal'.
>
> (Monahan, 2007:137)

Chapter 3

Mental disorder

Problems of definition and diagnosis

It would be possible to write an entire book on what is meant by mental disorder. Indeed, an excellent one has already been written on just that topic (Bolton, 2008). Its treatment here will necessarily be partial.

Mental disorder has been defined clinically, perhaps tautologically, perhaps simplistically, as 'a disorder that presents with mental signs and symptoms'. As will emerge more fully in the latter sections of this book, the current legal definitions are hardly more helpful. And there is a further fundamental problem, namely whether mental disorders are indeed distinct from physical disorders. Reputable opinion would argue not (see Kendell, 2001, Matthews, 1999). Indeed Kendell, a former President of the Royal College of Psychiatrists, has argued that

> ... if we do continue to refer to 'mental' and 'physical' illnesses we should preface both with 'so-called', to remind ourselves and our audience that these are archaic and deeply misleading terms.
>
> (Kendell, 2001:490)

That said, this is not the place to review what is a fascinating literature on the infusion of 'the mental' into physical illness and/or vice versa. Rather, the book takes as its premise a widespread recognition of the concept of mental disorder, even if that concept is itself of dubious value.[1]

The focus here is on a tension within the topic between an approach that emphasises a quasi-scientific basis, with all of the seeming certainty that that embraces, and one which places much greater stress on what is not yet known or understood (see Kendell, 2001 and Cheng, 2001, implicitly supporting the scientific view, and Turner, 2003, for a contrary view). The former approach might be typified by frequent resort to the accepted

---

1 As Kendell points out (2001:490) even DSM IV objects to the term as representing an anachronistic and reductionist mind/body dualism.

international classifications of psychiatric disorders, namely the World Health Organization's International Classification of Diseases, Edition 10 (ICD 10) and the American Psychiatric Association's Diagnostic and Statistical Manual, 4th Edition (DSM IV). ICD 10 has 17 categories of disease, with 'mental and behavioural disorders' being but one of these categories. It adopts a uniaxial approach. DSM IV relates only to those disorders treated by American psychiatrists and clinical psychologists, and is a product of the work of those professional bodies. It adopts a multi-axial approach.[2] But both ICD 10 and DSM IV encourage the presumption that a disease is present, even if it has not yet been identified. Both classificatory systems, as is revealed by their not infrequent revisions, have been subject to clarification and extension. One illustration of this would be the emergence of social anxiety disorder. Not officially recognised until 1980, this disorder only achieved an adequate definition in the 1987 revision of DSM; yet now social anxiety disorder is reported in the US to be the third most common psychiatric diagnosis after alcoholism and depression. As with the discussion of crime, the boundaries of mental disorder are subject to expansionary pressures (Horwitz and Wakefield, 2007).[3]

In contrast, and arguably at the polar opposite, is a much more hesitant approach, which would stress the relative historical newness of psychiatric diagnosis and reject any notion of hard and fast classifications that are in any sense akin to our ability to diagnose other disorders, such as diabetes or smallpox (see, for example, Bentall 2003). Indeed, Turner has argued that 'the claim that mental illness is the same in all cultures is an implicit assumption, rather than an empirical finding' (2003:472). In so doing he draws on the work of the American philosopher Donald Davidson, who has argued that 'there cannot, in any useful sense, be a science of the mental because of the impossibility of either strict psychological or strict psychophysical laws' (ibid); in essence, it is implausible to think of a science of mental states. Trying to disentangle the inevitably tangled web of what one means, when one says something, from what one believes, makes hazardous any claims to the elements of scientific rigour traditionally associated with diagnosis. Where the assessment of minor mental disorders and personality disorders is based on how people live their lives and what they believe in and value, then it is problematic to reduce these to an agreed vocabulary. If diagnosis

2 DSM IV, as a multi-axial diagnostic tool, has five axes; the first relates to clinical disorders and the second to personality disorders and 'mental retardation'. The fourth axis relates to psychosocial and environmental problems: the potential for diagnostic confusion with this system is inherent. ICD 10 is a uniaxial system, in that each diagnosis is classified under only one parent code, which ensures statistically that each patient is only diagnosed under one coding classification. Different kinds of errors will arise here.

3 Whether depression, social anxiety disorder and mere shyness are truly distinguishable is subject to debate: indeed, the medical treatment for each can be much the same.

inevitably depends upon assessing how an individual perceives and experiences the world (the phenomenological aspects of their being) then applying some scientific evaluation is a fraught and vulnerable exercise.

Another preliminary issue concerns the reasons for diagnosis. Diagnosis is generally held to fulfil four purposes: descriptive (a labelling function, to assist communication and as an aid to accessing information about a disorder), aetiological (implying information about the cause of the disorder, albeit that the cause might not be known), therapeutic (to guide decisions about treatment and management) and prognostic (to aid the process of forecasting the course of a disorder). As standard texts on these medical practices reveal, some diagnoses convey more information about these purposes than others: thus, a diagnosis of migraine is helpful for communication about symptoms and the likely progress of the disorder, but it is not definitive as to treatment and has little to say about the causes, given that these remain complex and uncertain. In contrast, diabetes mellitus is a diagnosis conveying clear information about the cause and recommended treatments, and even gives some information about prognosis, but it tells one very little about how the patient may present with symptoms, since the clinical presentation of diabetes mellitus varies considerably. It is often argued in psychiatry that diagnostic labels are usually more of the symptomatic kind than the aetiological kind. Indeed, having rigid classificatory systems, like DSM IV and ICD 10, may impede the development of aetiological understanding.

It is, of course, possible to diagnose a disorder based on the observation of a cluster of symptoms without knowing or understanding the basis for that disorder. Or at least this is possible for clinicians. I am not a clinician and my partial understanding has been gleaned to a great extent from my former research and teaching colleague, Nigel Eastman. In a course we taught jointly to doctors and lawyers, Professor Eastman attempted to elucidate clinical matters to the lawyers, whilst I and other legal colleagues tackled the doctors' understanding of the law. One of Eastman's examples would be the diagnosis of the condition 'thyrotoxicosis'; this was recognised long before the thyroid gland was identified as its source, and that occurred before a detailed pathological understanding of the thyroid gland emerged. Disorders can similarly arise both from problems with the structure of, for example, an organ, or in its function, or in the manner of its functioning, perhaps where a normal physiological mechanism operates to an abnormal degree (as in an anxiety state). Thus, there is a distinction between organic disorders, where there is an observable abnormality in the brain, or another structure affecting it, or in the way in which it operates, and a functional disorder where a normal brain functions abnormally. The situation is further complicated in that some disorders, which are associated with clear physical abnormalities, for example Alzheimer's disease, can be classified as both, or either of, a neurological disorder or a psychiatric disorder. Until quite recently the plaques and tangles evident in brain tissue associated with Alzheimer's were only evident at autopsy; yet PET scanning has now indicated the possibility of much earlier diagnosis (Small et al, 2006). Formerly, diagnosis was based on the signs and symptoms that are associated with the disease; signs being the observable sequelae, like memory loss, and symptoms being those matters about which patients complain, like forgetfulness and confusion. In some disorders, like Alzheimer's, the underlying physical signs, the plaques and tangles, can be present without any evident symptoms; and the symptoms can be present seemingly without any physical signs. And some disorders, like schizophrenia, have both physical and functional causes, with the balance between them shifting; and yet others, like the personality disorders, do not have any identifiable physical cause of which we yet know, beyond perhaps some argument about genetic predispositions, although complex classificatory and diagnostic tools exist to enable clinicians to diagnose the condition.

There has also been, as Eastman explained, a historical shift in emphasis in psychiatry from an approach – the psychoanalytic – which focused on an attempt to understand the human mind but which generated hypotheses which were not scientifically verifiable, to a phenomenological approach, namely one that stresses observable features emanating from the mind. It is this latter approach that has dominated post-war British psychiatry and its attempts scientifically to validate the process of diagnosis and treatment. As Eastman explained to our students, the difference between the two approaches can be captured in the sentence 'I did it because the voices told me to'; the phenomenological approach would diagnose an auditory hallucination; the psychodynamic approach would place the stress on *because* as a basis for explaining the behaviour. In practice, the most common clinical approach is an eclectic one, drawing idiosyncratically on a combination of experience (what is useful), information (what is known) and currency (what is believed at that time).

In the latter sections of this book more emphasis will be placed on legal classifications of disorder. These are not coterminous with psychiatric classifications, for example, psychopathic disorder (the legal classification under the (unamended) MHA 1983) was not a generally recognised psychiatric diagnosis: nonetheless, psychiatrists would give evidence as to its presence or absence based in large part, presumably, on their experience with various forms of personality disorder. For the moment, the analysis will focus on psychiatric definitions of disorder. Moreover, when thinking about the relationship between symptoms and criminal behaviour, it is important to separate out that body of literature concerned with the legal attribution of responsibility in those with mental disorders. This will also be touched on in later chapters of the book: the issues involved, such as establishing fitness to plead, diminished responsibility and automatism, raise different questions to those around causality. Such assessments of legal responsibility will govern, or partly govern, the issue of disposal. What concerns us here is the relationship between symptoms and behaviour, not how that behaviour is ultimately evaluated and judged.

Whilst this is necessarily crude, for our purposes psychiatric diagnoses can be divided into three types: those relating to mental illness, to learning disability or mental handicap, and to personality disorder. Whilst the nature of the concept of learning disability was less troubling to students, understanding the difference between mental illness and the personality disorders was more problematic. Eastman helpfully described the difference between these two categories by analogy to a raspberry ripple ice cream with a cherry on the top. If one conceived as the cherry being a mental illness, something added on to the person, which might be excised through treatment, then personality disorder was more akin to the ripples; it ran throughout the person and was integral to them, rather than being an optional extra. In this sense, the personality disordered person's current mental state cannot be defined as abnormal in relation to his or her own previous state, but rather only with reference to the population as a whole; and that deviation needs to be perceived as dysfunctional. The problems involved in both obtaining agreement on the diagnosis, where judgments have to be made both about an individual's personality and its impact on his or her life and the lives of others, and the likely effectiveness of treatment, are immediately apparent. Achieving change, beyond mere maturation, is also problematic: demonstrating that change has been achieved, equally problematic.

To avoid the evident difficulties that emerge once one uses the term mental disorder to embrace mental illnesses, learning disabilities and personality disorders, many in the field of 'mental disorder and crime' confine their interest to those suffering from the major disorders of thought or affect that form a subset of Axis I of DSM-IV-TR.[4] That is, typically, schizophrenia, major depression and bi-polar disorder. Some would argue that these major disorders are not as distinct as their designations imply, being rather labels for constellations of symptoms which, to a large degree, overlap in individual patients. Furthermore, because the personality disorders have played such a major role in the debates in England and Wales, to discount these Axis II disorders from discussion here would be misleading. And for other reasons that will emerge below, it may be unduly simplistic to separate Axis I and Axis II disorders; for as John Gunn, one of the UK's most influential forensic psychiatrists, has asserted, UK psychiatrists do not diagnose psychiatric disorder principally with reference to either DSM IV or ICD 10.

It is also evident that disorders come with differing severities: for example, mental illness is manifest across the severity range as neurotic disorders,

4 *Diagnostic and Statistical Manual of Mental Disorders*, 4th edn, Text Revision (2000) American Psychiatric Association.

where insight is retained, and psychotic ones, where there is a breakdown in reality testing. Again, an Eastman analogy is helpful; it is in short a difference between 'building castles in the sky' and 'living in them'. The term serious mental illness has also gained some currency and is used, as its terms imply, for the most severe cases. It has been variously defined, but the common ground seems to be that people with serious mental illness are significantly functionally impaired for an indefinite period (hence, the key factors being diagnosis, disability, duration); at least one per cent of the population are thought to be seriously mentally ill. Whilst serious mental illnesses have been recognised, and classified as diseases, since the time of Hippocrates under the broad headings of melancholia, mania and hysteria, this has not been without controversy or dissent within and outwith the medical profession. Historically, the treatments have been largely physical, and based within a medical disease model. Again, this is not the place to try to do justice to that (for a brief review see Kendell 2001); rather what is required is a broad, if simplistic, appreciation of some of the major features of the mental disorders.

Sub-classifications of mental disorder

In terms of the sub-classifications of serious mental illness one approach would be to conceive of it as a triptych of depression-mania-schizophrenia. This would thus entail first clinical depression, akin to a slowing down of all modalities of behaviour; second, mania, which involves behavioural overactivity, with excessive and abnormal patterns of speech, elevated and irritable moods and grandiose thoughts and perceptions; and third, schizophrenia, both acute, with its positive symptoms of delusions and hallucinations and chronic, with its negative symptoms like loss of motivation and function. Chronic personality deterioration can also ensue. The manifestations of these serious disorders are complex, permeable and culturally contingent. Whilst we would probably all recognise bi-polar disorder (colloquially known as manic depression) there are also the less recognisable schizophreniform illnesses, which present as acute schizophrenia, but do not develop into the illness itself. And schizoaffective disorders, which fall between schizophrenia and some of the manic disorders. Making these diagnoses, particularly where patients have been subject to medication, can be as much an art as a science; obtaining an agreed diagnosis in psychiatry is not straightforward, and as Coulter (1973) illustrates, is subject to a number of 'rules of thumb' (see also Peay, 2003).

Similarly, if taxonomies of mental disorder are but a list of conditions currently treated by psychiatrists, it can be a matter of luck, convenience, and local custom and practice as to whether disorders get treated by psychiatrists or by more physically-oriented clinicians. For example, Alzheimer's can be defined as a mental illness but it is as likely to be dealt with as a physical illness where patients are seen by a neurologist. It is, of course, less stigmatising to be treated by the latter than by a psychiatrist, but it probably makes very little difference to treatment. And where the diagnoses of particular disorders lie on the continuum between mental disorders and neurological disorders may be as much a reflection of their historical genesis and development as of any hard and fast distinctions between them (see generally Wootton 2006 on the development of understandings in 'physical' medicine).

Similarly, personality disorder is classified under a number of different types: schizoid, explosive, affective, obsessional, borderline etc. Borderline personality disorder is most frequently diagnosed in women, and can entail pseudo-psychotic manifestations. It is also the disorder most commonly seen amongst general psychiatric services in the UK. Whether any personality disorder, or all personality disorders, amount to a mental disorder is a controversial question. As touched on above, personality disorders have been presented as being categorically different from mental illnesses: but whether 'deeply ingrained and enduring behaviour patterns, manifesting themselves in inflexible responses to a broad range of personal and social situations' (ICD 10) are a disorder, or a difference, is a moot point.

Two issues arise. First, all those with mental illness will also have a 'personality', so the possibility not just of co-morbid disorders exists, but also of some diagnostic confusion, since the symptoms displayed by those with different diagnoses may be very similar. As Mullen (2006:242) notes, when drawing comparisons between those with schizophrenia and those with psychopathic disorder, 'both groups can be irritable, dissocial, unconcerned about (or blind to) the feelings and interests of others, grandiose, suspicious and negative, can hold unrealistic beliefs of entitlement and fail to learn from experience'. Second, how extreme do the deviations from accepted ways of thinking, perceiving, feeling and relating to others have to become before such deviations would be recognised as a personality disorder? Is it, indeed, primarily the associated offending behaviour that causes such differences between people to come to be deemed a disorder requiring specialist intervention? This is not an easy question to answer. But it should be stressed that for at least some people with recognisable personality disorders the levels of personal distress they experience are not so far apart from those who would conventionally be accepted as mentally ill.

> Dangerous severely personality disordered people often do not get the help they need to manage the consequences of their disorder. Most have a lifelong history of profound difficulties from an early age – many are the children of violent, abusive or inadequate parents, some may have been removed into care. Many are poorly educated and have a history of difficulty in finding work and housing. In adult life they have difficulty forming meaningful relationships with others, frequently become

involved in substance misuse, and suffer from depression or other mental illness. They are more likely than others to die violently by suicide or in accidents. So far no effective strategies have been identified to prevent development of severe personality disorder.

(Home Office and DoH, 1999:5)

Embodied within this quotation are the seeds of the difficulty. Whilst those with severe personality disorder may well be more likely to die violently by suicide, which can be taken as strong evidence of the existence of personal distress, and whilst it is true that those with personality disorder have an increased risk of co-morbid mental illnesses, it is also the case that the personality disordered per se do not feature heavily in our detained psychiatric populations, although they do make considerable demands on primary services, as any GP who has a double-slot booked at the end of the day by a familiar patient will testify. Why specialist services have not similarly grappled with large numbers of personality disordered patients is not clear: is it an inability or unwillingness where such people do not have a co-occurring mental illness, or because such people do not seek out services, whether because they don't experience the distress attributed to them, or because the services are not obviously accessible or available? But their confused status as 'mentally disordered' is evident, not least in the recent history of policy initiatives and legislative reform in the UK.

It is further instructive to read the Home Office and Department of Health's definition of what constitutes personality disorder:

Personality disorder is an inclusive term referring to a disorder of the development of personality. Personality disorder is not a category of mental illness, but a diagnosis of personality disorder, like mental illness and other mental disorders, can potentially be regarded for legal purposes as a cause of 'unsound mind'. It includes a range of mood, feeling, and behavioural disorders, including anti-social behaviour. These may separately or in combination, contribute to identification of severe personality disorder. Those with severe personality disorder generally have an inability to relate to others, poor control of impulses, and difficulty in learning lessons from previous experience. Not all people with severe personality disorder present a risk to society or to themselves. The severity of the disorder may, or may not, be related to the risk posed.

(Home Office and DoH, 1999:5)

Whilst this quotation somewhat plays down the role of offending behaviour, and stresses anti-social behaviour (suggestive of something of a less criminal nature) it is persistent aggressive behaviour that is most likely to lead to a clinician diagnosing anti-social personality disorder. It is also important to emphasise that the diagnosed disorder does not explain the aggression, it simply describes it. It may help to us to understand the disorder's development, progression and remission, and maybe even how it relates to particular offences; but it is not explanatory (see McMurran, 2004). And it bears re-iterating that whilst personality disorder can be regarded for legal purposes as a cause of 'unsound mind', in the absence of offending this is very rarely the case.

Moreover, it was not until the amendments made by the Mental Health Act 2007 to the MHA 1983 that personality disorder became legally a form of mental disorder for which one could be detained compulsorily beyond 28 days. This is an issue that will be dealt with later, but for the moment it is worth questioning whether those decision makers charged with the responsibility for finding legal responsibility (or not) are less enthusiastic about the mitigating persuasiveness of evidence of disorder, when that disorder appears to represent an individual's habitual or 'normal for them' behaviour. And whilst true mental disorder, if it interferes with an individual's thought processes, might properly be deemed as a relevant factor when considering the autonomous choices exercised by the 'reasoning criminal', character traits, features that are much more unlikely to be subject to change, are considerably less enticing as a basis for excusing an individual from the normal processes of the criminal law.

There is also a category of disorders induced by stress and by an acute reaction to it. Many of the symptoms may be identical with those in a psychiatric disease (the individual feels anxious, depressed, manic, amnesic, hallucinating etc) but they arise as a response to extraordinary stress. But both acute stress disorders and personality disorders need to be distinguished from psychiatric disorders 'proper'. There is, then, an interesting parallel with the definition of crime; true crime or real crime is regarded as the 'core business' of the criminal law and the criminal justice process. Yet the vast majority of offences fall on the margins of 'real' crime; such regulatory offences do not have the full stigma associated with 'real' crimes, sometimes because they involve no element of *mens rea* on the defendant's part. But often they do, and yet are still categorically distinguished from 'true' crime. Similarly with psychiatric disorders: there is a central core and then a potentially expanding, and certainly expandable, penumbra. And it is this combination of malleable borders for both mental disorder and crime which constitutes one source of the contentious nature of the relationship between them.

There is also a series of issues about vulnerabilities, which can further confuse the diagnostic picture. People who suffer from a mental disorder will have a prior history and a future, both of which may be relevant to the way in which the disorder manifests itself, confusing any bald criminological interpretation. For example, people who suffer from schizophrenia may have experienced various developmental difficulties which will influence their career prospects; the onset of the disorder itself may be associated with a breakdown in family relationships, increased drug or alcohol use and with breaks in employment patterns; treatment for the disorder may induce side-effects and lead to periods of self-imposed or state-imposed isolation. All of these may influence the possibility of being diagnosed as co-morbid with respect to various personality disorders or to substance abuse disorders. But it is not easy to tell if these are genuine expressions of co-morbidity, or that the underlying disorder simply makes one more vulnerable to the effects of substance abuse or the strains of everyday life. In turn, these may affect one's risk of engaging in criminal activities. The consequence of course is that it makes it problematic when trying to assess, for example, the relationship between schizophrenia and violence, to be confident that one is dealing, for the purposes of a research design, with a 'pure' form of the illness. As Professor Stephen Rose has noted, when responding to research suggesting that the brains of psychopaths were diagnostically distinct, if one focuses on the brains of imprisoned 'psychopaths' one can never be certain if one is looking at an original difference or at the long-term effects of exposure to alcohol, drugs and the prison environment.[5] And, as critically, it is equally problematic for health professionals who need to treat not just an illness but rather a whole person suffering from what may be a complex array of interacting and independent symptoms.

Finally, and leading on from this, there is a question about distinguishing symptoms that may be part of a normal experience, and those that derive from disorder. Psychiatric symptoms are like physical symptoms – not all pain or nausea is a sign of physical illness. Similarly, not all mental symptoms are morbid. This will be self-evident, but normal people have thought processes and normal people have personalities. In the same way that one's personality can deviate from the norm, one's thought processes will equally show a range of variation, and vary under particular conditions, whether affected by age, tiredness, different levels of consciousness, or drugs and alcohol, to name but a few of the relevant factors. Mental disorders rarely affect mental processes absolutely, only relatively. This, of course, poses a very real challenge to those who would seek to connect mental disorder and offending, since it is very hard to be clear about exactly what one means when one refers to a mental disorder. For just as it is probably unproductive to think about mental disorders as being somehow separate from physical disorders (Matthews, 1999; Kendell, 2001) it is certainly unproductive to think of them as being separate from the person: 'In reality, neither minds nor bodies develop illnesses. Only people ... do so, and when they do both mind and body, psyche and soma, are usually involved' (Kendell, 2001:491).

However, it is not my intention here to provide an exhaustive list of diagnostic labels with descriptions, partly because no one system is definitive, and

5 BBC Radio 4 Today programme, 3 September 2009.

partly because, for my purposes, it is more important to focus on symptoms, and, in particular, active symptoms, and their potential relevance to criminal behaviour. This is a course recommended by Mulvey (1994), together with a recommendation that the focus should be on traits, like, for example, impulsivity, rather than diagnoses. Notably, this is an approach that has been tried in criminological research, but has seemingly now been relegated with preference going to a holistic approach to offending. Indeed if personality to some degree influences everyone's behaviour then variations in personality, whether constituting disorders or not, together with the psychological nature of people's internal world and the meaning any offending behaviour has for them, are as likely to prove central to understanding the behaviour as any specific mental disorder.

Disorders and symptoms

A cursory examination of the main forms of psychiatric disorders in DSM IV (American Psychiatric Association, 1994), ranging alphabetically from acute stress disorder to voyeurism, would draw one's attention to some obvious candidates where an association with offending behaviour is almost inevitable; pyromania – 'deliberate and purposeful fire setting on a least two occasions' – would be one such example. Other disorders on the list, such as trichotillomania – 'the recurrent pulling out of one's own hair' – seem much more benign, at least insofar as the criminal law is likely to be involved. Similarly, if one were to look at the categories of psychiatric disorders organised by symptoms and signs, again some categories would strike even the lay observer as being more likely to be associated with conflict with the criminal law: impulse control disorders, such as intermittent explosive disorder, which is characterised by frequent and often unpredictable outbursts of anger occurring, albeit rarely, and mainly in younger people, would be one such candidate.

Perhaps the obvious contenders from such list of disorders would be: confusional states (because of the related inability to recognise the restraining influence of legal and moral norms); frontal lobe syndrome (see Sellars et al, 1993) where people seem to act without thinking of the consequences, and then, if arrested/imprisoned, are very distressed;[6] various addiction states (where the law criminalises the purchase, possession or use of particular substances, making them attainable largely only through illegal means, and increasing the probability of conventional offending for financial gain); psychotic disorders (those who believe, even if wrongly, that they are under threat and who may act disproportionately on such beliefs, taking them outside the

---

6 See *Masterman-Lister v (1) Brutton and Co (2) Jewell & Home Counties Dairies* [2003] 3 All ER 162 illustrating the implications of executive dyscontrol syndrome in a civil context.

remit of any defence they might otherwise have if their behaviour was merely governed by a mistaken belief, as opposed to a psychotically mistaken belief); depression and its specific association with homicide followed by suicide in a domestic context; delusional jealously, which combines elements of psychosis and depression, and its associated violence towards one's partner (see Mullen, 2006); states of mania which may lead to grandiose behaviour, again setting the individual outside the normal social and legal restraints; disorders of sexual drive (problems of excessive drive with no lawful outlet); sleep disorders; personality disorders; and developmental and emotional disorders associated with childhood and adolescence (which is anyway the peak age for offending). But, it is also evident that a number of disorders will have a protective effect, making it much less likely that people would become involved with the criminal law because their opportunities for offending are much more limited (for example, dementia, depressive disorders, obsessive-compulsive disorders – particularly, for example, agoraphobia and social phobias – eating disorders, and a number of the anxiety disorders).

As for symptoms, morbid states of elation might contribute to living beyond one's means (although it is fair to say that many psychiatric symptoms can prove problematic for sustaining job stability and economic well-being); thought disorders that interfere with one's ability to communicate can lead to problematic social interactions; beliefs about thought insertion, and the content of various delusions, particularly where paranoid or persecutory, can bring one into conflict with the law; grandiose delusions may lead an individual to believe that the law does not apply to him or her; visual and auditory hallucinations may again make people feel under threat; and disturbances in one's cognitive functions, of memory, attention, and intelligence, can simply make life more difficult to lead; finally, self-neglect, or its appearance – failing to comply with conventional norms – may invite victimisation.

In short, drawing lines between disorders and symptoms may be artificial: disorders are largely diagnosed on the basis of patterns of symptoms. And it is the focus on symptoms that is likely to prove the most productive.

What causes mental disorder?

This is a much shorter section than that on 'what causes crime'. For mental disorder the causes are sometimes known and sometimes not; and occasionally, the seemingly most likely cause of the mental disorder is crime, or an involvement with the criminal justice process. This thus creates an interesting reversal of the discussion of crime: for here, as will have been evident above, the bulk of the literature concerns the definition and diagnosis of mental disorder, not its causes. In essence, aetiology is the least well-developed part of psychiatry. And whilst the situation is somewhat more developed with respect to organic disorders, for even those disorders establishing true causation is problematic.

To take an analogy, if one were to consider what causes Alzheimer's disease one might be looking at genetic information; am I more likely to develop the disease if there is a history in my family? Or environmental factors; does exposure to particular toxins or the consumption of particular foodstuffs increase my risk? However, these questions pall when one looks at the statistics. One in five of people over 80 will develop Alzheimer's; one in three of those over 90. Thus, this is a disease that is so widespread that it is largely a matter of chronology: if you live long enough, your risk of brain deterioration and failure increases significantly. What causal associations there may or may not be will simply be buried by the correlations between two frequently occurring phenomena; old age and dementia.

My objective here is not to write a text on the causes of mental disorder: indeed, I am not qualified to do so. But rather I want to set out some of the relevant problems, and will do so briefly by reference to personality disorder, because here the ground becomes extremely muddy, and it helps to illustrate the stickiness of the field. For example, personality disorder has widely been held to be causally related to dangerousness, and particularly the antisocial/ psychopathic variants of personality disorder. Yet Rick Howard (2006) has hypothesised that the assumption may be misplaced, and that, insofar as a relationship may exist, it is mediated by a prior factor; namely, the abuse of alcohol at an early age. This is interesting not only because of the insights it may provide into the causation of personality disorder per se but also because it tilts at something of an icon (namely, that those with personality disorder are more likely to be dangerous). As Howard observes 'there currently exists very little, if any, scientific evidence to support such a causal link between personality disorder and dangerousness' (2006:703); indeed, as he argues, verifying any such link is likely to be problematic given the definitional overlap between specific personality disorders and criminal behaviour, and the transition from an association to causality.

Proponents of the relationship between PCL-defined psychopathy and criminality have argued that even when indices of anti-social behaviour are excluded from the measurement of psychopathy (Cooke et al, 2004) other psychopathic personality traits continue to be associated with anti-social behaviour. These cover the constellation of interpersonal, affective and behavioural traits, embracing, amongst other characteristics, glibness, lack of remorse and impulsiveness. Howard, however, argues that a history of early alcohol abuse is a confounding factor and, perhaps most interestingly, points to the literature on successful psychopaths. For example, a study by Board and Fritzon (2005) noted that in their (admittedly small) sample of 39 senior business managers, there was evidence of significant elements of a personality disorder profile. In particular, the managers displayed those elements referred to as the 'emotional components' of psychopathic personality disorder, whilst not showing those relating more to a socially deviant lifestyle, for example, impulsive acting out, physical aggression, mistrust or passive aggressive tendencies. The senior business managers displayed the following personality traits: histrionic (superficial charm, manipulativeness); narcissistic (grandiosity, exploitativeness); and compulsive (perfectionism, stubbornness and dictatorial tendencies). The authors concluded, amongst other things, that personality disorder could be measured as a constellation of traits across normal populations, rather than being categorical states; and in so doing supported the work of Morey et al (1985). Further they argued that it is misleading to describe individuals in terms of single diagnoses of personality disorder, when the presence or absence of underlying traits, and their relative strength, can not only be measured, but also provide a more useful way of understanding personality differences. Exactly why those with a personality-disordered profile should end up as successful business managers rather than in some socially deviant lifestyle perplexed the authors. However, they did stress that looking to the medical model for explanatory assistance seemed wrong-headed.

But what is important here is that a categorical approach to personality disorder, for example that of DSM IV, which represents personality disorders as 'qualitatively distinct clinical syndromes', is misleading. Individuals can succeed with extremes of personality dimensions in other walks of life, without engaging in the dangerous behaviour seemingly associated with a disordered personality, or in anti-social behaviour generally. Or at least in anti-social behaviour as it is conventionally conceived.

If it is indeed the 'impulsive acting out' component that distinguishes unsuccessful from successful psychopaths, this would cast some doubt on any hypothesis that propounded a causal link between psychopathy and dangerousness. Rather, Howard (2006) advocates the role of early-onset alcohol abuse, because of its role in impairing the prefrontal cortex during adolescence, a critical period in its development; such early damage to the pre-frontal cortex can be irreparable. This leads to interference with goal directed behaviour and emotional self-regulation, in turn contributing to greater alcohol abuse. The whole is depicted as a vicious upward spiral of personal destruction, heading ultimately towards adult offending. Of course, this also looks a little glib; but one can see the persuasive weight of arguing that the early use of alcohol (as opposed to its later use in successful business managers) may pre-dispose to a deviant lifestyle, whilst also nurturing the impulsive and irresponsible behaviour that goes with both alcohol abuse and anti-social violent behaviour.

The implications of this hypothesis are that, in order to prevent the development of personality disorder, the early use of alcohol should be rigorously controlled; the hypothesis would point to a worrying failure in today's climate. The alternative perspective is to argue that the personality traits precede the drinking, and that drinking just acts as a trigger to mental disorder (in the same way that the experience of war can do likewise in vulnerable individuals). For my purposes though, the saga simply illustrates, yet again, the problems of thinking about causality on this kind of grand scale.

Chapter 4

Are mental disorder and crime related?

Is there a relationship between mental disorder and crime?

The short answer is yes. But what is its nature? Is it largely a perceived/attributed relationship? Is it an association? Is it causal? And in which direction does the relationship primarily flow? Moreover, if there is a relationship, is intervening in one side of that relationship, possibly with treatment for mental disorder, likely to reduce the incidence of the other, namely criminal behaviour? However, the key questions, adverted to earlier, are why should mental disorder make a difference to the probability of criminal activity, and in what ways; that is, either to increase or decrease its likelihood?

Three illustrations will serve as a reminder of how complicated all this is likely to be. First a report of an exceptional case in which a brain tumour 'caused' a man to engage in paedophilia (BBC News, 2002). The report dealt with a man with no previous history of sex offending who began to show an obsessive interest in child pornography; he also solicited prostitutes at massage parlours. After conviction for molesting children and further persistent inappropriate sexual behaviour he was found to have a brain tumour the size of an egg. The tumour was removed; the man's behaviour improved. At some later point his interest in pornography returned and it was found that the tumour had re-grown; it was removed and the behaviour disappeared. Notably, the two neurologists dealing with the case found the tumour to be located in the right lobe of the orbifrontal cortex, an area of the brain believed to be tied to 'judgment, impulse control and social behaviour' (Choi, 2002). The compromised functioning of this area has also been characterised, somewhat more dramatically, as causing people to be 'biologically disadvantaged in developing a conscience' (see generally Raine, 1993). Of course, the validity of such an explanation is highly vulnerable, as indicated by the comments of a behavioural neurologist, also cited in Choi's article in the *New Scientist*, who questioned whether there may have been hormonal changes due to the tumour. What is exceptional about the report is the chronology of the changes: normal behaviour – tumour – abnormal behaviour – tumour removal – normal behaviour; and then the pattern repeated. The second illustration concerns dopamine agonists.[1] These are administered to treat Parkinson's disease and have been found to have, in rare cases, the curious side effect of producing compulsive behaviour in people who had no history of the relevant behaviours; typically gambling, excessive alcohol and food consumption, and hypersexuality. Taking patients off the medication led to an abatement in the behaviours. Warnings about the drugs are now included in the accompanying information leaflets. Both of these illustrate the potential for changes in the brain to be associated with changes in behaviour: these can in turn be deemed criminal according to the nature of the behaviour expressed. Yet even demonstrable changes in the brain, not in themselves mental disorders but physical changes, do not necessarily cause changes in behaviour. And here the third illustration is helpful. Evidence from positron emission tomography (PET scanning) suggests that the kinds of neurological changes in the brain associated with the development of dementia in older people can be shown amongst much younger people who have none of the relevant behaviours: testament either to considerable plasticity in the brains of younger people or to more complex explanations of the relationship between cause and effect. Or both. It is appropriate to remain cautious about any suggested associations between brain pathology and criminal behaviour.

Does crime cause mental disorder?

The relationship between mental disorder and crime is conventionally thought of in terms of the disorder contributing or leading to crime. But it can be explored in other ways. Are mentally disordered people more likely to be the victims of crime? Certainly, mentally disordered people are as likely to be victims as perpetrators (Teplin et al, 2005) but are they also peculiarly vulnerable to being victimised?

Amos et al (2006:9) assert 'While the media strongly associates mental illness with violence, people with mental health problems are more likely to be the victims of violence than perpetrators'. Even in situations where it might be hoped that people would feel safe, namely, in acute psychiatric hospital wards, high levels of violence are experienced, with 15 per cent of adult patients reporting physical assaults in the year 2006–7 (Healthcare Commission, 2008). Notably, Silver's (2002) study of violence committed against people who had recently been discharged from psychiatric hospitals indicates the important role that conflict in social relationships can have on the likelihood of subsequent violence. Mind's (2007) survey found 71 per cent of those with mental health problems reported having been victimised

---

1 This is a compound that activates dopamine receptors.

in the previous two years. Although this was based on a small sample of 304 respondents (and a response rate of less than six per cent), it should be stressed that 22 per cent reported having been physically assaulted, compared with under four per cent reporting violence, with or without physical injury, in the British Crime Survey (Moley et al, 2007).

Similarly, although also only a small qualitative study of the experiences of 25 community-based service users with schizophrenia, the work of Tony Colombo (2007) gives a critical insight into the experience of victimisation. Almost two-thirds of his respondents had been victimised sufficiently seriously during the previous year to report the incident to the police or their support worker.[2] Moreover these incidents of victimisation took place during everyday activities and included both physical and sexual assaults, together with more routine verbal threats and bullying. Nine of the perpetrators were identified as 'friends' or relatives, with only four of the sample of 23 incidents being attributed to strangers. In turn these incidents led to negative consequences, including depression, alienation, and perhaps most crucially, aggression. Indeed, that the perpetrators were so commonly identified as being within on-going relationships with the victims increases the probability of the perpetuation of such incidents – on both sides. In these circumstances, the problem of unpicking the chicken and egg phenomenon is laid bare.

Protecting those with mental health or learning disabilities from criminal victimisation, and potentially from its sequelae, has received some legislative support with the implementation of those sections of the Criminal Justice Act 2003 which deal with the increase in sentences for aggravation relating to the offender's hostility towards the victim based on disability or presumed disability.[3] But the true extent of such behaviour is very hard to quantify, albeit that there are examples of the most tragic kind. One case would be the suicide of Fiona Pilkington, and the death of her severely disabled daughter then aged 18. Their deaths followed years of abuse allegedly from youths within their locality. It is an example that may yet come to be seen as the 'Lawrence moment for disability hate crime' (see Williams, 2009). At the inquest, the jury identified poor information sharing between

2 See also *R (on the application of B) v DPP and Equality and Human Rights Commission (Intervener)* [2009] EWHC 106 concerning the unlawful discontinuation by the Crown Prosecution Service of a case where the victim, who suffered from a mental disorder, was deemed by the prosecution not to be capable of being a reliable witness. The court attributed this either to a misreading of the medical report or to being grounded on an unfounded stereotype of the witness based on his history of mental problems.

3 In February 2007 s 146(2) and (3) of the Criminal Justice Act 2003 made this a requirement; courts must treat as an aggravating factor any hostility shown towards a victim based on their disability or presumed disability. The difficulty remains that where victims believe that they will not be believed, they are less likely to report offences against them in the first instance.

the police, who had been contacted about harassment no fewer than 33 times over a seven-year period, and the council, who also failed to respond appropriately to her circumstances. That Fiona Pilkington was held to have unlawfully killed her daughter by setting fire to the family's car when they were both occupants, and whilst she was herself not always the willing recipient of help, the context of disability is telling. This case, of a depressed single mother with borderline learning difficulties experiencing repeated victimisation, is unlikely to be an isolated one, albeit that the profoundly shocking nature of the consequences must be unique. The relationship between learning disability, victimisation and criminality remains a fundamentally under-researched area.

Similarly, does crime cause or contribute to the development of mental disorder? Again, there is evidence that involvement with the criminal justice process, and in particular, being subject to imprisonment, justly or unjustly, can precede the development of mental disorder. Anyone familiar with the stream of miscarriage of justice cases will be aware of the damage done to the psychological health of those unjustly convicted (Peirce, 2007). It can, of course, be argued that these were individuals whose initial psychological vulnerability contributed to their confessions, and hence their conviction, but it is equally true that those who did not falsely confess still evidenced the negative effects of imprisonment on their mental health. One such example would be Paddy Hill, who was one of the six wrongly convicted Birmingham bombers. As noted by Peirce, Hill had, on the Gudjonsonn scale, a highly resistant personality but this did not seemingly offer him protection from subsequent mental health difficulties. The mental health of the Guantanamo detainees, and of those foreign nationals interned without trial in Belmarsh Prison under the Anti-Terrorism, Crime and Security Act 2001, is testament enough to the potentially damaging effects of custody. In her obituary for Jim MacKeith, perhaps the most influential forensic psychiatrist working in this field, Gareth Peirce tellingly notes:

> The legislation was repealed, but not until 2005 and only after half of those detained had been driven into serious mental illness. Indefinite detention, as the conscientious joint analysis of 48 separate psychiatric reports demonstrated, was largely responsible for having endangered the mental health of those detainees.
>
> (Peirce, 2007)

Moreover, the findings of the Sainsbury Centre's study of the effects of Imprisonment for Public Protection would similarly point to the damaging effects of indeterminacy (Sainsbury Centre, 2008; Rutherford, 2009). Although it is the case that those selected for IPPs are likely to have a higher incidence of pre-existing mental health problems (higher both than those on life sentences per se and significantly higher than the general prison population), the levels of mental health difficulties disclosed by the research are indicative of the additional detrimental effect of an indeterminate prison sentence on the mental health of those prisoners (see Rutherford, 2009: S49–50). Finally, the incidence of mental disorder in the prison population is significant in both the remand and sentenced populations; and at least some of this will post-date the commission of the offence (Singleton et al, 1998). Whether disorder may be a reaction either to the offence, or to the processes of justice, or to the conditions of imprisonment is explored in greater depth elsewhere (see Grounds, 2004, 2005). But Shalev's (2008) review of the impact of solitary confinement on, amongst other matters, an offender's mental health is testament to the powerful effects of imprisonment on all offenders, mentally vulnerable or not.

Another area where the process of involvement with the law and with courts suggests that mental disorders may be caused by such involvement concerns that of nomogenic disorders (Tyndel and Egit, 1988; Mendelson, 1995, 2007). Nomogenic disorders, as defined by Tyndel and Egit, are 'those conditions in whose development and/or maintenance the law and its implementation play a significant role'; they can include dissociative pseudodementia, drug addiction, alcoholism, PTSD, psychosexual disorders and functional somatic syndromes, namely those in which physical symptoms do not have an objectively demonstrable organic basis. These personal injury litigants have sometimes been disparagingly described as suffering from 'compensation neurosis'. But the clinical basis of the disorders now appears to have a firmer footing, since the evidence shows that even after their litigation is concluded, symptoms can persist in some sufferers (Mendelson, 1995). Mendelson notes that in a follow-up study of 760 claimants for compensation, of the 264 subjects who were not working at the time of conclusion of litigation and who could be traced, 198 (75 per cent) were still not working after an average of 23 months following the completion of their cases. Whilst there are obviously a number of possible explanations for this, the fact that the disorder has persisted even after compensation has been awarded suggests that a purely instrumental basis for the disorder may portray an incomplete picture.

Another pertinent statistic arises from sudden unexplained deaths amongst in-patients, reported by the National Confidential Inquiry into Suicide and Homicide by People with Mental Illness (Appleby et al, 2006). Over a five-year period 235 deaths were identified as being attributable to 'sudden unexplained death'. At first sight this would imply that psychiatric hospitals are curiously unhealthy environments. Notably, but perhaps not surprisingly, of the 235 deaths 78 per cent of the patients had been given psychotropic medication within 24 hours of their death. Other potential factors identified by the inquiry team included the use of restraint and seclusion: six patients had been restrained within 24 hours of their death, of whom four had also been subject to seclusion. The number of homicides committed by people who were described in psychiatric reports as having mental illness at the time of the homicide was 261 for the same five-year period (Appleby et al, 2006:105).

Finally, evidence is emerging, albeit somewhat contradictory, that there appears to be a raised incidence of mental health problems amongst those returning from war. Such an observation perhaps falls into that category of things that one simultaneously knows, and does not know. 'Shell-shock' from the First World War would be my own starting point. More recently there has been coverage of the suicide rate amongst those who fought in the Falklands War (their deaths now exceed those killed in the fighting at the time: Gould, 2007) and of Gulf War Syndrome. Notably, in the UK the latter is not considered to have been brought about by a toxic mix of chemicals administered to the troops to protect them against the possibility of biological warfare, but rather one having psychiatric components.[4] Perhaps most tellingly, a Pentagon task force reported '38% of soldiers, 31% of marines, 49% of national guard members and 43% of marine reservists showed symptoms of post-traumatic stress disorder or other psychological problems within three months of returning from active duty' (Tisdall, 2007). And, of those returning permanently, the mental health of soldiers who find themselves variously unemployed, unemployable and homeless indicate that a war environment is unhealthy way beyond the physical wounds inflicted. The role of homelessness has been well-charted (Fleisher, 1995) but its intersection with mental health and veteran status has become more prominent as a greater number of soldiers are discharged. To illustrate, a report by the National Association of Probation Officers (2009) documents a doubling of veterans in the prison population over the previous six years (constituting approximately 8.5 per cent of the prison population in 2008); over 70 case studies illustrate the toxic mix in veterans of mental health problems, alcohol and drug abuse, and violence, most frequently of a domestic nature: with alcohol seemingly the principal mediating factor. Although it is acknowledged that this population of young men were at risk of offending before entering the military, their mental health at that point was presumably sufficiently good to have been accepted into the services; in the intervening period something has contributed to the development of their problems. As Professor Robbins, the former head of traumatic stress services at St George's Hospital, commented:

> If we are asking people to do appalling things, to take part in regular firefights and hand-to-hand combat, you get to the stage where it

---

4 See Iversen A. et al (2007) with reference to the first Gulf War; Hotopf et al (2007) report that the 2003 Iraq war appeared not to have markedly deleterious effects on health outcomes, except for reservists.

de-sensitises them to violence. It is not just these specific things, but also [for soldiers] there is the constant rising and falling of the levels of tension. In combat, they are constantly on edge and after a while they become constantly on edge.

(The Guardian, 25 Sept 2009:1)

In civilian life, such violence would constitute crime. The argument is not straightforward, for it is the case that unpicking cause and effect, and separating them from pre-existing and on-going factors is tortuous, and that involvement with a cohort of military buddies can have a protective effect. But questions can still be posed about the consequences of involvement in war for the mental health of the participants. Is it involvement in an unjust war; or exposure to scenes of terrible violence; or the direct commission of violence; or a sense of being tarnished by involvement in a war without full support, which is damaging? Indeed, the consequential waves of destructiveness seemingly manifest themselves in ever more complicated ways, as may yet be revealed by the carnage inflicted by Nidal Hasan. Hasan was an army psychiatrist who carried out a mass killing at the military base Fort Hood, in Texas, where he had dealt professionally with returning soldiers; such vicarious traumatisation has already been noted by psychiatrists (Bisson, 2009). Whatever the causes of this particular tragedy, and of the countless lives degraded in less obvious ways, and whatever part mental health difficulties may or may not have played, the manifestations of them are indeed manifest.

Problems with perception?

During the summer of 2008 two novels, *Engleby* by Sebastian Faulks and *The Outcast* by Sadie Jones, were widely available in paperback. Both dealt with similar themes; the influence of childhood experiences on the subsequent development of mental disorder and with redemption; *Engleby* emphasised the psychotic elements of mental disorder and *The Outcast* personality disorder. Both protagonists committed serious criminal offences. Being narrated very much from the perspective of the 'disordered offender' one is struck by the interconnectedness of the issues; of how events rarely have single or simple causes; and of how easy it is to believe of an incident what we wish.

It is therefore not surprising that the commonly held belief of some relationship between mental disorder and crime is long-standing (see, for example, Pescosolido et al, 1999; Philo, 1996 and Pearson, 1999). Long and Midgley (1992), for example, have argued that the historical associations between the two concepts stem in part from a time in the nineteenth century when the boundaries between crime and mental illness were blurred, resulting in even greater definitional overlap than currently exists. Insanity was much more broadly defined so as to include the physically deformed, the socially inept, and some of those who offended. There is, of course, a considerable literature (see for example Scull, 1984; Lowman et al, 1987; Arrigo, 2001) which examines the decarceration and transcarceration theses – the relationships between the shifting populations in prisons, mental hospitals, care homes and the community; and even a 'law', namely Penrose's law, dating back to 1939, which attempted to demonstrate an inverse relationship between the number of mental hospital beds and the number of prisoners. All of this would support the notion of fluidity between these defined populations and their vulnerability to being collapsed together or cut apart; but it is a fluidity that is difficult to establish on a categorical statistical basis (Hartvig and Kjelsberg, 2009).

However, as Long and Midgley further observe, seeking common causative ground between the disordered and those who offended was to the advantage of neither group, as the negative attributions which abounded, of dangerousness and unpredictability, were mutually re-enforced (see Sellars et al, 1993). Even in the twentieth century the same tendencies persisted with Article 5 of the European Convention on Human Rights (ECHR) – the right to liberty and security of person – having exceptions for the deprivation of liberty with respect to criminal matters, but also under 5(1)(e) 'the lawful detention of persons for the prevention of the spreading of infectious diseases, of persons of unsound mind, alcoholics or drug addicts or vagrants'. Moreover, and as will be discussed later, dealing with both disordered non-offenders and disordered offenders under the same statutes, for example, the Mental Health Act 1959 and MHA 1983, can similarly disadvantage both groups. Visionary humanitarian aspirations with respect to the treatment of mentally disordered offenders were laudable in their intentions, but may have produced unintended consequences in respect of the perception of the wider body of mentally disordered people. Detaining the mentally ill alongside mentally disordered offenders in mental hospitals may be more detrimental to the public's image of mental illness, than it is to their image of offenders as rational risk takers.

Similarly, in the early part of the nineteenth century mental illness and criminality became associated partly because of attributions concerning their common causes: environmental issues were thought to be critical in their causation (Long and Midgley, 1992:64–5). If the root of these linked problems lay outside the individual, then they were presumably rectifiable; professional care in the tradition of the medical model was the remedy and the rise of 'moral treatment' the method of delivery. The York Retreat, opened by the Quaker William Tuke in 1796, abjured the use of restraints or medicaments for the calming of those afflicted with disorder of the mind. John Connolly, at the Hanwell asylum, also promoted a humanistic approach; by the early 1840s a number of the other new institutions had adopted similar tactics (Hunter and Macalpine, 1963; and for a comprehensive mental health time-line, see Roberts, 2004). Yet by the 1870s the public mood had changed: disappointment had arisen over the curability of mental illness with moral treatment, and the dominance of physicians in the treatment of what had become to be seen as 'diseases of the brain' returned. Perhaps Scull (1979) was right to argue that this disappointment and the perceived failure of Tuke's approach was attributable to the factory-like scale on which institutionalisation had been introduced; in any event, the stigmatic associations that mental disorder evoked became dominant and remarkably persistent thereafter.

It is not my intention here to deal with the arguments about stigma and its ramifications for those with mental disorder; these have been admirably reviewed by Graham Thornicroft (2006) in *Shunned: Discrimination against People with Mental Illness*; the disproportionate media coverage of mental health and violence is also widely accepted (Shift, 2006, 2008); its detrimental effects are hard to calculate, albeit that significant efforts to counteract this are now underway. But two matters about the relationship between stigma and mental disorder are worth stressing. First, issues of discrimination are central to the argument about the nature of risk and whether those with mental illness are primarily the objects or the subjects of risk. The disproportionate representation of the mentally disordered amongst penal populations has been one such source of methodological confusion and public angst. And secondly, the process of visible 'othering' of the mentally disordered is intimately tied up with the criminalisation of the mentally ill. One thesis would suggest that the process of institutionalisation created the stereotypical criminal type, who was then 'identified' by the professionals (through surveys of such populations) and subsequently 'recognised' by the public. Even as recently as 1980 it has been shown that people carry around an idea of what constitutes prototypical criminal faces (Bull and Green, 1980); the belief that the insane can be visually recognised is long-standing. Ironically, separating the effects of institutionalisation or the side-effects of medication from these prototypical stereotypes is not easy; as Goshen (1967) notes, observable signs of cerebral pathology, for example haematoma of the ear, were as likely in some cases to have their roots in blows by attendants to the individual's head as in any underlying pathology.

Mental disorder and violence: selective perception and reality

It is important to recognise that the literature on the existence and strength of a relationship between mental disorder and crime has ricocheted between positions of scepticism and conversion. A modest emerging consensus is that there is a relationship between some crimes and some forms of disorder, or rather, some people experiencing some symptoms, but that the relationship is slender. There is also an important difference as to the appropriate response to this relationship, which derives in part from differing perspectives on the nature of the harm that can result. The two perspectives can be crudely summarised with reference to how the data concerning the relationship between mental illness and violence might be portrayed; they are the Maden (2007) and the Thornicroft (2006) positions.

Tony Maden's book *Treating Violence* is, paradoxically, not about treating violence at all, since there is a ready acknowledgement that the evidence is too thin to suggest that we can do this. Rather it is a book about clinical risk management and, as Louis Appleby says in his foreword, 'pseudo-liberal attitudes and the mess they have got us into'. It starts from the notion that even if the numbers are small, the harm that can result in individual cases and the ability that clinicians have to predict and intervene in these cases would make clinicians negligent if they did not act forcefully. Indeed, as Professor Appleby asserts in his foreword 'it is an undeniable fact that mental illness is associated with an increased risk of violence'.

In contrast, Graham Thornicroft's book *Shunned: Discrimination against People with Mental Illness* accepts the evidence for a link, but argues that it is not only the incidence of the link that should concern us, but also the perception of the link, since it is the latter which will define our response to this topic. Thus he observes 'by far the strongest defining feature of mental illnesses, according to the popular portrayals in the mass media, is the link with violence' (2006:126). And, of course, it is important to stress that when Thornicroft talks of 'our response' he arguably means not only society's response, but that also of clinicians, researchers and writers. Since when one looks at the interpretation of the data, it is evident that even academics are not immune from a tendency to put a gloss or spin on particular findings. Indeed, I would not absolve myself from this failing; the selection of material for this book and the interpretation I have placed on it will inevitably reflect my own prejudices about the field. So the argument is not that there is not a higher risk, just that our preoccupation with this group's 'risk' is disproportionate and discriminatory. And this in turn may exacerbate the risk by discouraging early and voluntary access to treatment.

Of course, one might argue that these two experts (and both are researchers, clinicians and academics) will inevitably have arrived at conflicting conclusions, given the nature of the place from where they started; namely, Maden's preoccupation with violence and Thornicroft's with stigma. Both agree that violence by mentally ill people is rare; quite how rare is not clear. This is not surprising since reported violence, like reported crime per se, is both an under-reflection of the true incidence of violence and is subject to fluctuations. What is true for ordered violence will be true for disordered violence. But what is important for the argument here is that Maden starts from the premise that risk management and assessment as a part of routine clinical care does not add to the stigma patients' experience; whereas Thornicroft sees it as a potentially damaging preoccupation. It is arguably a bit like the gulf between those who believe that routine breast screening, even though it is damaging in itself, is worth it for the ability to pick up the rare cases that it does.[5] Appleby uses the analogy of plane safety; crashes are rare but we still expect the highest standards. Whether the analogy is wholly apposite, partly because the risk and the harm are not proximate, and partly because a failure in plane safety can have catastrophic results, is debateable, but the fact that it is made is pertinent, since it speaks to the height of the stakes some perceive.

The problem with a 'mental illness causes crime' approach, when based in the individual positivist tradition, is that all one can ever sensibly ask is what difference, if any, to the multiplicity of factors that influence criminal behaviour, might mental illness make – either to increase or decrease the likelihood of its occurrence? There is no doubt that the position is complex. As Graham Thornicroft concludes:

> Whether or not there is any additional risk depends upon the type of diagnosis, the nature and severity of the symptoms present, whether the person is receiving treatment and care, if there is a past history of violence by the individual, the co-occurrence of antisocial personality disorder and substance misuse and the social, economic and cultural context in which an individual lives.
>
> (Thornicroft, 2006:139)

This conclusion is not a reflection of mere academic angst. Rather, it underlies why no grandiose claims for the benefits of treatment are ever likely to be realised. But such a conclusion is also not likely to undermine a prospective belief held by an individual clinician when faced by a particular patient that a difference can be made; for this is one of the golden nuggets motivating therapists. Similarly, prospectively one can argue that a man in a temper with an axe raised who has made threats to kill a named individual, and that named individual is within striking distance, is likely rightly to be predicted to be violent. But that in turn says little about the generality of one's ability to predict given the occurrence of just some of the factors associated with violence in any individual. It is the difference between what we know statistically about groups and what can be known clinically about any individual.

---

5 See, for the conflicting arguments, the Scottish Breast Cancer Campaign: www.scottishbreastcancercampaign.org/screening.htm and Jørgensen and Gøtzsche (2009).

Chapter 5

Types of crime

Mental disorder and non-violent crime

It is a peculiarity of both the research literature and the case law that, in respect of non-violent offending, mental disorder does not feature prominently even though non-violent offending constitutes over 80 per cent of crime (for a contrary example see Amos et al, 2010). There are a number of reasons for this. Not only does the process of pre-trial diversion help to filter away from the criminal courts a proportion of the less serious offences (see Lennox et al, 2009 on the variety of diversion schemes) but also, for those cases that do emerge through to trial, the limited nature of our mental condition defences means that psychiatric evidence has more relevance to disposal than it does to conviction. For example, diminished responsibility is only a defence to a charge of murder; the defence of insanity tends to be raised only in relation to the more serious cases of violence (although it is equally applicable to run-of-the-mill offences) where the potential stigma of a hospital-based disposal following such a finding of not guilty by reason of insanity can be outweighed by the absolution from culpability. Unfitness to plead, discussed later in the book, is progressively diverting potentially culpable offenders away from trial into treatment;[1] and guidance for Crown Prosecutors on the exercise of discretion in respect of the prosecution of those with frank mental disorders who become involved in more minor offending also serves to reduce the numbers of such people in the process. Finally, it is not uncommon for mental health problems only to be revealed on reception in prison, making their relevance to the trial process for those not held on remand problematic. All of this means that despite the inevitable presence of many people with mental disorder in the offending population (see Lord Bradley, 2009) mental disorder does not feature as it arguably should as a relevant factor in determining guilt in non-violent crime.

---

1 The latest tranche of research by Ronnie Mackay and colleagues, commissioned by the Law Commission, is to be published alongside their forthcoming consultation paper on unfitness to plead.

As to the research literature, the bulk of research effort has gone into the more high profile end of offences of violence. Information about non-violent offending does emerge from those studies which have looked at criminal behaviour across the spectrum, but largely what the literature reveals is that those with mental health problems offend in the same way and at much the same rate as 'ordered' offenders. This may, of course, be an artefact of the statistical procedures, in much the same way that some doubt can be cast over the assertion that there is a documented relationship, even if small, between mental disorder and violent offending. So it may be that a 'positive' relationship – a relationship between mental disorder and non-violent offending – exists but is hidden.

The tendency, however, to focus almost exclusively on violence is regrettable. Not only does it contribute to the stigma associated with mental disorder, but it may also impede the development of a fuller theoretical understanding of the nature of any relationship between mental disorder and crime.

What follows is a short analysis of some of those areas where preconceptions abound about the probability of a significant relationship. And, of course, it bears noting that these research efforts will not be completely free of the influence of the preconceptions of researchers in respect of the areas selected for research. Two categories of research are evident reflecting different questions. Are particular offences committed more by those with mental disorder? And do those with particular diagnoses (or particular symptoms) commit more offences than their ordered counterparts? And in each case one can descend to a level of specificity and particularity.

Offence-based studies

Three offence types will be discussed; arson, baby and child stealing, and shoplifting.

Arson

For reasons that probably have as much to do with popular mythology as with any informed analysis, stemming, in my case, from the likes of Jane Eyre and mad Bertha's antics in the attic at Thornfield Hall, arson seems to have some primeval links with mental disorder. Associations have been reported between arson and mental handicap, but there has been little attention in research terms. What studies there have been of the involvement of mentally handicapped and non-handicapped arsonists reveal that they have similar motivations – vengeance and pleasure – and that over half of fires are started at home or in the workplace. This would be consistent both with opportunity theory and with the notion that a proportion of arson is instrumental rather than hedonistic; for example, those seeking better living conditions or wishing to make fraudulent claims on insurance policies can resort to arson seemingly as a quick-fix to what might be regarded by the perpetrators as intolerable pressures.

Soothill's (1990) critical canter through the literature is a helpful starting place. Soothill quickly dismisses any psychopathological all-embracing explanation for arson; indeed, he asserts that the historical search for one has created blinkers on the evolution of an understanding which has to be located not only in individuals, but also on the symbolic role that fire, and in particular arson, plays in different cultures. He argues that it is misguided to think of the arsonist as primarily a source of interest for the psychiatrist; rather the major dimensions for understanding arson are likely to be found in 'structural inequalities in wealth, power and privileges ... it is a crime committed by persons who are relatively powerless and arson may be the way that they articulate their protest about their position in society' (1990:786). That is not to say that there are no differences between the types of arson committed by normal offenders, and for example, arsonists suffering from a psychotic disorder. The former tend to set fire to homes and buildings; the latter, objects that are unlikely to endanger life. As noted above, much of 'normal' arson is instrumental, motivated by revenge, excitement, and/or the desire to achieve particular objectives, such as an improvement in housing conditions, or to claim insurance monies or to cover up other crimes. Interestingly, placing arson within a normalised context draws attention to the fascination that fire holds for us all, and hence the likelihood that much firesetting results from an inability to control one's impulses. Soothill also observed in 1990 that whilst there may then have been some emerging clarity about the nature and treatment of juvenile firesetters, the same could not be said about adults.

So, what is known about juvenile firesetting? Kolko (2004:177), writing about the topic in the US, noted that juvenile firesetting accounted for the majority of arrests in 1994, making 'arson the only crime to have had a higher proportion of juvenile than adult involvement (US Federal Bureau of Investigations, 1995)'. Moreover, arson appeared not to be a crime peculiarly associated with those with mental disorder, in that the only difference noted 'between delinquents adjudicated for arson or another crime was a greater history of past firesetting in the arson group' (Kolko, 2004:180). As interesting are the figures on prevalence for arson, with well over a quarter of children, in both patient and non-patient groups, reporting firesetting or matchplay. The continuity of firesetting over time is also remarkable. The significant predictors of repetition were first, the age of onset, for both patient and non-patient groups (Kolko and Kazdin, 1995); and thereafter, for non-patients, exposure to fire models and parental psychological control; and for the patient group, fire competence, complaints about the child, parental distress, harsh punishment and social service contact. Kolko is worth quoting at length:

... the precipitants for a child's recent incident of firesetting may or may not be related to any of these documented variables, nor reflect the potential influence of other features, such as the child's interest in or attraction to fire, exposure to fire materials, idiosyncratic motives, and limited fire competence ... also, there is considerable variability in the clinical pictures of firesetting youth, given that the behaviour has multiple motives, antecedent conditions, and consequences. Thus it is important to understand that firesetters may vary significantly in level of personal dysfunction, parental effectiveness, family integrity, and exposure to fire-related factors. We know even less about differences between children who present with varying forms of involvement with fire, such as those who set fires, play with matches, mix chemicals and create bombs, or just smoke.

(Kolko, 2004:180–181)

And this is the nub of the problem: arson is a legal category, but it disguises a multitude of different forms of behaviour. Both Soothill and Kolko are pointing to the same paradox: the use of fire is a central human activity and yet its abuse is regarded as somehow unusual and the proper domain of psychiatrists. But this simply may not be the case. Indeed, if one takes the variety of forms of behaviour and then tries to match them with the variety of presentations of factors associated with the perpetrators it is little wonder that no consistent picture emerges of a relationship between mental disorder and firesetting. And why should it, when the attractions (and dangers) of fire are evident to all?

Baby and child stealing

Where arson is an unusually common offence, child stealing is extremely rare (it needs, of course, to be distinguished from those cases where parents snatch children in domestic or cross-border disputes). In a study of 24 female cases by d'Orban (1976) one quarter were by women with mild mental handicap, eight suffered from schizophrenia and the bulk had a primary diagnosis of personality disorder. A tri-part typology of motivation was developed by d'Orban; the offences being (a) comforting – due to deprivation or loneliness – and prompted by a 'normal' desire to play at mothering; these offences usually involved taking the child of a friend or relative (b) manipulative – to control an interpersonal crisis – and tended to involve the taking of a stranger's child (c) psychotic – committed in an acute psychotic state, sometimes as a result of delusional ideas. Whilst this latter group would clearly satisfy any notion of mentally disordered offending, it is notable that amongst d'Orban's 24 mentally disordered cases, a 'normal' motivation could and most probably did underpin some of the offences.

Our sense of the scale of what constitutes 'child stealing' has perhaps been warped by the cases of Joseph Fritzel in Austria, who imprisoned both his daughter and then subsequently three of the children he had by her, and Philip and Nancy Garrido in California, who were charged with kidnapping an 11 year old girl and confining her thereafter for 18 years; whilst atypical in their appalling longevity, it should nonetheless be stressed that approximately half of the offences of child stealing are committed by men. Here, as d'Orban notes (1990) the children are largely older and a sexual motivation is at the heart of the offence; the offenders are not mentally ill and, if they were detained under mental health legislation, had been diagnosed as suffering from psychopathic disorder. Finally, it is important to remember that the great preponderance of child abduction is committed by a parent in a domestic dispute, and, insofar as any offence of this nature can be described as 'normal', it is evident that 'normally' motivated offending prevails.

Shoplifting

This is a category of offence that can truly be described as non-violent. As a type of criminal behaviour, shoplifting raises some archetypal difficulties. It is, first, a very common phenomenon: in 2007 the British Retail Consortium (inthenews.co.uk, 30 Oct 2007) reported detected thefts to the value of £205 million in its survey of British shops, and a rise of 8.5 per cent over the previous year. But 75 per cent of losses went undetected. In 2005, Group 4 Securicor noted that 700,000 people admitted shoplifting from British retailers each year, stealing on average £105 of goods per person.[2] Accordingly, most people who shoplift are successful in evading detection; and most are 'normally' motivated by greed, a lust for excitement or the need to finance a drug habit. The last immediately and necessarily raises issues about the relationship with addiction, arguably making mental disorder, broadly defined, a determinant of offending. The obvious riposte might be that were drug taking not illegal, and the price of drugs fell within the financial reach of the law abiding (like alcohol) then the offending might not occur.

Whilst those with advanced dementia are unlikely to find themselves in a situation where shoplifting might occur, albeit that their mental state would in itself prevent any such 'offence' occurring since the prosecution would be unable to make out the mental elements of the offence (dishonesty and an intention permanently to deprive), the issue of the stereotypical image of the middle-aged, menopausal, absent-minded female shoplifter persists. Whilst this image seems ingrained there is little empirical support for it in the psychiatric literature (Bluglass, 1990). But because shops vary widely in

2 G4S Security Services (UK) 28 November 2005: reporting an OnLineBus internet omnibus survey of 1,204 British adults aged 16–24.

their response to those they catch shoplifting it becomes difficult to disentangle the effects of the exercise of discretion by shops not to pursue perpetrators and the influence that the stereotype has on the exercise of that discretion.

Cases where those who have taken items, and are prosecuted, but who are then acquitted because the prosecution has failed to make out the necessary *mens rea* of the offence are interesting. In cases of absent-mindedness, age-related confusion, or incidents which occur during periods related to an epileptic attack or hypoglycaemia, the prosecution can struggle to establish any positive intention permanently to deprive; or indeed even of dishonesty. In some cases they may fail to demonstrate that the offence was voluntary, and not a case of non-insane automatism. Equally, but facilitating conviction rather than acquittal, some offenders plead guilty, perhaps because they feel guilty or ashamed or just because they want the case resolved, even though the prosecution would not have been able to establish *mens rea* and the individual would have been acquitted had the case been contested. All of that conceded, it is evident that because of the frequency of shoplifting, it is inevitable that some of those who shoplift will be concurrently suffering from a mental disorder. Whether the two are related other than by temporal proximity is what is at issue. Wilkins's (1971) research is pertinent. Of 382 shoplifters apprehended, less than half were charged and, of those who were convicted, the majority ultimately were fined. One male and three females were sectioned under the Mental Health Act 1959. Thus, less than two per cent had manifestly psychiatric disposals, with a further 21 being placed on a probation order.

This would not be wholly to deny the role of mental disorder in shoplifting. Bluglass (1990) helpfully reviews the role of schizophrenia and of depression in shoplifting, where attempts at concealment are rare and it is hard to conceive of these as criminal offences at all. Stealing particular items of clothing in association with a neurotic or sexual dysfunction does occur, but again its frequency in no way reflects its place in popular imagination. Kleptomania, where people have a compulsion to steal, is dismissed as being all but non-existent: although failing to resist an impulse to steal is a little more common, particularly as part of a personality disorder. Finally, there are offenders who appear to have engaged in extensive collecting and hoarding activities, who are then at a loss to explain their motives when apprehended. Such offences can often take place over a prolonged period of time, but not seemingly for an obvious gain.[3]

3 One such example arose in the Isles of Scilly where a woman, who had for many years served this small community in its newsagents, was found to have been taking coins on a systematic basis and hoarding them.

In short, mentally disordered people do commit non-violent crimes, but there seems to be little that is out of the ordinary about this offending; and much that is all too much in keeping with normal offending. And when it is 'out of the ordinary' it looks to be primarily an idiosyncratic symptom of the perpetrator's disorder, rather than a consequence of it.

Diagnosis based studies

Thinking about diagnoses rather than particular offences, Day (1993) conducted a helpful review of the literature on crime and mental retardation. A shift was noted from a general acceptance in the early twentieth century that mental handicap was a major causative factor in crime, attributed to the erroneous use of verbally based IQ tests, to a recognition that there is a very low prevalence of frank mental handicap in delinquent populations. It is also notable that those with disabilities are as likely to be victims as offenders; and when offences are committed against them, they historically have been less likely to be seen as viable victim-witnesses so prosecutions are rare. Day's (1993) analysis raises interesting questions about the relationship between overly protective attitudes to those with learning disability and the more recent focus on inclusivity. Undoubtedly protective attitudes will reduce the opportunities for offending, but may at the same time reduce the opportunities for engaging in other normal activities, for example, sexual activity. Day asserted that 'the overall pattern of sex offending in the mentally handicapped is similar to that in the non-handicapped' but that the former:

> ... show far less specificity in relation to offence type and victim characteristics than their non-handicapped counterparts, the victim's age and sex being largely a matter of circumstance and opportunity rather than an indication of a particular sexual preference or orientation.
>
> (Day, 1993:124–125)

Day also observed a difference between those mentally handicapped sexual offenders whose offending was confined to sexual offences and those for whom it was part of a wider pattern of lawbreaking. The former group tended to show less psycho-social pathology and their offending was attributed in large measure to a lack of 'normal' outlets for their sexual drive. As Day concluded, a more enlightened attitude to the sexuality of this group could significantly reduce the incidence of offending. Thus it is not only legal boundaries that serve to define the incidence of offending, but also social attitudes.

The Camberwell study of detected offending and mental health (Wessely et al, 1994:483) showed that convictions for women with schizophrenia, compared to other mental disorders, increased for most categories of offence (rate ratio 3.3) but the absolute numbers were small and offence categories included prostitution. For men, schizophrenia made no overall difference, although it increased the rate of conviction in African-Caribbean men, and reduced it for other ethnic groups. With respect to violence, discussed in the next chapter, the picture was more complex. But with respect to offending generally the analyses indicate a considerable sensitivity to the role of other factors. Thus, whilst there is an increased risk of conviction amongst those with schizophrenia, it is small; or as the authors put it 'slender'. Whilst not wanting to ignore these findings, since low risk and no risk are not the same, the point is made on the basis of the findings, that yet again, 'The strongest predictors of crime in those with schizophrenia are the same as those in subjects without psychosis' (1994:500).

Chapter 6

Mental disorder and violence

Given the discussion above about the complexity of the behaviours that make up specific legal classifications of crime it is critical to recognise that 'violence' is another term which embraces a multitude of behaviours. Common assault, for example, may entail no more than the apprehension of unwanted touching.[1] Wounding requires the continuity of the whole skin to be broken, but a relatively minor cut could suffice.[2] And robbery (theft with the use or threat of violence) can be satisfied where one 13 year old says to another 'give me your mobile phone or else ...' This is not to diminish the fear and distress that can be caused by these offences, merely to note that offences of violence are distinguished as much by their differences as by their similarities. This caveat is critical when thinking about the validity of statistical assertions.

The discussion will start with a synopsis of some of the methodological difficulties which bedevil interpretation of the data. It then shifts from an analysis of non-fatal violence to the literature on homicide. And it is important to remember throughout that suicides committed by those with mental disorder outnumber homicides by a factor of ten to one. In parts the analysis that follows entails unpicking statistical information, which will be demanding for some and tedious for others. But the claims based on the literature are influential, so going through this exercise is important if a judgment is to be made about whether these claims have any substantial merit.

Problems of methodology

The literature on the statistical basis of the relationship between mental disorder and violence covers much common ground (although that common ground will be contested here). There is an accepted critique explored below that many of the studies are empirically deficient as a basis for drawing

1 *Savage and Parmenter* [1991] 1 AC 699.
2 *Moriarty v Brookes* (1843) 6 C&P 684.

conclusions; hence, much reliance is placed on a limited number of studies, and on meta analyses.

Again, it is difficult to be confident or precise about the nature of the relationship. At times, assertions have been made for a positive and causal relationship; at others, that those with mental illness have no greater tendency to violence than those without. The difficulty which dogs the interpretation of the evidence is that neither mental illness nor crime occurs in a vacuum, and it is difficult to disentangle the various factors that make real world occurrences so messy to deal with. Thus, too much of the historical research has used convictions as a measure of incidents of violence; yet we know that the criminal justice process only partially, and then only in a very selective way, convicts perpetrators. Pressures at court to obtain guilty pleas can result in the downgrading of charged offences, so that an individual who may have committed a s18 offence (causing grievous bodily harm with intent)[3] may plead to a s 20 (infliction – no intent) offence, making any subsequent analysis of the meaning of conviction statistics problematic. Similarly, whilst the relationship between conviction and all crime committed would indicate a conviction rate of between 2–3 per cent (Ashworth, 2005) the figures for violence are significantly higher. Even so, most violence perpetrated does not end in a successful criminal conviction. Hence, the better studies use self-report measures of violence and seek confirmation from third party informants (for example, the MacArthur studies discussed below). Even then, definitions of what constitutes violence can vary considerably across different studies, so rarely are like cases dealt with alike.

Second, compared with non-violent offences, the occurrence of violence is rare; it has a low base rate. Violence by those with mental disorder is similarly infrequent. Making associations between rare events is problematic. There is somewhat greater confidence about the associations between drug/alcohol use and violence, albeit that, as Collins (2008) observes, most people who drink are not violent. But when they are violent their tendencies to incompetence make them easier targets for subsequent identification. These associations between substance abuse and violence are as true for those who do not have a mental disorder as for those who do. So, separating out the influence of the mental disorder element is tricky. And this becomes even trickier when 'mental disorder' is taken to embrace either drug addiction or drug dependence or alcoholism or all three, raising the further problem of whether the distinction between use and dependence is consistently applied.

Third, the greatest association between crime and a single factor is that of gender, so should we always separate out mentally disordered men and women, in order to ensure that it is not maleness that is having the greatest effect? On the other hand, there is evidence that whilst the disparities

3 Offences Against the Person Act 1861.

between male and female offending are considerable in 'ordered' populations, the same may not hold true for disordered populations, or at least in
women with mental health disorders. For example, one prospective study of
those with schizophrenia in the community, which included self-report
measures, noted that very similar proportions of men and women committed assaults during the two year study period (Walsh et al, 2004). Moreover,
Wessely (1997) found, on the basis of his longitudinal study in Camberwell,
that whilst men with schizophrenia have an enhanced risk of being convicted of violent offences, women with schizophrenia have an overall
increased rate of conviction: that is, their enhanced risk of conviction is not
confined to offences of violence per se (see also Robbins et al, 2003). Accordingly, the picture is complex and gender is a factor that requires careful
analysis when thinking about the statistics.

Fourth, economic and other structural conditions need to be taken into
account: for if these do have a major part to play, anything that predisposes
those with mental disorder to find themselves located amongst the economi-
cally or structurally disadvantaged may misleadingly enhance the seeming
influence of mental disorder. For example, and this point is frequently made,
the tendency of those with mental disorder to drift into conditions of instability, both in respect of their housing and their employment, may take them
geographically into high crime areas, making them both vulnerable as
victims and enhancing their prospects of becoming involved with violent
crime.

As with geography, chronology is also critical: if mental illnesses vary
over time in their severity, with symptoms both showing a natural variation
and a response to medication, then it is important when examining the evidence to determine whether one is dealing with someone who has a history
of mental illness or someone who is currently experiencing acute symptoms
at the point of the violent incident. And people with a history of mental
disorder will find that their opportunities to commit violent crimes vary
across time, according to their relative freedom. Too many studies, when
thinking about the natural chronology of people's lives, have focused on
populations who were easy to interview, easy to track or easy to document.
Using confined populations, rather than community samples, will inevitably
skew one's findings; confined populations will be those who have already
drawn attention to themselves, and are people who are more likely to have
been violent in the past. They will also be people whose opportunities to
commit violence, or rather documented violence, will be reduced because of
their periods of incarceration, resulting in their recorded offending being
probably an even greater under-representation of their true levels of violence than for non-incarcerated populations.

Finally, as Hiday (2006) has noted, factors such as the presence of drug
abuse, anti-social personality disorder, victimisation, community disorganisation, strained family relationships, lack of employment, low social skills

and homelessness can occur and co-occur, confounding any effects that the mental illness might be having. And Hiday makes this observation whilst acknowledging that most studies do control for the issue of gender, age and previous violence when attempting to disentangle what begets what. The implications are clear; for as she concludes 'It is too simplistic to think that treating the psychosis alone will be effective in reducing violence, given the complexity of causation' (2006:324).

Violence and mental disorder: a brief synopsis

Four conclusions can be agreed. First, the victims of violence by the mentally disordered are most likely to be, setting aside arguments about self-harm and suicide, their families and friends, not strangers. Second, the prevalence of mental disorder in incarcerated populations is disproportionately high. Third, there is a higher incidence of violence by those who are detained on grounds of mental disorder (frequently because violence has become one of the selective hurdles for access to beds). Fourth, the prevalence of violence after release varies: in some groups, for example those with long-stay records, it is significantly reduced; for others, especially where there was a prior record of violence and the period as an in-patient quite short, it is enhanced. Undoubtedly, those with mental disorder are likely to be more visible and less discreet in their actions, exposing them to a greater risk of apprehension (Stinchcombe, 1963); and thereafter arguably they are both less deferential to the police and more likely to be perceived as in greater need of intervention, both of which will enhance the prospects of arrest (for example, see Muir, 1977).

So what do the best studies suggest about the relationship between mental disorder and crime?

It has become something of an article of faith when discussing this area to note Monahan and Steadman's conclusion, following their extensive review of the field, that 'rates of true and treated criminal behaviour vary independently of rates of true and treated mental disorder'; and indeed that a higher rate of crime amongst the mentally ill and a higher rate of mental disorder amongst criminals tend to disappear once appropriate statistical adjustments were made for 'age, social class, and prior exposure to the mental health and criminal justice systems' (1983:181). That said, commentators then note Monahan's seeming retraction from this ten years later with his 'I now believe that this conclusion is at least premature and may well be wrong' (1993:287–88). The problem he identified lay with the original exclusion of socio-economic status; if having a mental illness did lead to a greater likelihood of downward social drift and this in turn contributed to the probability of violence occurring, then to exclude social class would be to confound the results. Similarly with institutionalisation: if mental disorder increased the likelihood of institutionalisation, then to control for institutionalisation would bias the results against the probability of finding an association. The difficulty of course is that in neither case is the excluded factor solely accounted for by the presence of mental disorder, so the issue becomes one of degree. To exclude completely will bias against establishing a relationship, to include will bias in favour. So the truth probably lies somewhere between the 1983 and 1993 positions. As Monahan subsequently observed:

> ... no matter how many social and demographic factors are statistically taken into account, there appears to be a greater-than-chance relationship between mental disorder and violent behaviour. Mental disorder may be a statistically significant risk factor for the occurrence of violence ...

but as he explains further:

> ... demonstrating the existence of a statistically significant relationship between mental disorder and violence is one thing, demonstrating the legal and policy significance of the magnitude of that relationship is another. By all indications, the great majority of people who are currently mentally disordered – approximately 90 per cent from the Swanson et al study – are not violent ... The policy implications of mental disorder as a risk factor for violent behaviour can only be understood in relative terms.

> (Monahan, 2007:144)

So Monahan's conclusion to this 24-year trilogy might be captured by his assertion that whilst there is largely agreement that 'active mental disorder is a modest risk factor for violence' (2007:146), there is also considerable disagreement over the policy and legal implications of this 'modest' relationship.

Violence and mental disorder: the evidence

I want to start by looking at one study in detail, Steadman et al (1998), because its design captures a number of the critical features that are missing from so many of the other studies in this field. Moreover, the study bears examination here as it will crop up at a number of points below. Even as part of the MacArthur programme (see generally Monahan et al, 2001) its design is not without fault. But critics of the programme (see, for example, Maden 2006:36–38 for a review of these limitations) are never loathe to pay tribute to its considerable achievements.

The Steadman et al (1998) study is of critical importance since it takes a sample of 1,136 in-patients from three sites in the United States and prospectively follows them into the community for their first year after discharge. During that period interviews were conducted every ten weeks with the sample to ascertain the occurrence of violence. The design is notable because it both includes for one of the sites (Pittsburgh) a sample of non-patients living in the communities to which the patients were discharged, and sought information on violence from three sources: official data, the participants themselves and collaterals of the participants. Despite the high initial refusal rates it is an admirably designed and executed study. Six features of the findings are worthy of comment here. First, the level of violence which emerges from agency records of the discharged patients was 4.5 per cent; yet by using the three independent sources of data the rate of violence rose to 27.5 per cent; that is six times higher. This speaks volumes about the inadequacy of any study that relies solely upon official records. It also speaks to the levels of unreported violence. The inherent limitations of all crime statistics have been fully documented elsewhere (Maguire, 2007), but it cannot be stressed sufficiently just how limited such statistics are. Second, the Steadman et al study notes that in the absence of symptoms of substance abuse there was no significant difference in the prevalence of violence between the patient sample and the non-patient sample. Third, substance abuse symptoms significantly raised the rates of violence in both groups. Fourth, the levels of violence in the patient sample declined over the year's follow-up; this may be indicative of the success of treatment, since violence levels were at their highest in the 10 weeks *before* admission. Fifth, a higher proportion of the patient group reported symptoms of substance abuse. And finally, violence in both groups was most frequently targeted at family members and friends and took place at home. All of this would seemingly point to the mediating relevance of the role of substance use in violence, rather than to the dominance of any underlying mental disorder.

So how could the picture have become so confused?

The sceptics

One attempt to address the difficulties arising out of this complex area, where the literature on the nature of the associations between mental disorder and violence is contradictory, was that of the Mental Health Division of Health Canada; they commissioned a critical appraisal of the literature (Arboleda-Florez et al, 1996) to determine whether there was sufficient evidence to conclude that mental illness causes violence. In essence, the authors argued that 'conclusions about a causal relationship between mental illness and violence may well be hasty and that the empirical evidence concerning a statistical association between mental illness and violence remains largely equivocal' (Arboleda-Florez et al, 1998:S39). As they note the literature is based on a number of different kinds of studies, using different sampling frames: the general population, tracked birth cohorts, psychiatric patients and imprisoned offenders. As will also become evident each kind of sample has its own peculiar methodological limitations. Although many of the more recent studies have come to the conclusion that there is a relationship between mental illness and violence, it is questionable as to whether one can effectively summate these findings, and assume that the methodological limitations cancel one another out, so as to argue that the picture is a consistent one, and thereby arrive at a causal association. Reservations have, of course, already been expressed about what is meant by a causal relationship, but Arboleda-Florez et al (1998:S39) go further to argue that such causal inferences could only be drawn once cohort studies of at risk individuals (namely those who have not already been identified as violent) had been done in representative populations including both the treated and untreated mentally ill. As they then observed 'To date no such studies have been conducted'.

To summarise this critique, the sorts of methodological difficulties encountered in these studies include:

– problems of defining and classifying both mental illness and violence
– a failure to determine the temporal order of mental illness and violence
– selection biases, for example the tendency to focus on institutionalised populations, and discharge samples from them, means that there will be pre-existing enhanced rates of violence. To compare these selected samples with the general population, where the denominator will include groups with historically lower rates of offending, will invariably bias results in favour of a positive association between mental disorder and violence
– failure to control for treatment effects in samples of the mentally ill
– failure to control for the effects of confounding – that is, confusing the effects of an extraneous variable with the effects of a study factor. This may occur either where the factor constitutes a link in a causal chain, or where factors co-occur and the presence of one makes it more likely for the second to be identified. Thus, the presence of violence has increasingly been influential in the classification and diagnosis of mental disorder;[4] similar difficulties have arisen with respect to the identification of dangerous severe personality disorder (DSPD) in England and Wales.[5]

Ideally therefore reliable evidence on which to draw conclusions about any relationship will come from studies that use unselected samples, tracked over time, where both the incidence of mental disorder and violence are carefully measured and all confounding factors are adjusted. That such

4 See Arboleda-Florez et al (1998:S41), and Harry (1985) on the analysis of the changes in the Diagnostic and Statistical Manual.
5 Whether the disorder has viability in the absence of violent offending is addressed later in this book.

studies do not exist, and are arguably unlikely to exist, makes the drawing of causal influences in this field highly problematic.

Good, less good and bad evidence

Over the last few decades there have been more studies of the relationship between mental disorder and violence than it would be sensible for me to list: but most of these, whether looking at rates of violence in populations who have been confined at some point, or at the presence of mental disorder in violent populations, have been methodologically flawed so as to make even their listing questionable. The analysis below focuses either on meta-studies, which attempt to combine data from different studies, or from reviews of reviews, or on the very limited number of studies based in the community on unselected or partially selected samples. Even these studies, as will emerge, are not wholly aproblematic, but they do tell a tale that is worth reviewing.

In 1999, Badger et al published a systematic review of post-1983 international literature on the epidemiology of mentally disordered offending, including studies in special hospitals and prisons. In the same year, a linked publication (Woodward et al, 1999), based on the same systematic review, focused on non-confined populations, a setting where unbiased and generally applicable results are most likely to be obtained. Distinguishing between confined populations and those who have never been admitted to a psychiatric hospital is critical, since the latter group show reduced levels of violence (Geddes and Kendell, 1995), whilst those patients with schizophrenia who have been admitted are more likely to have been violent (Castle et al, 1994). It may therefore be that it is the violence element that induces an institutional response, not the schizophrenia per se.

Three features from this international systematic review are notable. First, the authors acknowledge that any review in this area needs to handle data relating to the extremely complex interaction of three things, 'each of them ill-defined, culturally relative and subject to changes in conceptualisation and practice: mental disorder, offending behaviour, and the administrative systems set up to manage both of these' (Badger et al 1999: executive summary). Second, the authors of the non-confined studies draw attention to the relative paucity of epidemiological information (Woodward et al 1999:108), and its poverty in statistical quality due, amongst other factors, to the failure to consider confounding effects. Finally, all the authors stress that the prevalence of mentally disordered offenders in the psychiatric population is low (let alone in the population as a whole).

> Generally speaking, people who have been diagnosed with schizophrenia or learning disabilities are not dangerous to others, nor do they commit criminal offences at a greater rate than the general population.
> (Badger et al, 1999: Executive Summary, section 7)

But there are a small number who do.

Dealing first with the Woodward et al review of non-confined populations, details are included of the epidemiologic catchment area study in the USA (Bourdon et al, 1992). This entailed a survey of 18,571 adults, with interviews being conducted in five sites, with repeat interviews in two waves over one year apart. Other publications report data from subsets of the surveys: the mental disorder elements used DSM III, with violent behaviour being identified via five specific questions in the Diagnostic Interview Schedule, together with self-reports of arrests and convictions; Swanson et al (1990) is the most widely cited, and this subset was based on 10,059 adults, although, sadly, there was no independent verification of criminality since the estimates of violence were based on self-reported data. Whilst the chance of violent behaviour having occurred was greatest amongst those groups where it would be expected; men, the young, and amongst the most deprived socio-economic groups, of the 368 people who reported violent behaviour in the past year, 55 per cent had a psychiatric disorder compared with 20 per cent of the non-violent people. Tony Maden (2007:21–22) observes that this study 'asked a sensible question and chose a perfect sample' and found that 'violence was reported by two per cent of those with no psychiatric diagnosis, by eight per cent of people with "pure" schizophrenia, and 13 per cent whose schizophrenia was complicated by substance misuse or personality disorder'.

At first sight, this looks like persuasive evidence. Indeed, the Swanson et al study did conclude that those in the community with serious psychiatric disorders were more likely to engage in violence than those without; with violence being defined as having used a weapon such as a gun or knife or having been involved in a fight that came to blows with a person other than one's spouse or partner. But, when looking at criminality generally, where larger numbers were involved, the elevated rates for mental disorder embraced a multitude of diagnoses; and when unpacked, it emerged that antisocial symptoms and substance abuse had the strongest associations. Indeed, of mania/psychosis, panic/agoraphobia and depression, only mania/psychosis remained a significant predictor of crime once antisocial behaviour or substance abuse were controlled, and when combined, even this significant finding evaporated. And, of course, returning to the discussion of nomogenic disorders above, over the period of a year it was not always clear which came first, crime or mental disorder, so the study cannot reliably advance any causal hypothesis.

Thus, the Swanson et al (1990) catchment area study, described by Arboleda-Florez et al (1998:S43) as representing 'the state of the art in psychiatric epidemiology', impressively overcomes the problem of selection bias, but then encounters the difficulty of temporal order. Its measure of violence also overlapped with the diagnosis of mental disorder, since common interview questions were used for both. Indeed, using self-report methods may also encounter the problem that arises from a differential preparedness to report socially undesirable behaviour: maybe some people, whether due to mental disorder, criminality or some other shared underlying personality difference, are simply more prepared to report both behaviours, thereby disproportionately enhancing their seeming association (but see Link et al, 1992 below, where this factor was controlled). And finally, there is no means of knowing whether the individual acts of violence committed by those who had also experienced mental disorder was actually attributable to the disorder or to some other factor: the presumption prevails that if mental disorder has been present, the act will be attributed to that, rather than to any other potentially 'normal' motive.

The New York study (Link et al, 1992), among other analyses, compared 386 individuals who had never sought psychiatric help, with 111 who had had psychiatric treatment, but not in the last year. The latter group were between two and three times more likely to have been violent than the former group; and more likely to have been arrested during that year. The study is notable for three reasons. First, they controlled for an impressive range of factors that might otherwise have explained their findings. Secondly, they did, in particular, control for the subject's 'need for approval' on the basis that patient samples might be more willing to report deviant behaviour. But perhaps most interestingly, in respect of the discussion below in relation to 'what is it about mental disorder that might enhance the risk of offending?', they controlled for current symptomatology. And when they did this, there were no significant differences in recent violence between the two groups: most crucially, psychotic symptomatology was strongly related to aspects of violent behaviour, even when the factors of alcohol and drug use were accounted for. Actively experiencing psychotic symptoms, amongst both groups (that is both the 'known as previously mentally disordered' group and the 'never sought psychiatric help' group) was associated with violent acts.

Looking at the Scandinavian studies Woodward et al conclude (1999:108) 'All types of MD seem to be associated with all types of crime, but particularly violent crime'. This is an important sentence, since it will crop up again in the Bristol Review (Amos et al, 2006) discussed below. Notably though, its association there with the Scandinavian studies has been somewhat buried; so it is important to assess just how relevant these studies are. Woodward et al are cautious, since they recognise that bias can creep into the interpretation of data where different countries adopt different approaches to the practice of psychiatry and the organisation of a country's criminal justice process. To give one small illustration; if mental disorder is treated primarily on an out-patient basis, any hospital based data will inevitably be reliant on the more extreme cases which cannot be dealt with outside of the hospital. Sensitivity to such issues is not always apparent when summaries of research are reproduced. Similarly, the Scandinavian studies are based on official records, which have inherent biases. So caution should always be exercised when looking at data from other jurisdictions. Whilst similar in many respects to the UK, the Scandinavian countries are also very different in important ways: they have lower base rates of violence, they are relatively homogeneous societies, and they enjoy relatively uniform prosperity. And these differences are superimposed on what are detailed differences between the legal and administrative differences between our mental health and criminal justice systems.

On the positive side, the Scandinavian data do have the advantage of being based on large, virtually complete cohorts with information being routinely recorded. The Finnish study (Tiihonen et al, 1997) notes that of 5,636 men 2.1 per cent will have both committed a criminal offence (unsurprising) and been diagnosed with some kind of mental disorder by the age of 26; but that for 72 of these 116 men the crime will have occurred before the first positive psychiatric assessment (again perhaps unsurprising). The Ortmann Copenhagen study (in Danish) from 1981, and cited by Woodward et al (1999), demonstrated that 83 per cent of men with substance abuse or dependence had a criminal conviction; whilst 43 per cent of those with a major mental disorder and 35 per cent of those with no mental disorder had convictions, confirming again the widespread risk of criminal offending, but an enhanced risk in the presence of mental disorder. The Swedish Metropolitan Project (Kratzer and Hodgins, 1997), based on 12,717 subjects, found childhood conduct problems were associated with later classification as a mentally disordered offender. Generally crime was much more likely than mental disorder, there was an association between mental disorder and crime (especially for women) and that offenders with major mental disorder tend to commit more offences than do offenders with no mental disorder. However, the confounding effect here is that the data are based on convictions, a poor substitute for self-report data.

On the other hand, there are interesting findings about the nature of offending, with theft and traffic offences being the most common amongst both mentally disordered and mentally ordered men. Violent offences were elevated for both men and women, but particularly so for women where the base rate for ordered women was very low (one per cent) rising to six per cent amongst those with a major mental disorder. The Danish Study (Hodgins et al, 1996) had a sample of 324,401 people, and used the psychiatric register, itself based on psychiatric ward and conviction data. This study suggests again that drug use disorders are most likely to elevate the risk of criminal conviction; interestingly it also suggests that those with mental disorder might be more likely to have a raised risk of offending after 30 years of age (normally, the peak age for offending in the general population lies in the teens) and that 'criminals with mental disorder are more likely to commit crimes of a violent nature' (Woodward et al, 1999:107 interpreting the Danish study). Again, the caveats above need recalling: violence in the Danish study included 'unlawful threat and molestation' and was comparing those with mental disorder with psychiatric admissions against those with no psychiatric discharges on their records. The risk of selection bias is evident. Finally, there is the Stockholm study of 790 discharged patients with schizophrenia (Lindqvist et al, 1990); the cohort committed around four times as many violent offences (based on conviction data) as the general population, when controlling for age and sex. But again, these data need to be seen in the light of the fact that this is a discharged sample (so perhaps these individuals were being more carefully regulated by all who knew them than the general population) and that it is based on conviction data, which are a measure of unsuccessful offending. The Woodward et al (1999:108) review of these studies laments the lack of professional statistical input, noting 'confounding and interaction are barely considered and the cohorts described here are treated as fixed cohorts, rather than using survival analysis'.

Thornicroft (2006), citing Angermeyer (2000) who reviewed violent behaviour by people with schizophrenia in seven countries, notes that for men rates of violent behaviour were between 3.9–8.0 times higher than for the general population, and for women 4.3–4.4 times higher. Thornicroft also cites the same Danish study (using the 1944–47 birth cohort above), but he observes:

> when schizophrenia, bipolar disorder and organic brain syndromes were combined, criminal violence was higher for this group than for people never admitted for psychiatric treatment: 2.0–8.8 times higher for men and 3.9–23.2 times higher for women. These higher rates were explained in part by demographic factors (such as neighbourhood of residence) or by substance use, rather than by the type of mental illness.
> (Thornicroft, 2006:128)

Here we see the same data, albeit from a later publication involving the same authors (Brennan et al, 2000), being used, but a different interpretation being emphasised. Two further features emerge of note from this Danish record-based study (2000:495–6). First, violent offences were defined as including murder and attempted murder (at 18.6 per cent of total) and domestic violence was recorded at 0.09 per cent total. To my eye, the former looks high and the latter extraordinarily low. This might suggest either that Danish society is very different from British society, or that the figures are an artefact of some combination of legal and record-taking processes. Second, those with organic brain syndromes emerged as having the highest risk for violent crime amongst the male cohort; as the authors observe, this is consistent with other studies, but has drawn remarkably little attention in the 'mental disorder and violence' literature.[6]

---

6 See the earlier discussion of one man's history of brain tumours and sexual offending.

One of the problems in this area is that there is a multiplicity of studies on mental disorder and violence, many of them relating to schizophrenia, and many of them badly done. Cross-study comparisons can be highly confusing. So there is a natural tendency to rely on the limited number of studies that are thought to be well done, and on the reviews (or reviews of reviews) that attempt to summarise what is reliably known, or what can be gleaned looking across the data. But this understandable tendency brings its own drawbacks, one of which I shall refer to as the '45 minute' problem.

In the run-up to the 2003 Iraq war, in the government's dossier *Iraq's Weapons of Mass Destruction: The Assessment of the British Government* (September 2002 HMSO), the following assertion was made: 'military planning allows some of the WMD to be ready within 45 minutes of an order to use them'. In fact, this assertion was made four times in the document, including once by the then Prime Minister Tony Blair in his Foreword. Whilst mere repetition of a catchy phrase does not make it true, it may make it very influential, as events in the UK Parliament and Iraq subsequently proved.[7] And this is what needs to be guarded against when trying to make sense of the literature on mental disorder and violence. Thus, the most recent systematic review of reviews (Amos et al, 2006) asserts that 'All types of mental disorder seem to be associated with all types of crime, but particularly violent crime' no fewer than four times (at pp 4, 26, 87, 108). Yet this assertion comes, in the original, from the Woodward et al (1999) review of the Scandinavian studies above (Tiihonen et al, 1997, Kratzer and Hodgins, 1997, Hodgins et al, 1996). The same sentence notably also appears in the linked Badger et al (1999) review, which also cites the Scandinavian studies (Tiihonen et al, 1997, Hodgins, 1993, and Kratzer and Hodgins, 1997) all of which relied on information from official records, such as police records and psychiatric admissions, without self-report data. Thus:

> The major findings of the Scandinavian studies are that the prevalence of mentally disordered offenders up to the age 26–30 is between 2.1 and 2.8 per hundred for men and about half this for women. All types of mental disorder seem to be associated with all types of crime, but particularly violent crime. Conduct problems in childhood seem to be good predictors of future mentally disordered offenders.
>
> (Badger et al, 1999, Executive Summary, section 5)

---

7 Paul Rock kindly alerted me to the significance of Lewis Carroll's (1876) *The Hunting of the Snark* a poem which tells of the search for an imaginary creature. The Bellman, on landing the crew at a place he identifies as 'Just the place for a Snark!' observes 'I have said it thrice: What I tell you three times is true.'

Notably, both the 1999 Badger/Woodward reviews that made the original assertion above are hedged with caveats about the nature of the data; caveats that by the time of the Amos et al (2006) review are notably less evident.

Yet curiously, the executive summary to the Amos review, having made the assertion about 'violent crime', states:

> Major predictors of recidivism are virtually the same for mentally disordered and non-mentally disordered offenders with demographic and criminal history variables being the best predictors and clinical features being less good predictors.
>
> (Amos et al, 2006:4)

The final report of the review also asserts that 'Mentally disordered offenders were less likely to re-offend generally than non-mentally disordered offenders' (Amos et al, 2006:92). It is perhaps unfair to subject a systematic review to too detailed an analysis, since it is inevitable that there will be contradictions within the various studies reviewed. However, it is interesting to speculate why mental disorder would be particularly associated with violent crime, but not be a predictor for recidivism? One answer might be that these offenders have been treated, but the Amos study refutes the notion that we have good studies to show that interventions can reduce violence in people with mental disorder; and in any event the fact that clinical features are not particularly good predictors might suggest that intervening at this level is less likely to have any reliable impact on subsequent offending. Another explanation might have to do with the diversity of offending and the greater probability that violent offending, if it occurs, will be detected. But the overall picture is clearly confused.

To re-group briefly, the evidence presented so far on mental disorder and violence does not look overwhelming, albeit that those with serious mental illnesses seem somewhat more likely to be assaultive, in the Swanson et al sense above, than those without; but not as assaultive as those abusing drugs or, most problematically, abusing drugs in the context of a serious mental illness. And at this juncture it is perhaps worth adding some further difficulties to the pot. Whilst we have already noted the tendency to generalise in respect of 'violence' and to rely upon contentious data, there is another problematic tendency; namely, the tendency to particularise. As Hiday (2006) has eloquently illustrated, mental disorder is further refined in some studies as mental illness, major mental disorder, serious mental illness or schizophrenia. Moreover, these subgroups can be refined yet further by addressing, and just to give one example, those with paranoid schizophrenia who are no longer medication compliant. Is there an association, the proponents argue, between the people manifesting these criteria and violence? Quite how useful such questions become when so refined is problematic. The best statistical evidence, of course, is based on large groups. The bigger the group the better is the evidence when an association is demonstrated. But the question people really want answered relates to the individuals about whom specific decisions must be made: will this person go on and offend violently in the near future? And here the conflict is at its most stark between an individual/clinical approach – who I am holistically – where there are multi-factorial influences on what I do and who am I, and the scientific approach, which is trying to tease out those factors that are truly important by using large numbers.

Secondly, the more particular one becomes, the smaller the numbers get. Thus, as Hiday (2006:319) points out, looking at the Arseneault et al (2000) Dunedin study in New Zealand, it appears at first sight that those with schizophrenia-spectrum disorders are eight times more likely to be violent (this relates to relative risk) than those with no psychiatric disorder; but, when 'sex, socio-economic status and all other concurrent disorders are controlled, their relative risk of violence declines substantially'; namely, to 2.5 times that of controls. But, of the 39 people who suffered from schizophrenia spectrum disorders, only six were not co-morbid. And of these six, who constitute a very small number on which to draw any conclusions, although they may not have been dependent on alcohol or marijuana that would not exclude the possibility that these individuals were abusing such substances. Thus, as Hiday points out, the link between pure major mental disorder and violence begins to look somewhat unstable. And this is something that is acknowledged by all of the writers on mental disorder and crime: the most powerful associations are between drug and alcohol abuse and violence; or between those with particular kinds of personality disorder and violence. Manifestly criminogenic factors are thus sustaining the statistics. As even Maden (2007) acknowledges in respect of the MacArthur studies, once substance abuse is taken out of the picture there is little left on which to draw meaningful conclusions about mental illness and violence. In an attempt seemingly to rectify this, Maden cites the Swanson et al 1990 study discussed above; but, as has already been noted, this is a cross-sectional study where cause and effect cannot be disentangled.

And it is at this point that the 'weapons of mass destruction' analogy is most appropriate. Maden's seeming interest in proving his case produces a brief, but citation-rich, review of some of the published studies: having looked at the evidence of Taylor and Gunn (1984), Shaw et al (2006), Swanson et al (1990), Lindqvist and Allebeck (1990a,b), Link et al (1992), Stueve and Link (1997), Hodgins et al (1996), Brennan et al (2000) and Arseneault et al (2000), he asserts that it is 'unnecessary to quote further studies'. Indeed, he goes on to draw a parallel between the strength of the evidence relating to mental illness and violence in the community, with that between smoking and lung cancer:

In summary, there is a highly significant association between psychotic mental illness and violence in the community, of a similar order of magnitude to the association between smoking and lung cancer (Maden, 2004).

(Maden, 2007:23)

The earlier citation (Maden, 2004) is unhelpful since the same sentence appears, but with a change of 'in the community' from 'in society' and 'similar' from 'same'.[8] The identical phrase appears in the updated 2007 article in *Psychiatry*, but here it reads 'There is an association between psychotic mental illness and violence of the same order of magnitude as the association between smoking and lung cancer.' In the latter article the same evidence is cited as in the 2007 book. But is the comparison fair? First, smoking causes lung cancer, whereas the links between violence and psychotic mental disorder are associations – the problem of causality has not yet been overcome. Indeed the American Cancer Society (2007:34) asserts 'Smoking accounts for at least 30 per cent of all cancer deaths and 87 per cent of lung cancer deaths' and cites the seminal work of Doll and Peto (1981) and the US Department of Health and Human Services (1989). The Department of Health publication '*Smoking Kills – A White Paper on Tobacco*' estimated that in the UK smoking causes each year 46,500 people to die from cancer, and causes 84 per cent of deaths from lung cancer (1998:para 1.14). Secondly, even if one were only talking about relative risks 'the risk of developing lung cancer is about 23 times higher in male smokers and 13 times higher in female smokers compared to life long non-smokers' (US Department of Health and Human Services, 2004). To assert therefore, as Maden does, that the association between violence and a psychotic illness is of this 'order of magnitude' looks vulnerable when the Swanson et al study would make no greater claim than a broad doubling of lifetime prevalence. Indeed, when asked about this he retracted with the generous acknowledgement that 'The smoking comparison in the book is the only statistic in the book that is dubious and I regret using it now – if I had looked up the original work on smoking at the time I would not have used it'.[9] Whilst I have some hesitation in reporting this exchange, particularly since this current book will no doubt have plenty of errors on my part, I have done so because the significance of the claim lies in the fact that it was made in the first place. If it is a belief in the strength of the underlying association that led Professor Maden to cite the comparison, this belief will arguably colour his take on the literature. None of us can be free from the influence of our own preconceptions; but we ought nonetheless to ensure others are aware of them.

8 Maden (2004:2).
9 Personal communication 30 October 2007.

In conclusion, Monahan's (2007) careful review of the evidence and cautious assertion that acute mental disorder is a modest risk factor for violence must be right, and a modest one indeed when compared with the risks associated with alcoholism and drug abuse. Moreover, Monahan is always careful to stress that since serious mental disorder is relatively rare, its contribution to the overall rate of violence in the population is correspondingly small. And one might add that in the United Kingdom, where the base rate of fatal violence is much lower, the contribution of mental disorder will be even more marginal. This is peculiarly pertinent since it is these cases which invariably attract the greatest attention.

However, Monahan does place significant reliance on the data from the epidemiologic catchment area surveys (see Swanson et al 1990) as complementing or augmenting the other (methodologically limited) studies of discrete populations of patients or offenders, arguing, in effect, for the persuasive weight of the preponderance of evidence. Arboleda-Florez and others (1998) make the case against a causal relationship being established between mental disorder and violence, and do so by drawing on the methodological limitations of the studies Monahan promotes, namely the Swanson et al surveys. However, to be wholly fair, Monahan is not claiming a causal relationship; indeed he is very careful only to identify mental disorder as a risk factor, in that it correlates with and precedes violence. Although to be equally fair to Arboleda-Florez, he is critical of the Swanson et al study on precisely the grounds that it cannot claim temporal certainty. So I would suggest there is something of an impasse.

Mental disorder and the special case of homicide

Cautionary themes

Whether a homicide results from an individual's act of serious violence may be the result of factors outside the immediate control of that individual, rather than attributable to any desire intentionally to bring about death. Of 2,670 convictions for homicide noted by the National Confidential Inquiry (Appleby et al, 2006:102) for the period April 1999 to December 2003 only a bare majority (51 per cent) were convictions for murder, that is, intentional homicide. Moreover, the great bulk of the manslaughter verdicts are classified as involuntary manslaughter. In these cases, the perpetrator can most properly be described as a risk-taker where that risk has gone horribly wrong, either foreseeably (but not such as to constitute a virtual certainly) or unforeseeably to the perpetrator. Homicides classed as voluntary manslaughter in England and Wales, where a finding is made of not guilty of murder but guilty of manslaughter due to provocation or diminished responsibility, make up only a small proportion of manslaughter findings.[10] The outcomes are deemed a form of 'voluntary manslaughter' since the perpetrator intended the act of killing, but benefited from a defence to the full charge. Their rarity as an outcome is illustrated by the finding that diminished responsibility manslaughter constituted only 106 (four per cent) of the 2,670 convictions for homicide over the period April 1999 to December 2003. Notably during that period there were in relation to homicide a further (but only a further) five verdicts of persons found not guilty by reason of insanity and nine where there was a finding of unfit to plead.

Two important points emerge from this. First, dividing those who commit acts of violence (for example, the person who intentionally inflicts grievous bodily harm upon another, but where the victim does not die), from those who commit homicide, where the victim does, may be to perpetrate a categorical error. Similarly, to focus on the homicides where there was manifestly a 'mental disorder' element is to elevate in importance, and perhaps do so inappropriately, 120 of the total number of cases of 2,684 (four per cent of the total). When people with mental disorder kill, they tend to do so in broadly the same way, using primarily the same methods and attacking similar victims to ordered killers. The prototypical homicide is committed by a youngish man who attacks a female partner or relative at home using a sharp instrument. Gender differences reflect exactly what one would expect: men are more likely to use their strength than women, so that there is a greater tendency to strangle, use a blunt instrument or beat and kick a victim. But for both groups, a sharp instrument, easily available in most kitchens, is the weapon of choice.

But it is, and always has been, the case that a death alters everything. Arguably these should be treated as special cases, not only because of the fact of death but also because it is conceivable, even if not likely, that something might have been done by those involved in the mental health field to avoid the tragedies that occurred. A slender risk here is a slender risk of a terrible and fatal outcome.

Moreover, the following discussion about the relationship between mental illness and homicide needs to be read in the light of an open acknowledgement that drawing conclusions about the relationship is undoubtedly difficult (Appleby et al 2006:4; Taylor and Gunn, 1999). But to start, some recent statistics illustrate the problematic nature of these things. Coleman et al (2007:21) note that in 2005–6, for offences recorded as homicide in

---

10 The Ministry of Justice have not collected separate figures on successful provocation defences, so determining the exact number of involuntary manslaughter cases is problematic. Some insight can be gained from the study carried out by Mackay (2006) for the Law Commission. For the period 1997–2001 (a similar time period to the National Confidential Inquiry) there were 71 pleas of provocation, of which 24 were successful. If comparable, this would mean that the bulk of the manslaughter verdicts for the period April 1999–Dec 2003 would be neither diminished responsibility nor provocation findings.

which the apparent circumstance has been classed as 'an irrational act carried out by an apparently insane or disturbed subject', there were 25 cases out of 746 (ie 3.35 per cent) homicides. For the preceding years the figures were 4.5 per cent, 5.1 per cent, 4.4 per cent and 3.9 per cent. So, the first thing to stress is that around 95 per cent of homicides are not self-evidently committed by people who are 'insane or disturbed' at the time of the offence. Second, the absolute numbers are small. Third, the numbers look stable. And fourth, there are the further findings from another sample of homicide perpetrators (National Confidential Inquiry into Suicide and Homicide by People with Mental Illness, 2008); these note that during this four-year study period (leading up to 31 December 2005) of 2,053 people who committed homicide in England and Wales, 201 of them had been in contact with mental health services in the year prior to the offence. Notably, 50 of them were under the enhanced Care Programme Approach (CPA) at the time of the offence, suggesting ongoing and marked need.

However, even taking this broad definition of mental disorder, namely people who had been in contact with the mental health services in the preceding year, which of course says nothing about their mental health at the time of the offence, only ten per cent of homicide perpetrators fall into this category. Yet this ten per cent, as a result of the then mandatory requirement that a homicide inquiry be held, would most likely have distorted both public and professional perceptions of the links between homicide and mental disorder, and affected the landscape the public perceived of the association of mental disorder and extreme violence (Peay, 1996).

Finally, in this list of cautionary themes, the annual reports by the National Confidential Inquiry (National Confidential Inquiry, 2009) now enable us to chart fluctuations by year. Yet even these data present a mixed picture: this latest report notes an unexplained rise in the number of homicides by people with mental illness, whilst also noting a rise in the number and rate of homicides in the general male population (including a rise in firearm homicide) but no rise amongst those in contact with mental health services. As Professor Appleby, the Director of the National Confidential Inquiry, observed at the time of publication 'we now have to try and understand why this has happened'.[11]

Understanding homicide in the context of mental disorder

One place to start would be the longer term analysis, over 50 years, of mental disorder and homicide by Large et al (2008). Here, the picture is of a rising rate of homicide by both mentally disordered and mentally ordered

11 29 July 2009 (press release).

offenders until the 1970s, but a decline thereafter in the rate by offenders with mental disorder against a steady rise in homicide amongst the mentally ordered. Perhaps frustratingly, the authors come to no certain conclusions, pointing to a range of sociological factors which will have varied over that period, and to improvements in services, and to changes to the way legal tests are applied, even if the tests themselves have remained relatively static. And as helpful as it is to have access to this careful longer term analysis, the difficulties of understanding complex issues from such statistical data are immediately evident.

To begin with there is the familiar problem of slippery definitions. Monahan (2007:134) reports Shaw et al (2006) as noting that, of homicide offenders in England and Wales, '34 per cent had a mental disorder.' The figures observed by Coleman et al (2007) above suggest nothing like this order of magnitude. How can such stark differences in the figures be reconciled? First, the Shaw et al figure, drawn from the National Confidential Inquiry into Homicide and Suicide (see Appleby et al, 2001, and further Appleby et al, 2006), is based on a *lifetime* diagnosis of mental disorder. These figures derive from psychiatric reports prepared for either the court or the Crown Prosecution Service or from the questionnaire responses made by psychiatrists where it was known that the offender had had contact with the mental health services. In the psychiatric reports prepared for court purposes, given the seriousness of the offence involved, there may be a tendency fully to document the presence of any possible disorder. Psychiatric reports were available for 73 per cent of the homicide cases, yet only ten per cent of offenders were ultimately evaluated as having an abnormal state at the time of the offence.[12] Second, the Shaw et al (2006) study related to convictions during the period 1996-99 (see Appleby et al 2001) when nine per cent of homicides resulted in diminished responsibility findings; notably, such findings, for whatever reason, dropped dramatically in the third period of the National Confidential Inquiry (see Appleby et al 2006). Third, the definition of mental disorder covered schizophrenia five per cent; affective disorder seven per cent; personality disorder nine per cent; drug dependence six per cent; and alcohol dependence seven per cent, so the figure of 34 per cent is again an all-embracing figure. Further measures are revealing in respect of the difference between the life-time diagnosis, and the potential bearing that the disorder may have had on the homicide: ten per cent were thought to have an abnormal state at the time of the offence (62 per cent with depressive symptoms; 46 per cent with psychotic symptoms); nine per cent received diminished responsibility verdicts, indicating that the abnormal mental state

12 Since 2001, medical reports are no longer a requirement for those charged with homicide (*R v Reid (Sonni Lee)* [2001] EWCA Crim 1806). As a result, the numbers of cases picked up by the National Confidential Inquiry dropped in 2006 to 49 per cent of the total sample.

did have some effect in respect of the offender's full culpability for the offence; and by the time the point of disposal arrived, only seven per cent received hospital orders.

Thus, of those with a life-time diagnosis of mental disorder, most were not acutely ill at the time of the offence, and most had *never* received documented mental health care. Perhaps most remarkably, only four offenders suffering from schizophrenia were thought to be so disordered at the point of the offence that they fell within the terms of the M'Naghten Rules and gained a 'not guilty by reason of insanity' verdict; that is a quarter of one per cent of the sample. All of this makes the 34 per cent headline figure misleading. However, that figure is very much in keeping with those of general population studies where approximately a third of the population show a diagnosis of mental disorder based on life-time figures (Meltzer et al, 1995). What is not in keeping with the general population figures are the specific findings on schizophrenia and personality disorder, both of which show raised levels, and this is especially the case for schizophrenia. For example, Singleton et al (2001) report their highest prevalence for men with probable psychotic disorder as being in the 30–34 age bracket at a 1.3 per cent level for the previous year; this finding derives from their private household survey.

In an earlier article, Shaw et al (2004) examined the question of stranger killings, with particular reference to the role of mental disorder. These are important since stranger killings are perhaps, in the public's mind, the quintessential offence committed by those with mental disorder. Looking at a 30-year period from 1967 Shaw et al concluded that whilst stranger homicides did increase over that period the increase was not due to homicides perpetrated by mentally ill people. Stranger homicides were most likely to be related to drug or alcohol misuse by young men. Indeed, of 1,594 homicides reported in that study over a three year period, 85 were committed by people with schizophrenia and only 12 of those related to victims not known to the perpetrator, whilst 560 homicides were committed by those with a history of drug or alcohol misuse. The authors concluded that the advent of community care had not increased the risk to public: and that the public's growing fears of being the victim of a stranger killing by a mentally ill person were unjustified (Phelan and Link, 1998).

That knowledge however seems to do little to allay the media coverage of such issues. The extensive media coverage of the 'top-deck chip killer', the case of Anthony Joseph who killed Richard Whelan on a bus in July 2005, would be one illustration. Whilst one should be very cautious about relying on such coverage of these cases for an accurate portrayal, what emerges is both complex and illuminating. Joseph (also known as Anthony Peart) had a plea of diminished responsibility manslaughter accepted, and was sent indefinitely to Broadmoor hospital, after two juries failed to agree on a charge of murder in the context of conflicting medical opinion. Professor Eastman is reported as giving evidence that Joseph suffered from paranoid schizophrenia and was also in the early stages of a personality disorder in 2005, but another psychiatrist noted that Joseph had made no complaint about his mental health until he was on remand following the offence. Joseph had been taking both alcohol and crack cocaine. The family of the victim did not accept the basis for the psychiatric defence, observing that Joseph was 'an angry and vindictive man' (see *The Guardian*, 23 November 2007). After his conviction it emerged that failings in the justice system had permitted Joseph to be at large when he should have been in custody. An ensuing Criminal Justice Joint Inspection (2008) report also noted that there was nothing in the history of his prior offending which should have alerted the criminal justice authorities to his potential for extreme spontaneous violence. Quite what part his paranoid schizophrenia played in events remains unknown, or at least unknown in the public domain. But the association will no doubt have been made.

All of this would not be to suggest that there is not evidence for an elevated risk of homicide by people who suffer from schizophrenia: it is greater than would be expected by chance. But the figures are difficult to unpick. To assert, for example, that people with a diagnosis of schizophrenia are three times more likely to kill than people without this condition (Haffner and Bocker, 1982; Wessely and Taylor, 1991) looks both alarming and persuasive, until one remembers that these are relative risks. People are simply highly unlikely to kill per se. And since when people with schizophrenia kill, they are most likely to kill themselves, then a family member, partner or former partner, they clearly resemble 'ordered' killers; this would suggest that their motivations, and the factors that lie behind their offending, are probably in large part similar, with the mental illness element making a marginal contribution in some of the cases. Giving some support to this approach is the fact that of the 141 perpetrators in the Appleby et al (2006) study with a lifetime diagnosis of schizophrenia, only 74 had been in contact with services in the 12 months before the homicide. And supporting an approach that would give greater weight to the notion of a link, 32 of them had had contact in the week before the homicide. In fact, the major difference between those with schizophrenia who kill, and ordered perpetrators, is that the former are significantly less likely to kill a stranger (Appleby et al, 2006:124); and this may have as much to do with opportunity and proximity, drawing on routine activity theory, as to do with motivation. However, it is both the marginal contribution that receives public attention, together with an inappropriate emphasis on stranger killings.

Competing perspectives

The issue of perspective undoubtedly has an influence not only on the perception of the statistics, but also on their presentation. For example, evidence was given by the Zito Trust (2007) in a memorandum to the House of Commons Public Bill Committee (on the Mental Health Bill 2007).

> Since 1994 there have been over 300 published inquiry reports into homicide committed by people in contact with mental health services. Non-compliance with medication in the community is a consistent issue in these reports. As Professor Maden points out in his more recent review of inquiry cases, discussed in his book *Treating Violence* (published in 2007), 'Non-compliance with medication was a major problem and it featured in most of the Inquiry reports.' We recommend Professor Maden's book to everyone engaged in this debate. It quashes, for example, the idea that mental illness is somehow commensurate with other medical illnesses, such as diabetes and cancer, when it comes to defining and describing what powers should be available to clinicians under mental health legislation. How many people with diabetes who do not take their medication, he asks, end up killing members of the public?
>
> (Zito Trust, 2007 para 2.5)

Yet that quotation from Maden's book appears at page 147 where he is discussing his sub-sample of 25 cases of homicide by patients with severe mental illness who were known to have been previously violent: to qualify for this sub-sample the perpetrator had to be suffering from schizophrenia or other delusional disorder or bipolar affective disorder. It is thus misleading to allow the reader to elide the 300 cases of inquiry reports into homicide, where non-compliance with medication can be an issue but is not consistently so, with a selected sub-sample of 25 mentally ill patients where non-compliance with medication was a near consistent issue. Indeed, Shaw et al (2006) noted that nine per cent of their 1,594 homicide perpetrators had personality disorder, and only five per cent schizophrenia, these being life-time diagnoses (see also Appleby et al, 2006:115). Appleby et al (2006), drawing on the same data source (albeit for different years), observe that of those homicide perpetrators who had a primary diagnosis of personality disorder (five per cent) 71 per cent of them had had either no previous contact with mental health services, or no contact in the last 12 months. This would thus have excluded them from the mandatory terms of the 'Inquiries after Homicide' (Peay, 1996). By their exclusion, the issue of medication compliance becomes over-represented in the Inquiry reports; and similarly over-represented, albeit on a different basis, in the Maden sample. In fact, Appleby et al (2006:139) conclude that 25 per cent of *patient* homicides (that is, approximately 11 per year of the 30–50 'Inquiry after Homicide' cases) were preceded by non-compliance with medication.

Tony Maden has also argued that the occurrence of schizophrenia in five per cent of homicides, as opposed to one per cent of the population, would justify, in medical terms, the attribution of a causal link. He asserts that Paul Mullen's Australian figures themselves suggest that the occurrence is more around ten per cent.[13] Whilst these figures are based on a sample of identi-fied killers (and therefore unsuccessful ones) it is fair to concede that most homicides are 'solved', so they will be much more representative than a sample of convicted violence perpetrators. But it is also true that historically all homicide perpetrators in this country were referred for psychiatric assess-ments (although this is no longer the case). And there are good reasons for clinicians to err on the side of caution when diagnosing the possible pres-ence of mental disorder in their reports. Maden has also argued that even if schizophrenia was not responsible for most of the violence committed by people suffering from the disorder, then psychiatrists should still properly be interested in the violence, because that violence constitutes a risk, possi-bly of death, to third parties.[14] And that makes it exceptional, since few ill-nesses are associated with adverse events to third parties. But it remains the case that the five per cent figure is based on a life-time diagnosis. Appleby et al (2006:123) note that 141 people with schizophrenia committed homi-cide (five per cent of their sample); but of this group only 51 were mentally ill at the time of the offence. That would make the risk much more compa-rable to the general population rate (see Singleton, 2001 above). Again, this is a problematic denominator question.

Co-morbidity and homicide

One other interesting issue remains, which relates to issues of co-morbidity, and indeed, the other forms of serious mental illness that patients might experience beyond schizophrenia. It might seem self-evident that homicides committed by those with schizophrenia attract attention since they conform to fears and stereotypes, partly media inspired, of the crazed killer. But why is it that the relationship between other major mental disorders, such as depression or bi-polar disorder, and homicide attracts so little attention? And similarly, the relative neglect of personality disorder, and of those with alcohol and drug problems, and homicide. It is notable that Graham Thorni-croft (2006), in his book *Shunned*, does take the reader systematically through the literature on the assorted diagnostic classifications and their association with violence and homicide; and, in so doing, highlights an interesting and arguably neglected association between 'psychotic disorder, antisocial personality disorder and alcohol/drug misuse, which together substantially escalate the risk of violent behaviour' (2006:136). Of course, there are a number of complicating factors. For example, context can be

13 Personal communication.
14 Personal communication.

critical; discharge to a violent neighbourhood contributes markedly to the difference making a very toxic mix (Steadman et al, 1998). It has also been argued that the diagnostic boundaries between these conditions are not as robust as might appear (Bentall, 2003, 2009) or indeed, within a diagnosis such as bi-polar disorder that embraces both depression and mania at its extremes. Thus, the association may be between violence, where rates are raised for bi-polar disorder, without a raised rate for homicide (Thornicroft, 2006:130); or it may be that the target of the violence is different. Moreover, where homicide is followed by suicide, a not uncommon phenomenon amongst those who commit homicide, it is hard to disentangle whether the motivation is primarily suicidal rather than homicidal, but that the latter necessarily comes later in the offender's chronology. Certainly depression is much more widespread than schizophrenia, so it makes a larger contribution to the overall statistics (Thornicroft, 2006:31: see also Appleby et al, 2006).

Similarly, personality disorders are remarkably common and affect 20–30 per cent of the population. DSM IV R has ten types of disorder; ICD has nine. Antisocial (DSM), or dissocial (ICD), personality disorder are most relevant for violence and homicide, but there are overlaps between the definition of criminal behaviour and the diagnostic criteria. Again, with respect to its importance as a contributory factor to violence, the personality disordered group outweighs the psychotic group. But with respect to homicide the balance shifts somewhat. The Appleby et al (2006) sample of homicide perpetrators found 5 per cent had a primary diagnosis of schizophrenia and 5 per cent personality disorder (life-time diagnoses); yet the latter figure, as the authors note, is likely to be an underestimate (2006:128). Indeed, of perpetrators with personality disorder, 43 per cent had had no previous contact with mental health services; whereas for the schizophrenia group the figure was 35 per cent (itself surprisingly high). The consequence will have been that, with the methodology of the confidential inquiry, proportionately more of the patients with schizophrenia will have been picked up by comparison with those with personality disorder. Yet again this will have fed into any public association between schizophrenia and homicide.

So perhaps it is not surprising that psychotic conditions capture the greatest attention. Moreover, the general focus on schizophrenia may have as much to do with what is regarded as psychiatrists' core business; psychotic patients are self-evidently the domain of psychiatry, and conventional medical treatments (even if of variable efficacy) are available, as with the statistics. The alien nature of the disorder also fits with conventional stereotypes of 'madness'. But as has been urged repeatedly, this stereotype needs to be leavened by the reality: the numbers are small and the context is very complex; albeit that the stereotype will occasionally and tragically reflect the reality (Mischon, 2009).

That said, one final question arises, taking us back to the original issue as to whether homicide by those with mental disorder should be treated as a special case because it may have been possible to intervene and thereby avoid the particular tragedy. Are such homicides preventable? Appleby et al (2006:120) on this issue are revealing; first, of the 15 homicides committed by *in-patients*, the authors assert that four of them 'may have been preventable' (2006:130); this might suggest that the bar is set high for inclusion as preventable homicides. Notably, two of these patients were subject to close observation as in-patients. Second, six patients committed homicide after discharge but before their first follow-up. Third, 24 patients in the community were classified as having committed a preventable homicide. In total 34 cases, or 14 per cent of 'patient' homicides, were regarded as being in the most preventable group.

For the five year period, this made seven homicides a year by patients preventable. And the definition of 'patient' in the Appleby et al study related only to those who were in contact with the mental health services, or had been so during the previous 12 months. Interestingly, when questioned the clinicians themselves thought 41 homicides could have been prevented, indicating that clinicians are either harder on themselves or believe their predictive abilities better than those of the study group. At their last contact with services before the homicide, in 88 per cent of the cases the immediate risk was thought to be low or absent. But perhaps this is a self-fulfilling prophecy: had they been considered a high risk, contact would not have been lost with them. And finally, of course, the figure raised earlier of the number of patients subject to enhanced CPA who have nonetheless committed homicide is telling (NCI 2008); 50 of the 201 perpetrators in contact with mental health services were actually subject to the enhanced CPA regime. This was presumably for a reason, and yet still the homicide occurred. One might conclude that either the mental health services are not greatly skilled at preventing homicide amongst their client group, or that the homicides were themselves just not preventable. Indeed, are such questions even asked of the other approximately 1,878 mentally ordered perpetrators in the same study?

Concluding comments

Summarising such detailed information is not easy, but a few points are worth reiterating. First, most people who are violent are not mentally ill; most people who are mentally ill are not violent. Second, violence is relatively rare, but extreme violence is very rare in this country (albeit not in the US where much of the research is done); the risk of being a victim of homicide in England and Wales is 1:1,000 and the risk of being a victim of homicide by someone with schizophrenia 1:20,000. Third, there appears to be some increase in the risk of violence both by and towards those with mental disorder, but the mechanisms underlying this are unclear and the reliability of the data supporting the assertions open to criticism.

Chapter 7

Symptoms and causality

Symptoms as evidence of a causal mechanism?

What is the role of delusions in violence? This is another question where the evidence is confused, but we are beginning to edge towards some understanding. I would like to start with an illustration of a case where it might be thought that the offender's delusions had the clearest link with the violence he perpetrated, namely that of Eric Clark from the United States.

> Petitioner Clark was charged with first-degree murder under an Arizona statute prohibiting "[i]nten[tionally] or knowing[ly]" killing a police officer in the line of duty. At his bench trial, Clark did not contest that he shot the officer or that the officer died, but relied on his own undisputed paranoid schizophrenia at the time of the incident to deny that he had the specific intent to shoot an officer or knowledge that he was doing so.
> (Supreme Court, syllabus, *Clark v Arizona* (2006) 548 US 735)[1]

At the time Clark allegedly believed that aliens, impersonating government agents, were trying to kill him and bullets were the only way to stop them. Whilst this is a clear delusional belief on which Clark acted, it was seemingly not enough to provide him with a defence, for he was indeed convicted of murder. The prosecutor had offered circumstantial evidence that Clark knew the victim was a police officer and testimony indicating that Clark had previously stated he wanted to shoot an officer and had lured the victim to the scene in order to kill him. Clark was unable to establish either the defence of insanity (in Arizona, this would have required him to show that he did not know his criminal act was wrong) or to rebut the prosecution's evidence of the requisite *mens rea*, that he had acted intentionally or know-

---

1 The syllabus is the equivalent of an extended headnote. It is prepared by the Reporter of Decisions and issued at the same time as the opinion of the Court, but it constitutes no part of the decision itself: see *United States v Detroit Timber & Lumber Co* (1906) 200 US 321.

ingly to kill an officer. From the legal perspective it proved impossible to get agreement that either he had the delusion, or if he did have it, that he acted on it, or that if he acted on it, he still did not have a residual understanding of what he was doing. Admittedly the law has a high threshold of doubt in these matters – demonstrating evidence of a negative is never easy – but similar difficulties, of demonstrating what is going on in someone's head, applied to the clinicians. Why should it prove easy for clinicians to agree on the role of delusions in violence?

At this point it is worth stepping back briefly to consider again the problem of linking thoughts and deeds. In non-psychotic subjects the links are not always obvious: in psychotic subjects there is a further layer of difficulty. Under-reporting and over-reporting of both delusions and actions can confound the analysis. Work by Wessely et al (1993) nicely illustrates the problem: indeed, they did not attempt to assess the unknowable question of whether an action was the result of a delusion, but rather whether an outside observer would judge the action to be congruent with the (abnormal) belief. Taking a sample of 83 consecutively admitted deluded subjects, the researchers interviewed both the subjects and some informants. A number of factors are notable: first, only half the sample reported that they had acted in accordance with their delusions; second, violent behaviour was uncommon; third, there was a lack of congruence between the subject's reports of their actions, and those of the informants. Some delusions, because of their content, are necessarily nigh impossible to link to any kind of action; the example they cite is of a belief that thoughts were being put into someone's head from spaces in the air. And some beliefs would not result in behaviour that looked abnormal to an outsider; for example, wearing a green tie to give protection from surveillance by the IRA. Fourth, acting in accordance with delusions was more common than the existing literature suggested, but that could well have been, as the authors speculated, because the actions were themselves less visible; their innocuous nature, unlike violent or aggressive behaviour, simply did not attract attention. And finally, persecutory delusions were the only phenomenological feature associated with delusional action in general, on the basis of informant reported action. Of course, it is important to stress at this point that whilst such action included two cases of serious violence and 17 of minor violence before admission, the majority of 'harm' cases were of harm to self, largely deriving from disorders of appetite, and many were relatively innocuous activities: one case cited was of a woman making a complaint at the police station about her parents' use of diabolic powers. Thus, the relationship is thoroughly messy. The seemingly clear link between Clark's delusions above and his violent actions is the exception rather than the rule.

So does delusional symptomatology have anything to add when thinking about what mental disorder might add to the causes of crime? More starkly, does delusional symptomatology act as a trigger for violent behaviour?

Sellars et al (1993) have asserted that whilst most offending by those suffering from schizophrenia is not violent and when violent it is mostly trivial. But where it is violent the nature and function of delusional and paranoid beliefs appear to be of crucial importance. In contrast, Taylor (1982:280) has observed 'It is not unusual to find that the violent act of a schizophrenic cannot be directly explained by the current psychopathology. This does not, however, negate the relevance of the illness ... social and illness variables must be considered together'. And when taken together, it has been suggested that over 80 per cent of the offences of the psychotic were probably attributable to their illness.

Clearly, the nature of Clark's delusions would have served to dehumanise the police officer, arguably making such an act of extreme violence easier (see Young, 2007 above). Link et al (1992) have demonstrated that psychotic symptomatology was significantly related to recent violence, even after controlling for the most obvious factors such as alcohol and drug use. But whether psychotic symptoms are the critical variable and if so, how a psychotic belief might be transformed into a violent act, are questions which raise complex issues about the relationship between mental processes and behaviour. Are some psychotic delusions more problematic than others? Why, for example, should a psychotic delusion have any greater influence over behaviour than a true belief, or, for that matter, a mistaken belief? In law, both true beliefs and mistaken beliefs can constitute the basis for a complete defence; psychotic beliefs do not provide the same legal protection. Whilst a plea of not guilty by reason of insanity is always open to the defendant, bringing oneself within its narrow framework means that many of those experiencing delusions gain no protective benefit from them. This is, in itself, problematic, given our attempts both to explain crime from a person-oriented perspective, and in respect of the criminal law's emphasis on subjectivism. Even those defences that rely upon the notion of the reasonable man being invested with the defendant's characteristics have proved precarious (see, for example, the shifting grounds of the defence of provocation); and neither the subjective element in duress nor self-defence seem, in practice, to provide much cover to mentally disordered offenders.[2]

The influence of threat/control override

Setting aside the criminal law's limitations, how might these implied associations between psychosis and offending be explained? One approach is the 'rationality-within-irrationality' hypothesis (Link and Stueve, 1994:143);

2 *R v Smith (Morgan)* [2000] 3 WLR 654 and *Attorney-General for Jersey v Holley* [2005] 2 AC 58 on provocation; *R v Martin (Anthony)* [2003] QB 1 on self-defence and *R v Bowen* [1996] 2 Cr App R 157 CA (Crim Div) on duress; see also Buchanan and Virgo (1999).

this has been used to capture the notion of how an individual's behaviour might be understood even within a context of irrational beliefs. Link and Stueve, taking data from previously conducted studies, posited that psychotic symptoms that entailed the overriding of internal self-control and those that implied a specific threat of harm from others (threat/control override items) would be associated with violent behaviour, but that other psychotic symptoms, for example a belief that one's thoughts were being broadcast, would not be so associated (1994:143). The authors asserted that the results of their analysis lend support to just such an explanation: violence was mediated by psychotic experiences of either personal threat or that thoughts were over-riding an individual's sense of self-control. As they stressed repeatedly, their claims were modest: whatever effect there is, it was small, and small compared with the other correlates of violence; thus 'most respondents in our study who experienced threat/control-override psychotic symptoms had not engaged in recent violent behaviour' (1994:156). Again, the question that remains is what causes some to respond, what enables some to restrain themselves, and why is it some individuals can experience threat/control-override symptoms and not feel the need to do either? Finally, whilst Link and Stueve were appropriately tentative in their conclusions, given the acknowledged limitations in their analysis (1994:155), they did claim that their results overcome the limitations inherent within the Swanson et al (1990) study of temporal confusion and the possibility of differences in willingness to report undesirable behaviour (see above).

Whilst the initial studies in this field were broadly supportive of the threat/control-override thesis, two later studies questioned what was beginning to look like the received orthodoxy; namely, Appelbaum et al (2000) and Stompe et al (2004). Both are worth examining.

Appelbaum et al (2000:571), drawing on the MacArthur data, concluded that, 'Contrary to popular wisdom and to the results of several other studies, the data from this study suggest that the presence of delusions does not predict higher rates of violence among recently discharged psychiatric patients'. This is an important assertion because, unlike the studies that had indicated a positive association between delusions of the threat/control-override type and violence, the Appelbaum et al study was prospective: the data came from five face-to-face interviews over a one year period.[3] Moreover, in the first two follow-up assessments, participants with mind/body control delusions were less likely to commit violent acts. The MacArthur data-set is not without criticism, as noted above, being based on a non-forensic sample of patients admitted and then discharged according to the US model of comparatively short admission periods for what are likely to

3 See also Walsh et al (2004), another prospective study that failed to find an association between threat/control-override symptoms and violent behaviour.

be acutely ill patients.[4] Moreover, Appelbaum et al are careful to qualify their negative findings by noting that this does not disprove the clinical wisdom that deluded patients who have been violent in the past may be violent again; it is simply that delusions per se should neither justify admission nor preclude discharge. But for explanatory purposes it is notable that the significant results found were eliminated once anger and impulsivity measures were controlled. And this is interesting because of the association between active symptoms and inactivity generally; as the authors note, since delusions tend to be associated with chronic psychotic conditions, and since the latter tends to be associated with social withdrawal, people who are delusional may simply have less inclination and less opportunity to engage in the social interactions that can, in turn, lead to interpersonal violence (and arguably therefore, are less likely to turn up in the data-set).

Similarly, Stompe et al (2004), in a study based in Austria, came to largely negative conclusions in respect of the threat/control-override issue. They retrospectively compared 119 male offenders found not guilty by reason of insanity who had committed a 'severe' offence with a matched sample of 105 non-offending patients suffering from schizophrenia. Again their results confirmed the general findings above of a relationship between violent behaviour and substance abuse/lower social class, but threat/control-override symptoms were not generally associated with violence. However, there did appear to be some relationship between comparatively unspecific threat symptoms and the severity of an offence; and some differentiation of subtypes of schizophrenia with differing levels of severity of offence. Perhaps unsurprisingly, those with a paranoid subtype were over-represented in more severe violence, and those of a disorganised or residual subtype at the less severe violence end of the spectrum.[5] Notably, one feature that emerges from their paper, which chimes with the work of Cheung et al (2003) discussed below, is the need to insist on precise descriptions from patients as to the content and meaning of their delusions: indeed, Stompe et al argue that the inconsistent findings of Link, Swanson and colleagues with that of Appelbaum et al may be as much due to the incomparability of their data in respect of the precise definitions of threat/control-override symptoms. Stompe et al note that not only can control-override symptoms be volatile and brief, but they can also be experienced by the patient as negative, neutral or positive. Yet delusional threat symptoms are exclusively negative, and go beyond a generally suspicious attitude towards others to embrace, from the patient's perspective, ominous and dangerous aspects. Indeed, such

4 For example, in Steadman et al (1998) for the 391 enrolled patients at the Pittsburgh site the median length of hospitalisation was 15 days: for the three sites as a whole, the median length was 9 days for a sample of 1,136 patients.
5 Under Austrian law the definition of a severe offence is one that could attract a penalty of more than a year's imprisonment.

delusional symptoms can be evident not only in schizophrenia, but also in 'affective, organic, substance related, and personality disorders' (2004:41).

The influence of gender

A further perspective is provided by Teasdale et al (2006) who sought to re-examine the area in the light of these conflicting findings. One factor, the significance of which appears to have been overlooked in the original analysis, is that of gender. Do women and men respond differently to the experience of threat/control-override symptoms? Indeed, as Teasdale et al note (2006:650) other literature on gendered-based responses to stress suggest that men are more likely to respond with 'fight or flight' reactions, whilst women engage in 'tend and befriend' behaviours; that is, they seek out and nurture their social relationships. This parallels Appignanesi's (2008) argument that women, being more adaptable than men, are better at understanding both what is asked of them and what is required in response. Interestingly, whilst women's responses will decrease the likelihood of violence, since they are busy doing something else, men may either become more aggressive ('fight') or arguably, less present ('flight'), again potentially cancelling out any greater likelihood of violence. One area that the authors don't touch on here concerns violence in confined populations: here men experiencing the 'fight or flight' reaction cannot flee, and this may help us to understand levels of violence in confined male populations. Or is it that men are always more likely to respond by fight, if that is culturally expected of them? Of course, the reality is that most men neither fight nor flee, but simply endure the sense of chronic stress that results.

Teasdale et al (2006) used data from the MacArthur Violence Risk Assessment study (Monahan et al, 2001) to examine this gendered-based thesis further. Their definitions (2006:652) of what constituted threat/control-override symptoms were somewhat broader than the original Link and Stueve analysis, but they did separate delusions associated with threats from those associated with mind or body control. Interestingly, threat delusions included the belief that people were spying on the subject, that they were being followed or that they were being secretly tested or experimented on; it also bears recalling that these were post-discharge patients who were interviewed 5 times over a year at ten-week intervals.

A sample of 902 men and women who completed at least two waves of interviews was analysed. The majority did not engage in any violence, and of those who did, the incidence of violence decreased over time. The authors do not give details here of the extent to which these participants were either on medication, or were medication compliant; but it is worth remembering that, in the US, periods of in-patient hospitalisation are quite short, and individuals can be discharged when their symptoms are still active. The results supported the hypothesis. They found a main effect of gender on violence, but when gender was controlled, there was no positive significant relationship overall between threat/control-override delusions and violence. Indeed, whilst for men there appeared to be no effect of threat/control override on violence, for women there was a negative effect, with women being less likely to engage in violence when they experienced such delusions. Breaking down control-override and threats, for neither men nor women was there an association between control-override and violence; but there was an association between threat delusions and violence.[6] For women, this was a negative association: when women experienced threat delusions they exhibited lower levels of violence. For men, when they experienced threat delusions they exhibited higher rates of violence. Again though, it is worth stressing that 'only a small proportion of subjects experienced a threat delusion (between 5 and 7 per cent) or a control override delusion (between 4 and 6 per cent) during the year following hospital discharge' (2006:653–4).

Of course, once one starts to embrace gendered effects, other questions emerge. There may be an effect in respect of medication compliance, which may have an effect on whether delusions are experienced, whether they are believed as real, and/or whether one feels motivated to do anything about them, even within the rationality-within-irrationality perspective. Or are men less likely to admit that they have experienced such delusions without responding to them aggressively? How confident can we be that these were actually delusions rather than true beliefs, or mistaken beliefs? For example, Boyd-Caine (2008), in her study of executive decision-making at the mental health unit (then at the Home Office), documents the case of a woman who had killed her husband and who became subject to the oversight of the mental health unit due to her detained status. At the time of her detention it was believed that she killed her husband because she was acting under the delusion that he was about to take her baby daughter to Pakistan. Subsequent inquiries suggested that the belief was indeed credible, even if the response was wholly unacceptable. Moreover, since the MacArthur study had not gathered the requisite data directly to examine the mediating mechanisms underlying the impact of threat delusions, the Teasdale et al (2006) analysis constitutes one more possible variant on the debate. Again, the authors stress the need for a sensitive approach to risk assessment; gender is but one of the factors that may be operating. Status characteristics, race/ethnicity, cultural differences and social class may all have a role to play. Whatever the role of mental disorder, it has to be evaluated in the context of these wider (and in some instances, much more powerful) characteristics.

6 See also Stompe et al (2004) above, who further distinguish between the delusional idea of being threatened by physical aggression or poisoning, and that of being followed.

Delusional beliefs and actions

Buchanan et al (1993) in their study of 79 patients with delusional beliefs had also commented on the relationship between delusional beliefs and action. Notably, not only were no associations found when the patients' behaviour was rated by informants between their delusional phenomenology and action, but also the majority of the patients reported not acting on their beliefs. Of those who did, namely around a third, factors positively associated with action included being emotionally aroused, seeking information and identifying evidence to confirm or refute the belief. What this would suggest is that taking action is based on a process and is not some irrational response to the belief per se. And whilst the numbers are small with respect to those with persecutory delusions, the authors maintain their earlier assertion (Wessely et al, 1993) that delusions of persecution are more likely to be associated with action by contrast with delusions of catastrophe, which are not; and that feeling frightened in association with the delusion is also associated with action. As Maden comments (2007:2) 'It is perhaps not surprising that the combination of persecutory delusions, lack of insight and emotional distress increases the risk of violence'. But he goes on to make a more important observation; namely, that if the risk of violence is increased in those with mental disorder and it is due to extreme distress arising from imagined threats and irrational fears, then psychiatry does have something to offer; medicine is, after all, in the business of relieving such distress.

The chronology of the relationship between delusions and violence also bears some examination. As Taylor et al (1994:177–79) note delusional symptoms tend to have been present for long periods before an act of violence occurs. This raises two issues: first, that the probable sequence of events in those patients where both delusions and violence are present is that the mental disorder does precede the violence. But secondly, that deluded beliefs do not invariably lead to violence; indeed, they most usually do not. Of the 83 general psychiatry patients studied, only 9 had acted violently at all, even towards themselves. Indeed, of 121 psychotic men interviewed in Brixton, only one 'gave a clear description of an autochthonous delusion leading rapidly to a seriously violent offense' (1994:179).

There is work that suggests that delusions and hallucinations are far more commonplace than might be thought if one were to associate them merely with people suffering from psychotic disorders (Peters et al, 1999; Honig et al, 1998: and Bentall, 2009:106–108 for a discussion of this literature). Hence, when thinking about any link between mental disorder and violence in the context of hallucinations and deluded beliefs it is important to consider the nature of the delusion. Delusions can be negative, but they can also be positive: do warm, loving delusions cause one to be violent? A study by Cheung et al (1997) throws some light on this. Whilst their matched violent and non-violent patients both experienced auditory hallucinations and delusions, the violent group were significantly more likely to experience negative emotions, such as anger and sadness, in association with their hallucinations and that the tone and content of the voices were consistent with this, whilst those in the non-violent group reported more positive experiences and reported greater success in coping with their voices. Moreover, the violent group experienced more persecutory delusions, the non-violent group more grandiose ones. No association was reported between command hallucinations and violent behaviour, although the violent group reported that their delusions were more likely to make them feel anxious and intruded on, whilst the non-violent group reported feeling comforted, unconcerned and even elated.[7] Thus, as the authors conclude, 'specific aspects of the phenomenologies of hallucinations and delusions ... should be clinically assessed to determine the likelihood of violence as a result of such psychotic symptoms' (1997:181). Delusions can thus be associated with both violence and non-violence.

Indeed, it isn't even just the content of the delusion that is important, but how it makes you feel, for it was angry affect that independently determined the violence not the content of the delusion per se. This would be consistent with other theoretical approaches explaining violence in non-disordered people, namely that action is largely a product of affectivity; emotions that are generated by external or internal stimuli precede violent behaviour (see for example, Bleuler, 1924; Karli, 1991). Cheung et al (1997) are modest in their conclusions, noting both their small study size and its cross-sectional design, which makes claims about causality impossible. But, the study remains an interesting initiative in helping us to understand what might lie behind Maden's (2007) examples where negative delusions appeared to be the only motivation for killing, and where treatment could have had a dramatic, positive effect on outcome. And what might not; for it is the possibility of underlying causal links which intrigues.

Maden (2007:26) recommends that we should be comparing violence rates by schizophrenic patients when they have delusions with rates of violence when they do not; he asserts no one has bothered to do such a study probably because we can guess at the result. But can we? If you have a delusion, it can be resisted (see above); similarly, if you have hallucination it can be remembered and acted on later, which just reverts us to the difficulty of ever disentangling cause and effect. Even if you think of using threat/control-override as a mediating factor, the evidence is patchy. Again, why would being emotionally affected by something delusional make you more likely to act on it than being similarly emotionally affected by something you have observed on the television (often designed to influence one's

---

7 For one man's account of the different kinds of voices he learnt to accommodate over the period of his illness see 'Experience: I talk back to the voices in my head' *The Guardian*, 4 April 2009.

emotions) or indeed, observed in real life? Indeed, is it possible to know that you have a delusion; and if so, what are the consequences? Is one less likely or more likely to act on beliefs one knows to be false?

One last study in this saga is worth reviewing, since it brings us back again to the importance of seeing the role, if any, of clinical factors in their appropriate non-clinical context. Swanson et al (2006) report the findings of their 56-site study of violent behaviour in 1,410 patients suffering from schizophrenia. The research design was that of a cross-sectional study with clinical assessments, self-report data and some collateral data. The authors were careful to note the limitations that stem from this design, including its inability to draw conclusions about causality: as they asserted, the data 'show statistical associations, which may be consistent with a given causal formulation' (2006:497). But it is a large study of capacitous patients on sub-optimal medication at the point at which they came into what was a randomised clinical trial. In general, violence in this group has been associated with multiple factors, including psychotic symptoms, pre-morbid developmental events, and aspects of contemporaneous social situations, such as the opportunities for violence arising from living with family members.

But it is the findings on psychotic symptomatology that are of particular interest here. They provide support for the notion, proposed by Appelbaum et al (2000) above, that since delusions are often associated with chronic schizophrenia (where patients also tend to experience social withdrawal and smaller social networks) it is possible that such patients have 'less desire and fewer opportunities to engage in the interpersonal interactions that can lead to violence compared with less severely ill patients' (2000:571). Swanson et al found that patients living alone were indeed less likely to engage in violence than those living with family and that:

> ... high negative psychotic symptoms were significantly associated with reduced risk of serious violence, and that they moderated the effect of the positive symptoms: violence was significantly increased by positive symptoms, but only when negative symptoms were low.[8]
>
> (Swanson et al, 2006:496)

8 Five specific symptoms were associated with serious violence: hostility, suspiciousness/persecution, hallucinatory behaviour, grandiosity and excitement. The combination of delusional thinking with suspiciousness/persecutory ideation was highly associated with serious violence. And five specific symptoms were associated with decreased risk of serious violence: lack of spontaneity and flow of conversation, passive/apathetic social withdrawal, blunted affect, poor rapport and difficulty in abstract thinking. The six month prevalence of any violence was 19.1 per cent with 3.6 per cent of participants reporting serious violence. What this means is difficult to interpret. For example, Coleman et al note (2006:16), based on the 2004 Offending, Crime and Justice Survey, that 16 per cent of 10–25 year olds had committed a violent offence in the previous year.

As the authors observe, to carry out a violent act one needs a degree of initiative, organisation, social contact and psychomotor activation, and these tend to be absent in patients experiencing the negative symptoms of schizophrenia. Moreover, the subtlety of the analysis is impressive. Living with family members can be protective as well as provocative: where patients felt that they were listened to by family members they were less likely to behave violently; a finding that resonates with the literature detailing patients' experiences of coercion (see Kjellin et al, 2001; Monahan et al, 1999; and for a more recent study, Iversen K et al, 2007). Where patients enjoyed what lawyers would call procedural justice, that is, they had a chance to say what they thought and have things explained to them, they were much less likely to feel coerced, even if they were subjected to the formal process of compulsory detention. Similarly, patients who were not formally coerced could experience coercion and believe that they were detained, even when they were not, where they were treated without respect. Positive pressure, such as persuasion and inducements, did not generate feelings of coercion, whereas negative pressures, threats and the use of force, perhaps not unsurprisingly, did. Moreover, the intersection of psychotic delusions and one's ability to communicate with a world perceived as threatening may be a further complicating contributory factor (Lemert, 1962). Interestingly, Swanson et al (2006:497) observe that, whilst persuaded of the need for positive symptom management through medication and strategies to enhance compliance, the risk of violence, and particularly of more minor violence, is increased by a series of other variables that require clinicians to 'focus on the whole person in the community environment'.

Symptoms and offending behaviour

What then does all this work on symptoms and offending behaviour enable us to conclude? First, it would be nonsensical to suggest that there are no connections between the ideas we have and the things we do. This is true for the ordered and the disordered. Second, that we have ideas does not inevitably lead to actions: Wessely et al's (1993) research suggests that in 50 per cent of cases the deluded don't act on their delusions. Third, that the quality of delusions and their impact is likely to be more varied and subtle than is immediately apparent: green ties could be worn as a matter of choice or on the basis of some widely held superstition or because of an individually-held deluded belief. At what point one merges into another is likely to be culturally contingent: and at what point any belief influences any action is likely to be still more inaccessible. Fourth, people with delusions who act on them can act as responsible citizens rather than perpetrators of violence as Wessely et al (1993) illustrate with their woman who reports her parents to the police station because she believes they have diabolic powers. Fifth, the research into threat/control-override, which initially looked so promising, has interesting lessons, even if not those originally anticipated. Thus, threat and control need to be divided in their impact; we need to build in some assessment of the emotional significance of the delusion; we need to look at the influence of the delusion over time, and at the chronology of the disorder, since in the latter stages withdrawal rather than action is more common; and finally, we need to think about the influence of gender. All of this would suggest that the statistics on violence and the active symptoms of mental disorder, which are already of small order, need to be further subdivided. This, in turn, is likely to undermine any assertions about causality.

The statistically viable studies, conducted at population levels, are relatively reassuring, whilst being simultaneously unable to elucidate further on the subject of specific symptomatology. For example, Fazel and Grann (2006:1042) observe, following their study of the population impact of severe mental illness on violent crime in Sweden (using a population of 98,082 patients with severe mental illness), that the contribution of this group between 1988 and 2000 was about five per cent (that is patients committed about one in 20 violent crimes); this they hoped 'would generate a more informed debate on the contribution of persons with severe mental illness to societal violence'. And even this figure assumes an entirely causal association; and does not separate out co-morbidity as the focus of the study was on severe mental illness, not psychosis itself. Perhaps what is most interesting from a criminological point of view is that, when broken down by age and gender, severe mental illness is much less prominent as a population attributable risk fraction for young men (because being young and male are significant risk factors for violence); but, in older women, whilst violent offending was very rare, the risk attributable to severe mental illness was much greater. This in turn would make focusing psychiatric effort on older female offenders appearing before the courts potentially more rewarding.

This chapter concludes with a brief review of the case of Christopher Clunis. Whilst I am reluctant to single out such an iconic case, its rarity as a stranger-killing and its subsequent developments have changed the landscape in this field. Christopher Clunis attacked and killed Jonathan Zito on Finsbury Park Tube Station on 17 December 1992. Jonathan Zito was unknown to Clunis, and was stabbed in the face from behind in an unprovoked attack; he died shortly thereafter. Clunis suffered from paranoid schizophrenia. At his trial he pleaded not guilty to murder but guilty to manslaughter, on grounds of diminished responsibility. After the court proceedings had concluded an inquiry was held, chaired by Jean Ritchie QC, into the care and treatment of Clunis. That inquiry reported in 1994 and made a number of recommendations for reform and identified numerous deficiencies in the care of Clunis prior to the homicide. These are all detailed in the Inquiry's Report (Ritchie, 1994).

Whether Clunis either knew what he was doing, or knew that it was wrong, can only be subject to speculation, since there is nothing in the public domain to explain what was in his mind at the time of the offence; and he curiously did not raise the defence of not guilty by reason of insanity at his trial. He subsequently refused to talk to the Ritchie Inquiry about the killing, although he apparently communicated with 'intelligence and humour' on other matters with them (Ritchie, 1994:para 41). Yet what can be gleaned from his bizarre behaviour immediately *after* the killing is suggestive of a cognitively disordered state. Witnesses reported that he boarded the tube train and sat in a seat between other passengers 'as if nothing had happened' (para 39.3.9). There was no attempt to hide what had occurred – there were a number of passengers on the platform at the time – or to effect an escape. Accordingly, one might at least question whether he knew that his actions were wrong, even if he knew what he had done. In so doing, his behaviour was not inconsistent with some of those who have major mental disorders: as Hodgins notes (2004:222) there is a tendency 'to stay at the scene of the crime and/or to confess to a crime that they have committed'. This obviously makes apprehension and conviction easier, but it does not necessarily assist in understanding just what was happening in the mind of the offender at the time of the offence.

Chapter 8

Causal mechanisms, criminology and mental disorder

> The minimising or dismissal of the correlations between schizophrenia and violence by researchers and academics is less easily explained. In part it is due to misplaced good intentions. Many of us began our research in the area attempting to demonstrate that the public's fear of the violence of people with mental disorders were ill-founded. This they are, in the sense of being exaggerated but not, as it has turned out, in the sense of being groundless. The move to put the increased violence in proper perspective has all too often slid into dismissive minimisation.
>
> (Mullen, 2006:240)

This chapter addresses the charge of dismissive minimisation. Descending to the level of detail in which the previous chapters have indulged will almost certainly have been tedious, off-putting and difficult to follow. However, it has been an important exercise in order to illustrate, even if not establish conclusively, that the bases on which claims are made about the causal impact of mental disorder on crime are fallible. The fact that contrary positions are adopted with some verve and passion is understandable: at heart, the same objectives are shared but how best to achieve these remains contentious. Of course it is right to argue, because of the rarity in medicine of adverse events to third parties caused (or contributed to) by patients with disorders falling within the domain of psychiatrists, that those psychiatrists ought to engage with the issue of mental disorder and violence. But it is equally right that in so doing the ultimate harm caused may be greater if caution is not exercised about how the relationship is to be explained and, if necessary, pursued. Discouraging potential patients from coming forward for treatment, or undermining the treatment's potential effectiveness by structuring the conditions of treatment in ways that may be counterproductive, could contribute to the resultant total harm. Since such effects cannot readily be measured a cautious approach has advantages, even if it may appear Luddite. Anything else can certainly mislead both the public and the media.

Yet even those who argue at length about the poverty of our understanding about the causal links between mental disorder and violence still re-iterate, as a starting point, the relationship's positive aspects. And that is problematic, for it reflects, I would argue, a worrying slippage into headline assertions; as I have noted above, these can then be reproduced without the necessary qualifying context. This embodies a potential to mislead, and in turn affects the perception and the construction of the possibilities of what it is possible to do. For example, Silver's highly persuasive and otherwise excellent article advocating a criminologically based theoretical approach for future research, begins by asserting that 'although most people with major mental disorder do not engage in violence, the likelihood of committing violence is greater for people with major mental disorder than for those without' (Silver, 2006:686). By 'major mental disorder' Silver means those disorders of thought and affect that constitute a subset of Axis I of DSM IV, including schizophrenia and major affective disorders such as depression and bipolar disorder.

The assertion of this positive link by Silver is curious for two reasons. First, it is made without the reservation that his earlier work with Steadman et al (1998) displayed; namely the demonstration that, when comparing a discharged patient sample with a general population group in Pittsburgh, the prevalence of violence amongst the two groups could not be statistically distinguished. Second, Silver asserts that 'substance misuse raises the risk of violence by people with mental disorder substantially'. It does, but the earlier work also showed that adding substance abuse into the equation raised the prevalence of violence in both groups. The key difference appeared to be that the patient group were significantly more likely to report substance abuse. This begs the question as to which people without major mental disorder Silver is referring when he argues that the likelihood is greater for those with major mental disorder. For he concedes that 'we know that the risk of violence is modestly elevated for people with mental disorder, particularly those who misuse substances' but doesn't mention the effects of substance abuse on the ordered population. Finally, the assertion is made that 'no clear understanding of the causal mechanisms that produce the association between mental disorder and violence currently exists'. On this I agree. And this forms a valuable starting point for Silver's excellent analysis of the possible relevance of some selected criminological theoretical explanations. For the essence of what he is arguing is that we need an 'embedded individual level approach focused on a range of theoretically and empirically valid risk factors that may increase the likelihood of violence either in conjunction with or independent of mental disorder and its treatment' (Silver 2006:689: see also Swanson et al 1998 for an illustration of this approach). And it is the essence of his argument that I am adopting and adapting here; I am indebted to him for much of what follows.

A criminological perspective

First, two general caveats. The context in which violence or crime occurs and the meaning it has for that individual will be critical. Mental disorder may play a part, but it may not; or it may be that the mental disorder increases the likelihood of other criminogenic factors coming into play. Accordingly, dealing with them may be as effective in reducing the likelihood of offending, as would be treating the mental disorder itself; indeed, treating mental disorder can have both positive and negative sequelae (Rice et al, 1992 on the treatment of psychopaths in a therapeutic community; and Barrett et al, 2009 and Tyrer et al, 2009 on the mixed early findings of the DSPD assessment programme). Suggestions that therapy can have counterintuitive effects are rightly likely to attract some scepticism about the robustness of the underlying data (see, for example, Skeem, 2008); and questions about whether the treatment is active or not at the relevant time (see generally Hodgins, 1998 and 2000). But in some situations assessment, intervention and treatment can make the situation worse, perhaps by raising expectations, failing to meet those expectations and then having also to counter the understandable effects of the frustration experienced by those undergoing intervention.

Second, it is important to remember that mentally disordered people are, first and foremost, people; which means all of the factors that bear on people in terms of their preponderance for offending will bear also on the mentally disordered. It should not be a surprise that the Walsh et al (2004:249) prospective study of violent behaviour identified four factors as predictive: 'assault over the past two years, a history of violent criminal convictions, receipt of special education, and alcohol abuse'. It is critical always to remember that people come with a history, with family and friends, with an economic, and (still) class environment. They have jobs and homes; they travel between them. They socialise, drink and take drugs. They are subject to accidents and illnesses and life events aside from whatever impact their mental disorders may have. In short, they live. And crime is intimately associated with living. Crime is all around us.

So, what might be the mediating criminogenic factors that have a peculiar bearing on those with mental disorders, either increasing or decreasing their likelihood of offending? The remainder of this chapter looks at those mediating factors and theories, and ends with an acknowledgement which is not dismissive, but rather strives to develop an argument about what could be fair, both to those with and those without mental disorder who have, co-incidentally or consequentially, offended.

Theory and practice

Proponents of social learning theory would emphasise a detailed examination of the social networks of those with mental disorder: to what extent do the beliefs, attitudes and behaviour of family members, caregivers, neighbours, friends and others increase or decrease the likelihood of criminal activity? Are those with mental disorder more likely to mix with a particular stratum of society where crime or the use of violence is more acceptable? Such an approach would historically resonate with theories that stressed the importance of the volatile and transient nature of some poorer communities – often located in what members of the University of Chicago Sociology Department used to call zones in transition – where weak controls, both formal and informal, operated and delinquency was nurtured over generations. And it is not that people in such communities are more criminogenic, but rather that the very nature of the community, with its vestigial levels of control, makes them feel more anxious and less inclined to establish the networks of interdependence which build strong communities (see, on the contribution of social disorganisation theory, Silver 2000). More recently, the work of the MacArthur group would emphasise the role of particular neighbourhoods in facilitating or reducing the likelihood of violence: 'violence by persons with mental disorders may be, in part, a function of the high crime neighborhoods in which they typically reside' (Monahan et al, 2001:60; see also Silver et al, 1999). Indeed, this work resonates with that of Sampson et al (1997) who have argued, based on a study of over 300 neighbourhoods in Chicago, that 'collective efficacy', a combination of the area's social cohesion and the preparedness of residents to intervene to promote the common good, is linked to reduced violence.

Are those with mental disorder exposed to more stressful life events and more likely to experience negative affective states like anger or fear? Feeling under threat, and the fear that it produces, can facilitate violence amongst the ordered; if a belief that one is under threat, and the negative emotional states that accompany that, are associated with particular delusional states, then the probability of violence may be enhanced. If such beliefs arise in the context of an environment where violence is regarded as a problem solver, then the route to enhanced rates of interpersonal violence can be mapped, if not necessarily followed. So, are mentally disordered individuals exposed to disproportionately more negative and stressful life events, perhaps partly through the process of victimisation, facilitated by a process of stigmatisation? And does the process of coercion or perceived coercion to which mentally disordered people are exposed add to their sense of injustice and grievance, in turn contributing to the precipitation of violence? Indeed, James (1995) has brought a number of these elements together in his argument that the neo-liberal policies pursued in the 1980s, and the economic damage done to working-class young men thereby, could contribute to levels of paranoia and subsequent violence. Whilst this is a heady-brew of interacting factors, the causes of violence are never likely to be straightforward.

Ironically, whilst those with mental disorder may be exposed to greater formal social control, through the processes of coercion and detention, are they equally subject to less informal social control because of the nature of their personal relationships? As Silver (2006) posits does mental disorder increase the likelihood of instability and breakdown in social relationships? Do such changes in social bonds increase the likelihood of violence? Are they subject to fewer interdependent systems of obligation and restraint? Are relationships infused with tension, leading to reciprocal antagonism and a greater propensity to be subject to victimisation? The exploratory work of Colombo (2007) above documents the day-to-day aggression and interpersonal violence to which those with mental disorder are subjected. And as we are frequently reminded, violence occurs in a context: it is rarely a unilateral event. Does the rejection that comes with the stigma of mental disorder lead generally to lower levels of social support? Is mental disorder therefore a risk factor for rejection by others?

That category of criminological theories termed 'control theories' (eg Hirschi, 1969) would start from the proposition that crime is inherently rewarding and that law-breaking is potentially widespread: the critical questions then surround the issue of what prevents people from offending. The strength of an individual's bond to society determines whether people comply with the rules: and that bond is based on elements such as their attachment to others, their involvement in society, their commitment to a conforming lifestyle and whether they believe they ought to obey the law. Subsequently, Gottfredson and Hirschi (1990) developed the thesis to include aspects relating to impulsivity and self-control, arguing that crime is facilitated in conditions of low self-control. This begins to resonate with the control-override thesis; and, whilst this has not been satisfactorily demonstrated to have an independent effect generally in offending by those with delusions of control-override, it has potential in respect of mentally disordered offending per se. Are such offenders more likely to be risk-takers, to lack sympathy for the victim (possibly, with respect to personality disorder, since this can be one of the diagnostic criteria), or to be less able to postpone pleasure? Or is it that some mentally disordered people, partly as a result of stigmatisation, live in an atmosphere where their social ties are significantly less strong or less stable than for the ordered population? Again, the thesis may be true for some individuals; but it is not true across the board. And control theory needs to take account not just of the effects of mental disorder, but also of the more commonplace effects of gender (for an excellent account see Hagan et al, 1979).

At first sight, rational choice theory might seem an incongruous application theoretically. But, as asserted earlier, there is no reason to presuppose that those with mental disorder routinely engage in offending behaviour for any more or less rational reasons than the mentally ordered. Whilst intuitively it has been attractive to portray those with mental disorder as irrational or out of control, there is no convincing empirical evidence to support this. In any event, rational choice theory places less emphasis on the nature of offenders and more on the contexts in which offending occurs: target hardening, controlling access to the opportunities for crime and increasing the risks of being caught apply equally to the ordered as the disordered. What then is required is an analysis of the costs and benefits of a particular course of action as perceived by the perpetrator. It may be that those with mental disorder weigh these costs and benefits differently, but perhaps the greatest mediating variable is likely to be the perception of surveillance: delusional disorders involving paranoid features may make people less likely to offend because they perceive themselves to be subject to greater surveillance. In practice, those with mental disorders may be less subject to surveillance because of the environments in which they live, whether due to isolation or because of the arguments about the nature of communities and neighbourhoods explored above. And whilst it may make sense to argue that most violence occurs within close relationships and that these might be more subject to fracture where those with mental disorder are involved, or that those relationships are inherently more proximate and continuous where caregivers are involved, both of these explanatory strands largely draw their power from the nature and intensity of the contact, rather than any irrational motives by the perpetrator.[1]

Does a criminal careers perspective assist? Yes. Much of the literature reviewed above on the relationship between mental disorder and violence has been criticised for being cross-sectional; and if you want to understand the sequence of events in an individual's life and their impact on subsequent behaviour, you need to follow people longitudinally. One very interesting finding cited by Silver (2006) as emerging from one of the few studies that has attempted a longitudinal approach (albeit over a relatively brief period following discharge) is that of Teasdale (2004); namely, that whilst social stress and social control were significantly related to violence within an individual's history, clinical factors, such as threat/control-override delusions, Brief Psychiatric Rating Scale scores and alcohol problems were not related to violence, but were related to victimisation. This would seem to imply that violence is 'normally' regulated, but victimisation attributable to mental disorder.

Finally, the etiological evidence, also noted above, illustrates that the offending patterns of early start offenders, whether mentally disordered or not, were indistinguishable; yet late starters did postdate the onset of major mental disorder (Hodgins et al, 1998). Whilst it is intuitively persuasive that early onset will be more influenced by prolonged exposure to criminogenic values, it clearly cannot be the case that all late start offenders suffer from

1 The emerging research from the MacArthur Foundation Network on mandated community treatment is pertinent here: the finding that violence within families is significantly increased where family members exercise leverage as representative payees for relatives with psychiatric disabilities is testament to the power of proximity and opportunity as explanatory variables in the occurrence of violence. See http://macarthur.virginia.edu with specific reference to the work of Eric Elbogen and colleagues.

mental disorder. Similarly, Mullen pointed towards growing support for two types of violence in schizophrenia: Type 1:

> ... have organised delusional symptoms that are related to the violence, do not have prominent histories of conduct disorder or adult delinquency, usually commit their first violent offence after entering treatment, almost always attack a carer or acquaintance and, perhaps most importantly 'look like' patients.
>
> (Mullen, 2006:241)

Homicide offenders may be over-represented in this group. Type 2 violence, which is responsible for the majority of violence in those with schizophrenia, have:

> ... disorganised clinical syndromes, have histories of conduct disorder, early-onset substance misuse, and, usually violent and non-violent offending prior to diagnosis, commit domestic and non-domestic violence and 'look like' criminals.
>
> (Mullen, 2006:241)

Perhaps these offenders don't just 'look like' criminals but simply have more in common with their offending cousins – those who offend in this way – than with their diagnosis cousins, namely their disordered counterparts. This would parallel the arguments of James et al (2002) about the difference between offenders with mental health problems and those with mental disorder who offend. Nonetheless, in emphasising the heterogenous nature of mentally disordered offenders, Hodgins, Mullen and others have reminded us of an important lesson: crime amongst the ordered is diverse, opportunistic and intermittent; and so it is amongst the mentally disordered.

All of this causes Silver (2006) to call for an infusion into the field of mental disorder and violence, and I would add mental disorder and crime generally, of an approach informed by criminological theory. Empirical studies in the field need to adopt designs that take account of changes over time both within individuals and across the risks to which they are exposed. For over time these risks will change, and it is their proximity to the occurrence of violence that is critical, not necessarily the presence of a person 'with mental disorder'.

Equally, in policy terms, Mullen (2006:246) is right to argue that whilst we might be able to identify small sub-groups of high risk patients, we are not able to identify within those sub-groups the very few patients who will be violent; this state of affairs 'mandates risk management strategies that augment care and treatment for the whole group, rather than justifying policies of coercion and incapacitation directed at selected individuals'. Yet, our focus seems to remain very much on the back end of psychiatric care and on its more controlling element, with early intervention and support in crises remaining way short of its targets (Carvel, 2007). It is nonsensical to approach the issue in this way. If positive psychotic symptomatology has a relationship with serious violence, then the arguments for facilitating effective treatment and management are clear: but, given the role of substance abuse and other interpersonal and social factors in offending generally, it is equally clear that the clinician's focus cannot be on medication alone. So to do may prevent a very small number of serious offences, but it will fail to address the much more common issue of general offending, and all of the consequences that trail in its wake, whilst potentially alienating the very patients for whom medication may help.

And finally, is it wrong to ask the general question does mental disorder cause crime, and right rather to question how much crime or violent crime can be attributed to mental disorder? Answering this question, with its estimation of population based attributable risk, produces a less dramatic and much less frightening response. Monahan describes mental health status as making 'at best a trivial contribution to the overall level of violence in society' (2007:144); and Wessely et al (1994), referring specifically to schizophrenia, term it 'slender'. Of course, not all will agree (see Maden, 2007). But, as Arboleda-Florez et al (1998) observe, clinicians' perceptions of risk may be based on the changing cohorts of patients with whom they are faced; as risk infuses the activities of others, those patients admitted to hospital may simply be amongst the more violent or more potentially violent. Equally, as the diagnostic criteria for mental disorder expand under DSM and under domestic legislation, academics' views, and in particular my own, may be based on cohorts that are increasingly less disordered and more reflective of the population as a whole.

Having detailed the complexity of the terrain, and charted a possible way forward, the discussion now turns to some of the practical manifestations of the status quo. The next few chapters look at some of the human rights issues, partly because they help to document the borderlines between disorder and deviance; with disorder seemingly permitting greater intervention than mere deviance. And partly because a human rights analysis throws considerable light upon the way in which mentally disordered offenders do experience a form of double discrimination. This discrimination is harder to justify if mentally disordered offenders are not, in some sense, an exceptional category but rather the exceptional meeting point of two characteristics with undoubtedly negative connotations; namely, disorder and criminality.

Chapter 9

Human rights and mentally disordered offenders

The logical consequences of the analysis in the preceding chapters are by no means straightforward. This chapter begins by exploring some of those consequences in preparation, in subsequent chapters, for an examination of some of the human rights case-law as a means of elucidating and illustrating the issues. The final chapters of the book explore particular responses to these difficulties.

Whilst the argument was made in the earlier chapters that the relationship between mental disorder and crime is slender, all the time there is a relationship for some individuals, the first consequence should be that we have in place robust mental condition defences. Such defences should ensure that people are not inappropriately convicted where they are not culpable for the offending. Moreover, any established relationship also requires that good treatment can follow for those whose disorder contributes to, but may not wholly account for, their offending behaviour. This also raises issues of ensuring that the right people (offenders, offender-patients, patient-offenders and patients) are in the right place at the right time and that there enough places of the right sort available, all of which requires good initial decision-making about allocation and disposal, and some subsequent flexibility between health care and penal systems. And since detention subject to the MHA 1983 brings with it a considerably greater potential for intrusive treatment, compared with detention for the purposes of punishment, the same person detained in either hospital or prison will experience very different levels of intervention. These may be wholly appropriate, but nonetheless very different.

Second, there are questions which arise from the recognition that mental disorder and crime co-occur, but are not related. This has consequences for issues such as the fairness of trial procedures and the appropriateness of punishing those who may not be fit to be punished, even though they were 'fit' in the sense of being held culpable for the offence. Here, questions arise over what constitutes humane treatment in a penal environment and about the prior appropriateness of fitness to plead provisions. Again, the same individual being dealt with under either essentially criminal or civil proceedings, or a combination of both as with unfitness to plead (Peay, 2010a), will enjoy or endure different levels of protection.

Third, over the period of time during which individuals are subject to punishment or treatment their mental health can fluctuate. This brings with it both the need for flexibility in the systems mentioned above, but also the possibility that inflexibility will produce what looks like arbitrary decision-making under either or both regimes where very similar cases will be dealt with differently and/or inappropriately according to their location. Perhaps the most telling example here concerns the response of the courts to those patients and prisoners who refuse food or otherwise wish to self-harm. Capacitous decision-making even if it leads to harmful consequences for the individual in a penal environment will largely be respected;[1] in a therapeutic environment the MHA 1983 provides a route for overriding capacitous decision-making. Additionally, such decision-making by those with mental disorders in a therapeutic environment is arguably more vulnerable to being judged incapacitous and thus overridden on those grounds.

There is also the issue of the position of victims. In earlier chapters the position of mentally disordered offenders as people who have been subject to victimisation has been raised, but it is important to stress that the victims of mentally disordered offenders have arguably been at a disadvantage in the way in which they have been dealt with by the criminal justice system, compared with the victims of ordered offenders. Some progress has been made in addressing these disadvantages but in other areas those difficulties stem from the ambiguous position of mentally disordered offenders.[2] As patients, issues relating to their treatment are rightly subject to questions of medical confidentiality, a matter some victims might find frustrating. However, this is the flip side of the greater intrusiveness that patients experience adverted to above; if these patient-offenders are primarily patients then they should be entitled to all those protections traditionally afforded to those in a doctor-patient relationship.

Accordingly, the chapters that follow will pick up on some of these specific issues; what follows now is an exploration of some of the general issues arising from the context of placing mentally disordered offending into a human rights context.

1 What constitutes capacitous decision-making is not straightforward, since whether or not one is deemed to have capacity will vary according to the nature of the decision to be made, and the context in which it is made. One definition is to be found in s 2 of the Mental Capacity Act 2005, namely that 'a person lacks capacity in relation to a matter if at the material time he is unable to make a decision for himself because of an impairment of, or a disturbance in the functioning of, the mind or brain'.
2 See, for example, ss 36–38 of the Domestic Violence, Crime and Victims Act 2004 which provides a right to victims to make representations about the conditions to be attached to a restricted patient's discharge or to receive information about any such conditions.

Mentally disordered offenders as perpetrators of human rights abuses

That the human rights of those with mental disabilities has been a central focus of activity is manifest, and rightly manifest, albeit that some of that activity is relatively recent (see Gostin and Gable, 2004; Perlin and Szeli, 2008; and the work, for example, of the Mental Disability Advocacy Centre in Budapest). However, mentally disordered offenders and mentally disordered offending are not prominent there, nor are they evident in the literature generally on human rights. Indeed, such offenders are amongst the least obvious candidates, as potential perpetrators of abuse against others, for public sympathy or the injection of limited resources. They also constitute a problematic and incoherent group for such initiatives, despite raising a multiplicity of relevant issues. From a human rights perspective mentally disordered offenders are not easy to portray as victims. What constitutes a victim is, of course, itself a contentious matter. This has been explored elsewhere (Rock, 1996, 1998; Peay, 2010b); and memorials to the dead are a poignant reminder that perpetrators are rarely regarded as victims.[3]

First, it is clear that offenders, disordered or not, come with a history of having already infringed the rights of others; and perhaps to have infringed those rights in the most serious and malign ways; in turn this makes the promotion of such perpetrators' rights more problematic. The 1950 European Convention on Human Rights and Fundamental Freedoms (ECHR) formally recognises that some rights are absolute rights, for example, the Article 2 right to life and Article 3 'prohibition on torture' provisions, albeit that these rights, as unqualified, are subject to high thresholds, with the result that they can be difficult to invoke (Richardson, 2008). There is scope to limit or qualify other Convention rights on the face of the ECHR, which again erodes the protections offered in particular to mentally disordered offenders, and the interpretation of these domestically have been contentious, even in the ordered-offending context. One such example would be the House of Lords decision on 'kettling' and Article 5, which in turn potentially has some probably unintended consequences for the disordered population.[4] The European Court of Human Rights (ECtHR) explicitly recognises necessary balances must thus be attained. As Lord Steyn observed in one of the first cases heard under the Human Rights Act 1998:

> In the first real test of the Human Rights Act 1998 it is opportune to stand back and consider what the basic aims of the Convention are. One finds

3 One example of this would be the memorial in Hyde Park opened in 2009 with its 52 steel columns; 56 people died in the London bombings on 7 July 2005.
4 *Austin (FC) (Appellant) & another v Commissioner of Police of the Metropolis (Respondent)* [2009] UKHL 5, problematically supporting the relevance of motive when considering whether Article 5 is engaged.

the explanation in the very words of the preambles of the Convention. There were two principal objectives. The first was to maintain and further realise human rights and fundamental freedoms. The framers of the Convention recognised that it was not only morally right to promote the observance of human rights but that it was also the best way of achieving pluralistic and just societies in which all can peaceably go about their lives. The second aim was to foster effective political democracy. This aim necessarily involves the creation of conditions of stability and order under the rule of law, not for its own sake, but as the best way to ensuring the well being of the inhabitants of the European countries. After all, democratic government has only one raison d'etre, namely to serve the interests of all the people. The inspirers of the European Convention, among whom Winston Churchill played an important role, and the framers of the European Convention, ably assisted by English draftsmen, realised that from time to time the fundamental right of one individual may conflict with the human right of another. Thus the principles of free speech and privacy may collide. They also realised only too well that a single-minded concentration on the pursuit of fundamental rights of individuals to the exclusion of the interests of the wider public might be subversive of the ideal of tolerant European liberal democracies. The fundamental rights of individuals are of supreme importance but those rights are not unlimited: we live in communities of individuals who also have rights. The direct lineage of this ancient idea is clear: the European Convention (1950) is the descendant of the Universal Declaration of Human Rights (1948) which in Article 29 expressly recognised the duties of everyone to the community and the limitation on rights in order to secure and protect respect for the rights of others. It is also noteworthy that Article 17 of the European Convention prohibits, among others, individuals from abusing their rights to the detriment of others. ... The European Convention requires that where difficult questions arise a balance must be struck. Subject to a limited number of absolute guarantees, the scheme and structure of the Convention reflects this balanced approach. It differs in material respects from other constitutional systems but as a European nation it represents our Bill of Rights. We must be guided by it. And it is a basic premise of the Convention system that only an entirely neutral, impartial, and independent judiciary can carry out the primary task of securing and enforcing Convention rights. This contextual scene is not only directly relevant to the issues arising on the present appeal but may be a matrix in which many challenges under the Human Rights Act 1998 should be considered.

(Lord Steyn *Procurator Fiscal v Brown (Scotland) at* para II)[5]

5 *Procurator Fiscal v Brown (Scotland)* [2000] UKPC D3.

This is an important analysis when thinking about mentally disordered offenders, for here the balance of rights is even more complex than in cases of mental illness alone. The way in which this balance of rights pans out is illustrated below.

It is perhaps also worth digressing briefly to consider some relevant, albeit commonly remarked on, features of the Convention. First, the ECHR is said to provide a floor not a ceiling: not only does this reflect the basic and low level of protection from which the Convention proceeds but it also explains why national law may set higher standards than the Convention. Indeed, the rights embodied in the ECHR are not only compromised rights, compromised in the sense that the very process of attaining them amongst a group of disparate countries required their compromise, but the rights are also largely uncontroversial ones. And whilst it is easy enough to acknowledge the rights of people who are well-regarded, it is not so easy to cede rights to those who are not, and it is they who need protection above all. In this context it is perhaps not unsurprising that the weight accorded to those with mental health disabilities, let alone, mentally disordered offenders, is not prominent on the face of the ECHR. Second, the Convention is described as a living instrument; it is an organic beast and its language and content need to be seen in their contemporary context.[6] Thus, previous decisions may lose their applicability, although applicants would not know that in advance, and arguments that have previously failed may succeed at another attempt. In this light, cases that are even only a decade old should be treated with some caution. Similarly, those that emanate from one jurisdiction may prove less applicable in another simply because the context can be fundamentally different. This also helps to explain in part the persistence of lawyers in taking cases on behalf of offenders with mental disorders. Third, the ECHR is intended to be interpreted so that its rights are practical and effective, not theoretical and illusory (see Starmer 1999; para 4.1); this necessarily entails a purposive interpretation of the Convention, and one that has constantly to address a changing resource landscape. In short, the ECHR has much more of a fluid feel to it than those familiar with domestic legislation might expect. Finally, it is important to stress, as Hale (2007) reminds us, that the very essence of the Convention is respect for human dignity and human freedom.[7] And it is arguably these values that are most jeopardised when considering society's dealings with those who both have a mental disorder and who have offended against the rights of others.

The balancing of rights referred to above is also explicitly recognised in the Convention, where a number of the Articles set out are not absolute rights, but qualified rights. For example, Article 8 – the right to respect for private and family life – states (emphasis added):

6 *Tyrer v UK* (1979–80) 2 EHRR 1.
7 *Pretty v UK* (2002) 35 EHRR 1.

1. Everyone has the right to respect for his private and family life, his home and his correspondence.
2. There shall be no interference by a public authority with the exercise of this right except such as is in accordance with the law and is necessary in a democratic society in the interests of national security, *public safety* or the economic well-being of the country, for the *prevention of disorder or crime*, for the *protection of health or morals, or for the protection of the rights and freedoms of others.*

(Article 8, ECHR 1950)

Thus, the state may interfere with Article 8 rights in order to secure certain interests; and, whilst the onus is on the state to show that such interference is in accordance with the law (by which it means that the law has a domestic basis and is sufficiently clear to enable a citizen to comply with the law), *and* protects a recognised interest, *and* that the action taken is necessary in a democratic society (that is that it meets some pressing social need), *and* is the minimum necessary to secure this legitimate aim, it can readily be seen that some groups will be more vulnerable to such interference than others. Thus, those who have offended, or who are thought likely to offend, or whose health is at risk, will be peculiarly vulnerable, albeit that the interference has to be justified according to the doctrine of proportionality (that is, the action taken is proportionate to the need to be met and the grounds given are sufficient and relevant). So those with 'cleaner hands' will find it easier to gain the protections offered by the Convention than some others. Mentally disordered offenders are triply jeopardised by this potential disadvantage (their own health, the protection of others and the prevention of crime); yet this triple jeopardy paradoxically provides greater scope for lawyers to challenge the extent and application of those qualifications.

Mentally disordered offenders: invisible, ignored or all too evident?

Having argued in the preceding chapters that those with mental disorder who offend suffer from too bright a light being focused on the limited association between mental disorder and crime it is ironic that this chapter largely adopts the opposite premise: namely, that in a human rights context mentally disordered offenders may suffer from their invisibility. Perhaps not their invisibility as such, but an aversion of gaze in terms of their not being regarded as the most 'deserving' of such attention. Thus, whilst the human rights issues arising in respect of civil patients are enthusiastically pursued, and the rights of offenders at least pursued with verve, the position of mentally disordered offenders, who straddle the disordered-offending spectrum, is a much less comfortable fit in a human rights context. And this discombobulation, deriving as it does from the confused moral status of mentally disordered offenders, is only one of a series of factors that contribute to the almost hidden presence of these offenders.

Part of this invisibility is structural and stems from the location of mentally disordered offenders within the scheme of the MHA 1983. On the one hand, this adopts an impressive approach by dealing with disordered offenders at the point of sentence primarily in terms of their disorder and not their offence. Thus, if given a hospital order under s 37 of the Act the offender will thereafter be treated by the detaining hospital for all intents and purposes on the same basis as if the admission were direct from the community on an admission for treatment section (s 3). The conviction becomes a part of the patient's history rather than the event that will determine their future. The position is, of course, markedly different if the offender receives a restriction order (see Boyd-Caine, 2010).

But on the other hand, the scheme of the MHA 1983 locates mentally disordered offenders in Part III of the Act; whilst this position is a logical one, coming as it does after the sections dealing with the compulsory admission of civil patients, it has had the consequence of relegating them to a form of secondary status. Indeed, during the various initiatives forming what was a labyrinthine reform process of the MHA 1983, mentally disordered offenders tended to be discussed by the various bodies involved in the reform process somewhat late in the day; indeed, sometimes such consideration actually took place late in any given day. Sometimes, such offenders did not feature at all in written submissions from assorted bodies. This affected, I would argue, not only the deliberations of the Richardson Committee on which I sat, but also those of the Joint Committee on the Draft Mental Health Bill and the Joint Committee on Human Rights; it also arguably affected some of the bodies which made submissions to these Committees.[8] So, the profile of mentally disordered offenders, and the problems they raised, remained relatively low throughout the reform process.

The invisibility is also attributable in part to the confused status of mentally disordered offenders: as neither wholly culpable offenders, for whom full criminal justice procedural protections apply (eg the Article 6 right to a fair trial provisions) nor as wholly incapacitous patients, for whom special procedures can be invoked where consent to particular forms of detention or treatment cannot be obtained. I would argue that if we had better mental condition defences and better provisions for separating those who are fit to plead from those who are manifestly not, then the existing human rights framework might be pursued more robustly where issues of culpability could be more clearly resolved. However, our current arrangements allow a different approach to the same individual to be determined according to

8 This is speculation on my part since I was not privy to these discussions, and could only observe the written products of such discussions.

where he or she is being detained; namely, hospital or prison. This can be justified but it does presuppose good and effective initial decision making concerning allocation of offender-patients between prison and hospital.

But the invisibility also stemmed in part from an aversion of gaze. It is inevitable that, in human rights terms, mentally disordered offenders pose real difficulties. All liberal democracies face, as Lacey (2008:3) has so eloquently illustrated, the problem of how to include those who threaten the critical features of such democracies. The extent to which a society's criminal justice provisions can be regarded as progressive is often taken as an index of how 'truly' democratic such a society is. But how do you accommodate threatening minorities without allowing them to exercise undue weight over the majority who do respect and adhere to the tenets of a democratic society? Those who are amenable to education, reformation and change are, of course, manifestly legitimate and worthy targets for these democratic endeavours. But the stereotype that many have of mentally disordered offenders does not fit neatly into such categories, and makes them harder to accommodate in a general context of ignorance and fear. Moreover, whilst respecting the rights as such individuals is a sign of good governance, the protection of those rights may be perceived by others to be at the expense not only of their current rights, but also as posing an unquantifiable risk to future interests, given that such offenders are all too readily perceived as presenting a high risk of future harm. Two matters are evident: ensuring a better understanding of the true nature of the associations between mental disorder and crime is critical; but it is also clear why the tension between our humanitarian desire to deal with such offenders in terms of their health needs can readily be subsumed into an inclination to deal with them in terms of their risk. Or put another way, to try to avoid thinking about the problem at all. Hence, the aversion of our gaze.

Energising the focus?

In practice, and somewhat curiously, there has been considerable human rights based activity in the field of mentally disordered offenders. Indeed, the very first declaration of incompatibility which occurred after the passage of the Human Rights Act 1998 was in a case concerning a mentally disordered offender;[9] and another mental health case came quickly thereafter with respect to the problematic right of a nearest relative to information about a patient.[10] This may be attributable to a number of factors: for example, mentally disordered offenders straddle the protections under the

9   *R(H) v London and North East Region Mental Health Review Tribunal (Secretary of State for Health intervening)* [2002] QB 1.
10 *R(M) v Secretary of State for Health* [2003] EWHC 1094.

ECHR which relate both to offenders and to those of unsound mind, which means that virtually all aspects of Article 5 can potentially be engaged. Similarly, the Article 6 (right to a fair trial) provisions, and Article 8 (right to respect for private and family life) have had an impact both on the trial proceedings and on the subsequent conditions of detention. The procedural injustices that can arise in respect of these Articles are an area that the ECtHR is arguably better at tackling than, as will emerge, substantive injustices.

Moreover, the bulk of mentally disordered offenders are not incapacitous, as is the case with many generally held to be of unsound mind; this means that their independent ability to challenge the circumstances of their detention or treatment through the law remains vibrant. Indeed, the statutory provisions under the MHA 1983 with respect to review by Mental Health Review Tribunals (MHRTs – now known as Mental Health Tribunals) entail, for most mentally disordered offenders, an on-going involvement with lawyers; and of course these offenders will have already had significant exposure to lawyers during the process of conviction. Thus, the fact that mentally disordered offenders can be acutely aware of perceived injustices, are in contact with lawyers, and are simultaneously not as helpless or as vulnerable as are many held under the civil provisions of the MHA 1983 on grounds of mental disorder, all contribute to the ferment in this field. A ferment that is notably in stark contrast to the position relating solely to those of unsound mind. Here the cases are few and far between domestically (even if remarkable in their import[11]) and the ECtHR's jurisprudence derives in large measure from the activities of small advocacy organisations such as the Mental Disability Advocacy Centre in Budapest (see also Bartlett et al, 2007; Perlin and Szeli, 2008) or highly committed carers, or competent, aggrieved and grieving relatives supported by a small coterie of dedicated lawyers.

So it is arguable that the historically low profile that the mental health field has had is now changing. The recent Criminal Justice Joint Inspection (2009) on work prior to sentence with those with mental disorders is one reflection of this. Another can be seen in the major report on mentally disordered offenders in the criminal justice system by Lord Keith Bradley (2009).[12] Whilst the report was somewhat delayed, its appearance and the seeming flurry of activity that has greeted it, at least in government response terms, is impressive. The Ministry of Justice (2009) produced a response to every one of the 82 recommendations (accepted; accepted in principle;

11 *R v Bournewood Community NHS Trust ex parte L* [1998] 3 All ER 289 HL and subsequently, in the ECtHR, *HL v UK* [2004] ECHR 471.
12 Lord Bradley, a former Labour MP who held junior ministerial positions in the Department of Social Security and the Home Office, was appointed a life peer in 2006.

under review) and has established the National Programme Board, which met for the first time on the 24 June 2009 to take forward these initiatives. A delivery plan was published in November 2009 (Department of Health, 2009).

Here is not the place for a detailed critique of the Bradley report, and it is too early to assess the impact it will have. But three matters are noteworthy. Lord Bradley commissioned an estimate of the financial costs and benefits of a number of the actions proposed by his review team (Tribal, 2008): the financial costs are eye-watering. For example, the cost per prison place per annum is estimated at £23,585 and the cost of a medium secure hospital bed £150,000. Moreover, although it might be possible to contrast reasonably accurately the cost of a prison place *vis à vis* a hospital place, the real problem with costs come from estimating how many offenders would be diverted or re-located from one environment to another were Lord Bradley's recommendations to be implemented, and in particular of the critical numbers transferred into hospital beds rather than being dealt with in the community. It is also notable that the earlier report by Jean Corston (2007) with respect to the position of vulnerable women in the criminal justice system similarly advocated, without much success, the diversion of women with mental health needs from the criminal justice system.

In this context the definition of what constitutes mental disorder becomes critical: if only serious mental illness is included a very different figure emerges from these reports than if those with personality disorders are also embraced. And it appears that the Tribal report (at p 12), relying on Bradley (at p 48) which in turn relies on Rennie et al (now published as Lennox et al, 2009, but see also Rennie et al, 2009) is using a much smaller figure for its estimates than might be realistic, so even Bradley may have misunderstood the true financial costs of his report's proposals. And this in turn is critical. In its response to Bradley, the Government noted:

> There is a need for further work to be undertaken against these recommendations to establish their full potential impact on resources and deliverability. Given the current economic climate, there is a strong possibility that no new resources will be available for this work and existing resources may need to be reprioritised.
>
> (Ministry of Justice, 2009, para 20)

And this message is reinforced when one examines the responses. For whilst the majority of the recommendations have either been accepted, or accepted in principle, and passed to the new National Programme Board to review, three are categorised as 'under review'; and these have obvious, immediate and significant cost implications. And these are not just financial costs but also entail significant opportunity and resource costs. First, that there should be a new minimum time target for the NHS to transfer a prisoner with acute, severe mental illness to an appropriate healthcare setting. Second, that this target should be a mandated item in the new Central Mental Health contract and included in the Operating Framework. And third, that the requirement for Criminal Justice Mental Health Teams should be included in the standard NHS contract for mental health and learning disabilities on a mandated basis, and not on the existing non-mandated basis. Notably, Lord Ramsbotham, the former Chief Inspector of Prisons, asked a question about these recommendations in the House of Lords on 1 June 2009. The reply was that the matters were being remitted to the new National Programme Board.

What canvas?

It is inevitable that people who have mental health problems and who have offended will find themselves, as the Bradley Report documents with respect to the criminal justice locations, being dealt with in a number of settings, both before and after conviction. These can include hospital (both secure, medium secure and local hospitals), prisons, police stations and the community in its various guises. The scale of this is hard to grasp. At one end of the spectrum, police-citizen interactions, identifying those with mental health problems looks like finding a needle in a haystack. At the other, custodial populations seem to be swamped by mental disorder. And to take just one point in the process, the Bradley Report (2009:59) estimates, on the basis of a study (Shaw et al, 1999) conducted on those over 21 appearing at one urban Magistrates Court, that there are some 9,143 people appearing at Magistrates' Courts annually with a serious mental illness having been bailed, and a further 8,081 with serious mental illness having been held in custody before their court appearance (out of a total of approximately 821,000 defendants making their first appearance); that is approximately two per cent of these defendants. But these defendants do not include amongst their number all of the classifications of mental disorder other than serious mental illness.

It is evident that human rights issues will abound both across the spectrum of disordered offending and be writ large at particular points in that spectrum. The focus here will be primarily on those who have been detained, where there has been a loss of liberty. This is not to argue that offenders dealt with in community settings do not raise critical human rights questions, just that in such settings offenders are dealt with largely either on the basis of their consent or on an equivalent, or indeed preferential footing, to those with mental health problems who have not been convicted, or who may not have offended at all. The work of James et al (2002) on the use of the hospital order and that of Seymour et al (2008) on the use of the community order and the mental health requirement are illuminating here.

There is also a powerful argument that our conception of human rights is currently too narrowly focused and that we ought also to be embracing socio-economic rights, such as the right to access health care services, to adequate housing and to a safe and healthy environment (Stavert, 2007). The European Union Charter of Fundamental Rights and other international instruments do, as Stavert illustrates, begin to embody such rights but they have generally been much slower than in the promotion of civil and political rights and 'particularly in relation to people with disabilities' (2007:187). The position of those with mental disorder who have offended lags even further behind. Indeed, whilst the Joint Committee on Human Rights (2008) has called for a public consultation on a new Bill of Rights to guarantee a legal right to an adequate standard of living, health and housing, the marginalised and vulnerable groups specifically identified are 'the elderly, children and people with learning disabilities' (Andrew Dismore, Chairman Joint Committee on Human Rights, 10 August 2008). And nowhere in the report is mention made of mentally disordered offenders. Perhaps this is because they are rightly not thought of as an identifiable group, but rather fall under the aegis of either the elderly or the young or the learning disabled. But I suspect not; and that neglect would be consistent with the notion of relative invisibility already advanced.

The discussion that follows will also not stray from the more developed terrain of human rights in their civil and political guises, and will be further limited by its concentration on issues arising out of detention. For those who have been detained the consequences of the intersection of both mental disorder and offending are multifarious. Four manifestations will be explored: namely, the detention of mentally disordered offenders in prison; the introduction of indeterminate sentences for public protection (which illustrate how a broader-brush politically inspired intervention can have consequences far beyond those intended); the imposition of compulsory treatment on capacitous patients; and implementation of the law and policy with respect to smoking in hospitals, which has had obvious consequences for some detained mentally disordered offenders. These four illustrations will be dealt with in the chapters that follow, but they are preceded by some preliminary observations about deprivation of liberty in the context of mentally disordered offenders.

Chapter 10

Deprivation of liberty

Deprivation of liberty, and of all the personal freedoms it necessarily diminishes, is qualitatively different from any other civilised form of punishment. It is recognised as such by Article 5 of the ECHR. Notably, it can occur both in a penal context and a therapeutic one. Its peculiarity stems in part from the series of other intrusions and deprivations of the most profound kind it brings in its wake: deprivation of contact with one's family, lack of control over one's future and, potentially, the pains of indeterminacy (which may itself be damaging to mental health). Its qualitative difference is recognised by those who send offenders to custody in a purely penal context. As one Scottish Sheriff remarked:

> Tagging and community service are supposed to be equivalent but they're not. Shutting the door and locking someone up is not the same. Jail is reserved for when you have tried everything else. There's something awful about taking away someone's liberty. People don't understand just how severe a punishment prison is.
>
> (Millie et al, 2007:252)

The decision to imprison an offender is a sufficiently complex process without muddying the waters by introducing the further complexity of mental disorder. Decisions to imprison ordered offenders embrace both notions of desert and issues of deterrence, incapacitation and rehabilitation. For mentally disordered offenders the equation similarly goes beyond what any direct application of desert would imply, even once account has been taken of the notion that mental disorder might mollify what is seen as deserving: depriving mentally disordered offenders of their liberty *may* reflect the perceived seriousness of the offence they have committed based on notions of desert, but it may also embody an approach that enhances the period of deprivation because of the offender's perceived increased dangerousness or unpredictability, attributable to their mental disorder.

Moreover, there is the additional factor of treatment for the disorder; this also goes beyond the traditional idea of rehabilitative efforts under a penal regime. Although sterling efforts have been made to rehabilitate offenders within such regimes, the suggestion that criminogenic traits could be *eliminated or cured* lay outside what has reasonably been anticipated to be the benefits of rehabilitation. And penal rehabilitation has recently embraced a new twist; namely that a failure to take a rehabilitative course may delay the possibility of release. The Court of Appeal even suggested that whilst treatment can have as its goal effecting change so that an offender is no longer dangerous (or no longer sufficiently dangerous to merit further confinement), it may also act as a platform for assessing dangerousness through exposure to treatment and the offender's response to it.[1] Rehabilitative efforts can thus both reduce and potentially increase the period of penal custody, either within a fixed sentence or, increasingly likely, on an indeterminate sentence. But for mentally disordered offenders the therapeutic desire that a period of deprivation of liberty should be of a sufficient span, and most usually be of an indefinite nature, so as to allow for or enhance the prospects of change through treatment of the disorder, has been commonplace. And although clinicians may approach treatment with the more modest goal of managing disorders, policy and the law still seem geared around concepts of more enduring change, albeit not complete cure.

Indeed, one of the first amendments introduced under the Mental Health Act 2007 to the MHA 1983, an amendment which was almost immediately brought into effect, was to abolish time-limited restriction orders (see s 40(1)). Under both the 1959 and 1983 Mental Health Acts it had remained possible for sentencers to give a restriction order but limit its duration, so that, once expired, offenders could only continue to be detained subject to satisfying the civil provisions for detention under those Acts. Under the amendments introduced by the Mental Health Act 2007 restriction orders can now only be given on an indefinite basis, thereby leaving the ultimate control over those offenders in the hands of the Secretary of State, albeit tempered by the protection offered by the MHRT to discharge the patient, either absolutely or conditionally. This oscillation between determinacy and indeterminacy has been a typical marker of penal regimes.

In bringing about this change, the concept of a 'tariff' period in detention to reflect the offender's culpability is abandoned, even though this was never officially endorsed with respect to those mentally disordered offenders dealt with under mental health legislation. This makes these indeterminate orders

---

1 See para 66 of *R (Walker) v Secretary of State for Justice (Parole Board intervening)* [2008] EWCA Civ 30. This was an observation that met with some curiosity in the subsequent appeal in the House of Lords *Secretary of State for Justice (Respondent) v James (FC) (Appellant) (formerly Walker and another) and R (on the application of Lee) (FC) (Appellant) v Secretary of State for Justice and one other action* [2009] UKHL 22.

exceptional. In contrast, in other indeterminate sentences, for example the IPP (Imprisonment for Public Protection) or life sentences, there is a tariff period set by the sentencing court (exceptionally even a whole life tariff). After that, detention is solely on grounds of attributed risk. If it is plausible to argue that the period of determinacy that formerly applied to mentally disordered offenders went to culpability for the offence, then a desire to avoid having to make and apply this assessment may stem from a political anxiety that one can seemingly never be too careful about the issue of recovery from mental disorder when it has previously been associated with a risk of serious harm. After all, under the previous regime, once the determinate period had expired control over the offender left the Secretary of State and was handed back to the clinicians. Perhaps clinicians were simply not to be trusted with this. Or as Boyd-Caine (2010) illustrates, clinicians do not, and do not have to deal with the same political repercussions that politicians and government officials face when 'things go wrong', albeit that those clinicians will face other consequences. What appears to be the objective of the new restrictions on restriction orders is maximum flexibility. This enables clinicians and, fundamentally, the state to ensure the complex interaction between mental disorder and potential dangerousness is fully managed.

A human rights perspective

So what might a human rights perspective contribute here? First, the special nature of deprivation of liberty, for the disordered and the ordered, is recognised:

> Everyone who has been the victim of arrest or detention in contravention of the provisions of this article shall have an enforceable right to compensation.
>
> (Article 5(5) of the ECHR)

Indeed, under the UK's arrangements this provision is particularly pertinent since the Human Rights Act 1998 controversially did not incorporate Article 13 of the ECHR, the right to an effective remedy (White, 2000). So in those cases where breaches of human rights have been found outside the confines of Article 5, our domestic courts have been disadvantaged by not having access to an effective remedy. The lack of an effective remedy has independently created grounds for complaint under the ECHR.[2]

---

2 *Paul and Audrey Edwards v the UK* (2002) 35 EHRR 19.

Second, Article 5, which concerns deprivation of liberty, states:

> Everyone has the right to liberty and security of the person. No one shall be deprived of his liberty save in the following cases and in accordance with a procedure prescribed by law:[3]
>
> (a) the lawful detention of a person after conviction by a competent court;
>
> ...
>
> (e) the lawful detention of persons for the prevention of the spreading of infectious diseases, of persons of unsound mind, alcoholics or drug addicts, or vagrants;
>
> ...
>
> Everyone who is deprived of his liberty by arrest or detention shall be entitled to take proceedings by which the lawfulness of his detention shall be decided speedily by a court and his release ordered if the detention is not lawful.
>
> (Article 5 of the ECHR)

What constitutes 'a procedure prescribed by law', 'speedily', and 'by a court' have all been subject to review.[4] And it is not uncommon for seemingly robust words from the courts to be qualified. Thus, whilst it has been observed that where the liberty of the subject is at stake an energetic and rapid approach is required, speedy did not mean immediate or at once.[5]

It is also critical for the discussion that follows to grasp why what constitutes 'unsound mind' has been so influential. In the early case of *Winterwerp*[6] the ECtHR declined to define what constituted an 'unsound mind' as the court asserted that its meaning was continually evolving as research in psychiatry progressed, and society's attitudes to mental illness changed. But the court did establish that for a person to be detained on grounds of 'unsoundness of mind', except in emergency cases, three criteria must be satisfied. The individual must:

(i)   be reliably shown to have a true mental disorder evidenced by objective medical expertise

---

3 Evidence from recent ECtHR cases (*HL v UK* [2004] ECHR 471; *Storck v Germany* [2005] ECHR 406) assert the state's positive obligations to take active steps to protect vulnerable people from breaches of their conventions rights, rather than relying on sanctions.

4 See, for example, *R (on the application of KB and others) v MHRT and another* [2003] EWHC 193, which concerned the speediness of access to a body that has the power to discharge (or terminate the period of the detention).

5 *R (Rayner) v Secretary of State for Justice* [2008] EWCA Civ 176.

6 *Winterwerp v the Netherlands* (1979–80) 2 EHRR 387 at para 39.

(ii) the mental disorder must be of a kind or degree warranting compulsory confinement

(iii) the validity of continued confinement depends on the persistence of such a disorder.

At one level, *Winterwerp* is not very demanding; all that is required to satisfy 'unsound mind' is objective medical expertise of a mental disorder of a kind or degree warranting compulsory confinement, and that it persists. But it has, in practice, proved relatively fertile ground and a raft of challenges has been brought on behalf of those suffering from mental disorder who have offended, whether convicted or not. Indeed, if an 'offender' is detained on grounds of unsound mind, following a finding of not guilty by reason of insanity, then the conditions of detention have to be in a hospital in order for them to be appropriate for the purposes of detention to be pursued.[7] But, if the detention is partly on grounds of punishment for offending, then those of unsound mind, namely offenders with mental disorder, can be detained in prison.

Two examples will suffice at this point to illustrate the power of the *Winterwerp* criteria. Most recently, and in response to the incorporation of the ECHR into domestic legislation, there have been developments in the guise of the Domestic Violence, Crime and Victims Act 2004 (DVCVA). This has tightened the criteria for admission to psychiatric detention, based on the *Winterwerp* criteria of the need for objective medical evidence to establish unsoundness of mind. No longer can those charged with offences, even the most serious offence of murder, be sent to a psychiatric hospital unless they meet the criteria for detention under the MHA 1983. Thus, sleepwalking, hyperglycaemia, epilepsy and other more obviously physically-based conditions will no longer suffice, unless doctors assert they are forms of 'mental disorder' which meet the criteria for admission. Of course, whilst these examples have been beloved by criminal lawyers pointing to the absurdities in the law, they rarely featured in practice. But it is good at least to have the law straight.

In brief, s 24 of the DVCVA 2004 is remarkable. We are all familiar with the notion that those convicted of murder receive a mandatory sentence of life imprisonment. The judge has no discretion as to the type of sentence, only discretion in respect of the tariff period offenders will serve before they become eligible for consideration for release on life licence. Even those who are acutely mentally ill at the point of sentence will receive this mandatory penal disposal no matter how inappropriate reception into prison may be, if they are convicted of murder. Yet if they are charged with murder, but found unfit to plead (or not guilty by reason of insanity) the judge no longer

---

7 *Aerts v Belgium* (2000) 29 EHRR 50.

has automatically to send the perpetrator (I am avoiding the use of the term offender here since although the act will have been committed the person's criminal culpability cannot be established because of their mental state) on an indefinite basis to a psychiatric hospital, but now has the discretion to order a community disposal. This may seem surprising in the context of such a serious event, but deprivation of liberty of those of unsound mind requires that they are suffering from a true mental disorder to be established on the basis of objective medical evidence. And it may simply be that those who have killed and yet are unfit to plead, perhaps because of a profound physical disorder or dementia, do not have a condition which would justify admission to a psychiatric hospital. Such individuals need no longer be sent to languish there on an indefinite basis but can be given a supervision order in the community or an absolute discharge.

Similarly for those found not guilty by reason of insanity. Where their 'disease of the mind' is based on an incidence of sleepwalking, or is perhaps attributable to arteriosclerosis, epilepsy, hyperglycaemia or some other curiosity in the legal annals formerly considered to be a 'disease of the mind' requiring admission to a psychiatric hospital, no such admission will any longer be possible. Unless two doctors are prepared to assert that such an individual suffers from a mental disorder requiring treatment in hospital, there will be no hospital disposal or confinement at all (since the perpetrator is not convicted but acquitted of the murder) but rather a supervision order in the community. And this makes good clinical sense since admission to a psychiatric hospital for arteriosclerosis, or one of the other diagnoses aforementioned, makes no sense where this is not an appropriate venue for such disorders to be treated.

The second illustration where Article 5 and the *Winterwerp* criteria have had a positive impact concerns the legality of detention, whilst simultaneously underlining the importance of the ECHR in determining the appropriate boundaries of the state's relationship with the citizen, and the need for the citizen to be protected from the actions of the state. The seminal case of *X v UK* in 1981 caused the UK to re-write the scope of what was to become the MHA 1983 so as to ensure that restricted patients (those offender patients who are thought to pose a risk of serious harm to others) had access to a body that could discharge them from hospital if they no longer met the criteria for therapeutic detention.[8] Until that point, discharge for these patients lay exclusively in the hands of the relevant Secretary of State. Notably, the influence of *X v UK*, in arguing that such decisions should not lie solely with the executive who may be vulnerable to undue political and public pressure, has spread far wider than just mentally disordered offenders. For executive discretion was subsequently curtailed or

8 *X v UK* (1982) 4 EHRR 118.

removed in the cases of children held at Her Majesty's Pleasure, discretionary life prisoners and finally, mandatory life sentence prisoners. However, the government has resisted all attempts to remove the Home Secretary's (now the Minister of Justice's) continued *exclusive* control over decisions about transfer or trial leave of restricted patients. In essence, this leaves the MHRT with a hard choice between either discharge or no discharge, when the former may be premature and the latter may unduly delay therapeutic progress. This is because controlling the movement of patients between hospitals is the real route out of high security for offender patients; thus, restricting the MHRT's discretion in this way effectively leaves the Minister of Justice with the final decision (Boyd-Caine, 2010, Srinivas et al, 2006 and Eastman, 2006).

Finally, it is important to recognise that detention embraces a multitude of sins. As the ECtHR confirmed in *HL v UK* detention is not a fixed concept: the distinction between detention and mere restraint was one of 'degree or intensity, not one of nature or substance'; although specific factors would provide the necessary degree or intensity, these factors could include the 'type, duration, effects and manner of implementation of the measure in question'.[9] Such fluidity leads to a number of paradoxes. Detention does not involve merely physical walls. There can be walls and no detention; if people have the wherewithal to get out, for example by the use of a key or the cognitive capacity to use a key pad. Thus incapacitous informally admitted patients can be 'detained' on the same ward where voluntary capacitous patients would not be considered to be detained. Similarly, there can be detention in the absence of walls, for example in an open prison where prisoners know that they cannot stray beyond a certain point – barrier or no barrier. Their detention derives from their knowledge that lawfully they could be returned and then detained possibly in more stringent conditions.

That this can lead to confusion even in the minds of those who are expert in dealing with these issues is illustrated by the case of *IT v Secretary of State for Justice*.[10] Richard Westlake, a casework manager in the Mental Health Unit at the Ministry of Justice, asserted with respect to a patient who required escorts that 'I consider the escort arrangements amounted to a deprivation of liberty equivalent to detention'. The Court disagreed.

9 *HL v UK* [2004] ECHR 471 at para 89.
10 *IT v Secretary of State for Justice* [2008] EWHC 1707 at para 9.

Chapter 11

Mental disorder and detention

A perspective from prison

What issues does the detention of mentally disordered offenders in prison raise? The first point to stress, as noted above, is that the detention of offenders in prison, whether they be mentally disordered or not, is partly an end in itself, in that the deprivation of liberty is imposed as punishment (and not for punishment, or arguably even necessarily for rehabilitation). Second, the numbers of mentally disordered offenders in prison is, on any measure, substantial. Singleton et al (1998) found seven per cent of sentenced men (and a higher percentage for remand prisoners) with probable functional psychotic disorders. This would mean with a prison population of 84,354 on 2 October 2009 (Ministry of Justice, 2009a) there would be some 5,900 offenders with the most serious of mental illnesses in prison, an arguably wholly inappropriate environment even though they are convicted as culpable offenders. Notably, the numbers of restricted patients in high security hospitals stood at 643 in 2007 with a further 3,263 restricted patients detained in other hospitals (Ministry of Justice, 2009b) so the notion that these prisoner offender-patients might seamlessly be transferred into the hospital system is a logistical nonsense. Moreover, the Singleton et al (1998) survey of psychiatric morbidity found, using a much broader definition of mental disorder than just probable functional psychotic disorder, that only one in ten of the prison population were likely *not* to be suffering from one of four diagnosable disorders (broadly, psychosis, neurosis, personality disorder, drug dependence and alcohol abuse); and 64 per cent of the male sentenced population would have some type of personality disorder (Summary Report:11). Of course, having no national agreed definition as to what constitutes a 'mentally disordered offender' makes it impossible to settle on consistent estimates as to the number of such offenders in any given place within the criminal justice system (Criminal Justice Joint Inspection, 2009); all that can be said with confidence is that the levels of mental health need within penal populations is much higher than in the community.

This finding is not peculiar to England and Wales. Fazel and Danesh (2002) conducted a systematic review of psychiatric surveys of prison populations in 12 countries. Their findings were similar to those of Singleton et al, with 3–7 per cent of men with psychotic illnesses, 12 per cent with major depression and 42 per cent with a personality disorder. As they observe 'Prisoners were several times more likely to have psychosis and major depression, and about ten times more likely to have antisocial personality disorder, than the general population' (2002:545). And Steadman et al (2009) in the United States found 31 per cent of women and 14 per cent of men being booked into local jails with current symptoms of serious mental illness. The incidence of mental disorder in prison is significant and probably universal; the problems that trail in its wake are rife. Indeed, it would be fair to say that prison populations are riddled with mental disorder.

What is prison for?

HM Prison Service's 'Statement of Purpose' asserts:

> Her Majesty's Prison Service serves the public by keeping in custody those committed by the courts. Our duty is to look after them with humanity and help them lead law-abiding and useful lives in custody and after release.

> Our Vision

> - To provide the very best prison services so that we are the provider of choice
> - To work towards this vision by securing the following key objectives.

> Objectives

> To protect the public and provide what commissioners want to purchase by:

> - Holding prisoners securely
> - Reducing the risk of prisoners re-offending
> - Providing safe and well-ordered establishments in which we treat prisoners humanely, decently and lawfully.[1]

A number of issues arise. First, under what sorts of duties are the prison service to protect prisoners from harming themselves, and, in particular, with respect to those known to be mentally disordered offenders? Second, what about harm caused to other prisoners, mentally disordered or not, by those who are detained and are known to have mental health problems? Third, what problems arise as a result of the detention of mentally disordered offenders in a prison environment once a decision has been made that

---

1 See www.hmprisonservice.gov.uk/abouttheservice/statementofpurpose/.

they should be held and treated in a therapeutic regime; that is, in hospital under the provisions of the MHA 1983? Thus, mentally disordered offenders detained in prison may be at risk from themselves, from the others with whom they are detained, and from negligent care by the state.

Suicide in prison

Having asserted that a prison environment is no place for a seriously mentally disordered offender it is worth briefly asking whether the Prison Service is able to hold such offenders safely? A definitive answer to this is, of course, not possible, but some insight can be gleaned by looking at the statistics on suicide in prison. In 2007 there were 92 apparent self-inflicted deaths among prisoners in England and Wales (Ministry of Justice, 1 Jan 2008): on 31 December 2007 the prison population was 80,067, of whom 10,419 were serving indeterminate sentences (either life sentences or IPPs). Of the 22 prisoners who committed suicide while on indeterminate sentences, four of them were on IPPs. In contrast, amongst the detained hospital population, there were 206 suicides in a five year period (Appleby et al, 2006:63) and 856 amongst in-patients generally (ibid:64); these would include those on the ward, those off the ward with permission, and those off the ward without permission. For crude comparison purposes therefore, of the 14,000 detained patients on 31 March 2004 (Department of Health, 2005) there were approximately 41 suicides. That is for every 341 detained patients there was one suicide, a rate that is two and a half times that amongst prisoners. And whilst the statistics on suicide amongst the non-detained would suggest that it is not the detention per se that is responsible for the suicide, and that rather the presence of mental disorder and the associated distress is likely to be the key factor, the very fact of detention is clearly no guarantee of safety. If anything, prisons seem better at preventing people committing suicide than hospitals, although markedly worse than the community. For, as the Bradley Report (2009:97) notes, the prisoner suicide rate in 2007 in England and Wales was 114 per 100,000: in the general population it was 8.3 per 100,000; notably, around 30 per cent of offenders engage in some form of self-injurious behaviour during custody.

The reason for this albeit crude analysis is to address in part the extent to which the prison service meets its own objectives of providing a safe environment for those they detain. Undoubtedly there is a legal obligation to protect the health of prisoners deprived of their liberty, especially where they are vulnerable and lack capacity to complain (Peay, 2010b).[2] Where the state

---

2 See *Keenan v UK* (2001) 33 EHRR 913 where a breach of Article 3 was established in the case of a mentally ill prisoner who committed suicide after being placed in solitary confinement following an assault: the ECtHR found significant defects in the medical care of Keenan.

exercises complete control over offenders and there is a special danger of them taking their own lives, there is a duty of care, insofar as is practicable, to prevent them from committing suicide.[3] As the ECtHR held in *Keenan*, following the reasoning in the case of *Osman*, persons in custody are in a particularly vulnerable position, there is a heightened risk of suicide, the state is responsible for them and thus the state is under a duty to protect them.[4]

The test posed in *Keenan*, which concerned a young man who committed suicide whilst held at Exeter Prison, was 'whether the authorities knew or ought to have known that Mark Keenan posed a real and immediate risk of suicide and, if so, whether they did all that reasonably could have been expected of them to prevent that risk'.[5] There is, of course, a general duty under Article 2(1) for the state to take measures and precautions when detaining others to diminish the opportunities for self-harm, and that this should be done without unnecessarily infringing personal autonomy; this can be achieved, for example, by removing sharp objects from prisoners and providing netting between the floors of prisons where there is a central atrium. This is because prisoners, as a class, do present a risk of suicide, so to comply with the general Article 2 duty prison authorities must take measures to diminish the opportunities for self-harm. But this is a separate duty to that relating to the operational duty which applies to protect particular individuals where there is a known risk to them. And, as Baroness Hale noted in the case of *Savage*, for prisoners this operational duty embodied more than just the obligation to have the appropriate system in place to diminish the opportunities for self-harm, but also entailed, under s 249(1) of the *National Health Service Act 2006*, an obligation on the relevant NHS bodies and the prison service to secure and maintain prisoners' good health.[6]

Homicide by mentally disordered offenders in prison

Prisons can be violent, intimidating and frightening places for ordered offenders. For disordered offenders such experiences are likely to be magnified, not least because such offenders may be more likely to be victimised where assumptions are made about the nature of their offences or the nature of their mental health status. Within any closed institution, the latent dangers that stem from that institution include exploitation, abuse and bullying. In this sense, the interaction between victim and offender, with all

---

3 *Reeves v Commander of Police of the Metropolis* [1999] 3 All ER 897.
4 *Osman v UK* (1998) 29 EHRR 245.
5 *Keenan* at para 92.
6 *Savage (Respondent) v South Essex Partnership NHS Foundation Trust (Appellants)* [2008] UKHL 74 at para 30.

of the potential it can bring as a contributory risk factor for further offending, may be peculiarly heightened within the prison environment. And shamefully, being in prison provides no guarantee that offenders can be wholly protected from even the most serious of offences.

The case of Christopher Edwards is one such example.[7] Paul and Audrey Edwards took action following the killing of their son Christopher by another mentally disordered man in a shared prison cell. The circumstances of his death were horrific and it is understandable why his grieving parents suffered further stress and ill-health given the frustrations they experienced in trying to pursue an effective remedy. For example, the non-statutory inquiry which was held in private into his death sat for 56 days yet his parents were only entitled to be present on the three days they were giving evidence. They were successful in their case before the ECtHR against the UK on three grounds. First, that there had been a violation of Article 2, the right to life, regarding the circumstances of their son's death, both in placing him at risk and in failing to pass on relevant information; most unusually, the ECtHR concluded that there had been a violation of the positive duty of the state under Article 2(1) to protect the lives of those within its jurisdiction. Breach resulted from the failure of virtually all of the agencies involved in the case (medical profession, police, prosecution and court) to pass on information about the perpetrator, Richard Linford, to the prison authorities. Indeed, the inadequate nature of the screening process at the prison when both prisoners were admitted compounded this violation of the state's obligation to protect Christopher Edwards. The sorry history of misunderstandings, miscommunications and professional lapses is not in itself unusual in this field (Bradley, 2009); that the circumstances turned out as they tragically did was.

Second, the ECtHR held that there had been a further breach of Article 2 insofar as there was a failure to hold an effective investigation; one important element of this derived from the fact that the inquiry sat in private and Christopher Edwards' parents were all but excluded, being neither represented nor able to put questions to witnesses. The ECtHR concluded that they could not be regarded as having been involved in the procedure to the extent necessary to safeguard their interests; moreover, mere publication of the Report did not satisfy the need for public scrutiny given the nature of issues thrown up by the case.

Third, the Court found that there had been a violation of Article 13 as Paul and Audrey Edwards did not have an appropriate means available to them to determine whether the authorities had failed in their duty to protect

---

7 *Paul and Audrey Edwards v UK* (2002) 35 EHRR 19. See also the case of Zahid Mubarek, who was killed by a violent and racist prisoner in his cell *R (on the application of Amin) v Secretary of State for the Home Department* [2001] EWHC Admin 719.

their son's life. Moreover, even had the inquiry not been deficient, it would still not have provided a means to obtain an enforceable award of compensation for the damage they suffered. Indeed, the Court acknowledged that breaches of Articles 2 and 3 of the Convention, which rank as its most fundamental provisions, should in principle have some provision for compensating non-pecuniary damage flowing from the breach. Damages were awarded under Article 41 to ensure just satisfaction, given that the internal law of the UK only permitted (very) partial reparation (namely, in their case, funeral expenses); this had constituted a breach of Article 13. Article 13 was notably not incorporated into the *Human Rights Act 1998*.

Of course, the duty to protect the life of others against homicidal assaults is an obligation to take preventive measures to protect an individual at risk from another; it should not impose a disproportionate burden on the state and that for breach there must be a failure to take reasonable measures to avoid 'a real and immediate risk to life'. Quite what would be regarded as a 'disproportionate' in any situation would be for the courts finally to determine. But, within a prison environment, it is clearly the case that the state's capacity to control the situation, and accordingly the reasonableness of the measures it might be expected to take, is much more evident; and thus more litigable. It is, indeed, the very fact of detention that crystallises the heightened duty on the state. And detention can occur not only in prison, but also in hospital under the MHA 1983. As Baroness Hale pointed out and then sidestepped in *Savage*,[8] it could equally arise with respect to the *de facto* detained, informal assenting patients lacking capacity, as in the *Bournewood* case.[9]

Detaining mentally disordered offenders in a prison environment

The prison environment is not one best suited to detaining people with health problems, even given all the recent changes in the administration and delivery of a prison health service, and it is particularly ill-suited to detaining those with mental health problems (see Wilson, 2004; Birmingham et al, 2006; Richardson, 1999). Being in prison may in itself damage an offender's mental health (Durcan, 2008, Jamieson and Grounds, 2002). There is, of course, some merit in the argument that many offenders have complex health needs and that, for equally complex reasons, they would not be getting the best care for these outside of prison. But, and as stressed above, once an offender is in the full-time care of the state different standards apply; that they have been breached repeatedly is an indictment of the prison

8 Savage at para 30.
9 *HL v UK* [2004] ECHR 471.

service, but it is also an indictment of the lack of political will to remedy the situation.

Such a remedy would entail a considerable expansion in mental health services and in the provision of beds, both secure and otherwise for what is undoubtedly a difficult and demanding population. The Bradley Report (2009) documents the unmet need; the government responded positively to this report; but the timidity in pursuing even, for example, more robust standards in effecting transfer from prison to hospital does not bode well.[10]

10 See Chapter 9.

Chapter 12

The intersection between penalty and therapeutic detention

Indeterminate sentences for public protection

Indeterminate sentences of imprisonment for public protection (IPPs) were introduced amidst controversy under the Criminal Justice Act 2003 (see specifically s 225 and chapter 5 of the 2003 Act on 'dangerous offenders'); they were brought into force in April 2005 and then amended via the Criminal Justice and Immigration Act 2008.[1] They may be imposed on offenders who have committed certain serious violent and sexual offences.[2] In essence, an IPP is made up of two custodial elements; a determinate term of imprisonment (the tariff element) to reflect the seriousness of the offence committed and an indeterminate element which ends at the point where it is considered no longer necessary for the protection of the public to detain the offender. As recently noted the statutory structure for IPPs provides for two purposes: commensurate punishment and public protection.[3] IPPs may be premised on giving prisoners a fair chance of ceasing to be dangerous (and demonstrating that they have ceased to be dangerous); but that is not synonymous with the purpose of the legislation. In short, rehabilitation per se is not one of the purposes of IPPs.

The 2003 Act quickly required amendment, with the 2008 Act creating a minimum tariff of two years to reflect the punitive element of the sentence; this was intended to secure an enhanced seriousness threshold. The speed with which these amendments were introduced reflected concern at the time that the use of these sentences was spiralling out of control, and contributing further to the growth of an already burgeoning prison system. Originally the government had predicted that only an additional 900 prison places would be required as a result of the new sentences; yet by October 2009 some 5,600 prisoners were serving IPPs, with 2,130 of them

---

1 See ss 13–18 and s 25.
2 See s 225 of the Criminal Justice Act 2003. The Sentencing Guidelines Council (2008) has published a guide for sentencers and practitioners which helpfully sets out the relevant offences.
3 *Secretary of State for Justice (Respondent) v James (FC) (Appellant) (formerly Walker and another) and R (on the application of Lee) (FC) (Appellant) v Secretary of State for Justice and one other action* [2009] UKHL 22 at para 105.

post-tariff,[4] and the government was estimating that there could be around 12,500 IPPs by 2014. This series of events is testament to the enthusiasm with which governments legislate after wise words from practitioners and academics urging not only a more cautious path, but also predicting the very problematic outcome which the government had then to address. Or as Lord Brown put it in the House of Lords case of *James, Lee and Wells* 'The maxim, marry in haste, repent at leisure, can be equally well applied to criminal justice legislation, the consequences of ill-considered action in this field being certainly no less disastrous'.[5] But that is not the story of greatest relevance here.

Two matters are of interest here. First, the argument that IPPs reflect a convergence between the disposal of mentally disordered offenders, and the sentencing of ordered offenders. As will emerge below, the IPP looks in many ways like the hospital order combined with a restriction order under ss 37 and 41 of the MHA 1983. Both the new penal disposal and the existing health disposal envisage a period in detention where treatment in its broadest sense will be offered with a view to effecting change in the offender; both forms of 'treatment' are offered under coercion, and in the health setting, this treatment can be given compulsorily; release from prison and discharge from hospital are both subject to the offender or offender-patient being deemed to be no longer a sufficient risk; and recall from the community can be effected where the offender or offender-patient's behaviour causes sufficient concern, provided in the latter that the offender-patient's health meets the criteria for recall;[6] the primary objective of the restriction order is protection of the public, as is the primary objective of the IPP, although the latter entails a prior punitive element. For IPPs 'rehabilitating the offender' as a specific purpose of sentencing, to which sentencers must have regard, was disapplied under s 142(2)(c) of the 2003 Act, together with all the other designated purposes of sentencing. Indeed, as the House of Lords observed, whilst the IPP legislation provided the government with the *opportunity* to introduce treatment courses, the provision of these to obviate risk was 'not amongst the specific legislative objectives' laid down in the 2003 Act.[7] For the restriction order, it is the hospital order which makes provision for treatment, not the restriction element per se. So in some respects the IPP and the hospital order with restrictions are similar devices; whether an offender who has committed a serious offence receives one or the other will be determined by the courts on the basis of a set of overlapping criteria.

---

4 Lord Tunnicliffe, *Hansard*, 28 October 2009, Column 1253. By October 2009 only 76 IPP prisoners had been released (Sainsbury Centre for Mental Health, personal communication).
5 In *James* at para 65.
6 *MM v Secretary of State for the Home Department* [2007] EWCA Civ 687.
7 Lord Brown in *James* in the House of Lords at para 49.

The second reason why IPPs are of interest concerns the differential impact that they have had, and will continue to have, on mentally disordered offenders (see Rutherford, 2008; Sainsbury Centre, 2008). For not only are IPPs used more with offenders where there are mental health problems, but having a disorder as such makes it more difficult for an offender successfully to complete the terms of the IPP and be released from prison. They will also invariably draw mentally disordered offenders and clinicians deeper into the quagmire that is the terrain of prediction of dangerousness (Bickle, 2008). This is because, under s 157 of the *Criminal Justice Act 2003*, where a court is considering whether an offender is indeed a dangerous offender for the purposes of making an IPP, the court must comply with the general requirements that precede the making of a custodial sentence; namely, to obtain a medical report where an offender is or appears to be mentally disordered. Although there is the saving provision that if, given the circumstance of the case, the court considers that such a report would be unnecessary, the expectation is that such reports would be routinely required.

As detailed above, the IPP is a sentence which fixes a determinate tariff period of imprisonment to punish the offender and reflect the seriousness of the offence committed. This period is then followed by an indeterminate term of imprisonment during which the offender will only qualify for release if the Parole Board is satisfied that 'it is no longer necessary for the protection of the public that the prisoner should be confined' (s 28(6) of the Crime (Sentences) Act 1997). IPPs are manifestly a risk-based sentence, and as such their introduction was consistent with what had become over the previous decade the growing influence of risk in criminal justice matters (Kemshall, 2003). Superficially IPPs were designed for 'dangerous' offenders who had committed a serious offence which did not carry a maximum sentence of life imprisonment; some 95 trigger offences fall into this category of having a maximum sentence of at least ten years. Conviction of such serious offences, combined with a prediction that the offender may commit any one of 153 specified violent or sexual offences and the court thought there would be a significant risk of serious harm to members of the public by the commission of such specified offences by the offender, would result in an IPP. Indeed, the provisions under the Criminal Justice Act 2003 mandated the courts to impose them on offenders once the criteria in s 225(1) were satisfied; and s 229 required the courts to make an assumption of dangerousness where there was a previous conviction for a specified offence, unless it would be unreasonable to conclude the risk criterion was satisfied. This is one factor that contributed to the steep rise in their use, by comparison with that predicted by the government.[8] Notably,

---

8 Although it is fair to note that the use of other sentences and orders, for example the suspended sentence and the community treatment order, has exceeded government expectations; indeed, any option that seemingly offers a more cautious path will, at times when risk is an ever-present agenda, be used with some abandon.

under the amendments introduced by the *Criminal Justice and Immigration Act 2008* the statutory assumption of dangerousness in s 229 was abolished and IPPs were henceforth only to be imposed where the determinate period of imprisonment would have been at least four years, leading to a minimum tariff of two years; the mandatory nature of IPPs was also abolished, giving sentencers greater discretion as to when they should be imposed, for example, as an alternative to a life sentence of imprisonment.

Before moving to a discussion of the problems with and legal challenges to IPPs one point of clarification is necessary. Section 225 of the 2003 Act refers both to life sentenced prisoners (for whom parliament has already determined that a life sentence is the maximum sentence for the offence category) and to prisoners on IPPs (which are indeterminate sentences – and could accordingly last for life – but which can be awarded in cases where parliament has fixed the maximum term for the offence category at ten years or more than ten years). I would argue it is important not to elide the two categories since in life sentence cases parliament has taken a particular view of the seriousness of the category of offence. In IPP cases parliament has said that the offence may merit up to ten years (or more) but that this period can now be extended indefinitely in the context of certain violent and sexual offences where there is a future 'significant risk of serious harm'. The two are not the same. Superficially they appear the same since even with life sentences a tariff will be fixed in order to mark out the period after which a prisoner can be released on parole; but they are different sentences. Indeed, one of the purposes of the legislation was to ensure that the public could be protected from offenders whose current offences did not attract a life sentence but who were nonetheless assumed to be dangerous, by giving them the new indeterminate sentence. And I would suggest they are not the same even though parliament added 'a defendant serving an IPP' to the ambit of the phrase 'life prisoner' in s 28 of the 1997 Act: this made administratively consistent the basis for release by the Parole Board – but did not necessarily imply the two sentences were the same. Parliament could, but did not, have ordered life sentences in all these cases, albeit if having to encounter judicial criticism along the way.[9] The relevance of the asserted distinction is further discussed below.

Problems with and for IPP prisoners

One consequence of this intersection of factors has been that the IPP population is much more similar in psychiatric terms to the life sentenced population, than it is to the general prison population: thus, 18 per cent of IPPs; 17 per cent of life sentenced prisoners and nine per cent of the general prison

9 See para 104 of *James* in the House of Lords.

population had received psychiatric treatment in the past (Sainsbury Centre, 2008). Add to this the way in which indeterminacy appears to have an independent impact on the distress experienced by prisoners, and the denial of access to courses that those with mental health problems report, and the IPP population begins to look like a particularly damaged and challenging group (Grounds, 2004, 2005). Indeed, the Lockyer Review (Lockyer 2007) established that the profile of IPP offenders, whilst being more like the life sentenced population than the general prison population, is in a sense more extreme than the lifer population; there are more high risk offenders, they are more likely to suffer from personality disorder (and be deemed psychopathic or DSPD) and there are more sexual offences and robbery amongst them. Indeed, their criminogenic needs were greater; and, whilst they had lower recorded psychiatric histories at the time of their offence than lifers, they were found to have higher levels of current psychiatric and psychological problems (Lockyer, 2007:44).

The immediate problem is that these sentences were used in a high proportion of cases where offenders had mental health problems. This was not necessarily because the problems were overt, or because they were brought to the attention of the courts, but rather because when asked to consider whether an offender posed 'a significant risk to members of the public of serious harm occasioned by the commission by him of further specified offences' (s 225(1)(b)) it was likely that mentally disordered offenders, particularly those with personality disorders where issues of worry and risk intersect, would be caught by the application of the measure.

Other problems arose from some of the relatively short tariff periods set which, in the context of an overcrowded prison system, meant that offenders for whom rehabilitative efforts would be required before the Parole Board would be satisfied that a significant reduction in risk had occurred did not have the opportunity to engage in the requisite rehabilitative endeavours. These had, in recent years, become to be seen as deliverable through the medium of particular courses, such as anger management, sex offender treatment programmes, the enhanced thinking skills course etc. Moreover, the Parole Board was specifically required to consider, amongst other matters, and where the information was relevant and available, 'whether the lifer has made positive and successful efforts to address the attitudes and behavioural problems which led to the commission of the index offence'.[10]

The problem for prisoners on IPPs quickly became apparent; indeed, it had been widely predicted. The courts loyally applied the legislation, finding themselves satisfied about the requisite criteria, and the prison system had no choice but to accept this new category of prisoners on indeterminate

10 Direction 6(d) of the Secretary of State's directions to the Board on the release and recall of life sentenced prisoners pursuant to s 39(6) of the 2003 Act.

sentences. However, because the seriousness of the offences committed were not necessarily of the most heinous, short tariff periods were set, and prisoners quickly passed into the indeterminate part of their sentence. However, the Parole Board could not be satisfied that the risk of re-offending had been sufficiently reduced, because the prisoners had not had the opportunity to complete, or in some cases even undertake, the necessary courses to address their 'dangerousness'. The situation was aptly captured by Laws LJ when he remarked 'In consequence the prison population is swollen by persons whose incarceration retributive justice does not require and whose release executive management does not allow'.[11]

Legal challenges

The early challenges to IPPs have a convoluted history, and one which is not yet complete since *James* was, in 2010, being pursued in the ECtHR with respect to violations of Article 5(1) and (4). It is not necessary to review these cases at length, since the judgment in the House of Lords ultimately rejected all the appeals; and the Secretary of State conceded there that he had been in breach of his public law duty to give IPP prisoners every opportunity to demonstrate their safety for release – a conclusion already reached by the Court of Appeal in *Walker and James*.[12] In essence, it was accepted by the Secretary of State that it was not rational for him to have introduced the new scheme and then fail to provide sufficient resources to permit offenders to complete the requisite courses, which the Parole Board would have used as part of the evidence to determine whether a prisoner's dangerousness had been reduced. The actions of the Secretary of State thus constituted a breach under *Padfield*,[13] in that he was frustrating the policy and purposes of the statute under the terms of which he acted; he was described in the House of Lords as having 'failed deplorably'.[14]

However, this breach of his public law duty did not make detention of the prisoners after their tariff had expired unlawful. As the House of Lords concluded, IPP prisoners are held subject to the provisions of s 28 of the Crime (Sentences) Act 1997 and cannot therefore be held 'unlawfully at common law', since the Act, in effect, trumps any common law breaches. Indeed, under s 28(6)(b) the Parole Board can only direct the prisoner's release on licence (a direction the Secretary of State has a duty to effect) where the Board 'is satisfied that it is no longer necessary for the protection

---

11 *Walker v Secretary of State for the Home Department* [2007] EWHC 1835 Admin, Divisional Court para 31.
12 *Walker and James* [2008] EWCA Civ 30.
13 *Padfield v Ministry of Agriculture, Fisheries and Food* [1968] AC 997.
14 Lord Hope in *James* in the House of Lords at para 3.

of the public that the prisoner should be confined'. This presupposes that the issue of dangerousness was properly determined by the sentencing court, but we will return to this later.

Article 5(1) and Article 5(4)

As to the intersection with the position of mentally disordered offenders the first issue concerned whether post tariff detention (during the period of systemic failure by the Secretary of State) was in breach of Article 5(1). Article 5 – the right to liberty provision in the ECHR – permits under 5(1)(a) the lawful detention of a person after conviction by a competent court, but there has to be 'a sufficient causal connection between the conviction and the deprivation of liberty'.[15] Detention which was lawful at the outset can be transformed into an arbitrary deprivation of liberty if the grounds for the continued detention have no connection to the legislature's objectives.[16] Detention can be solely for the purpose of protecting the public; and life imprisonment has been approved by the ECtHR where 'mental instability' led to dangerousness;[17] similarly for 'character and mental state'.[18] But conviction is a prior requirement under Article 5(1), and the detention must be in order to achieve the required objective (in these cases to protect the public by offering secure confinement). It is not permissible to use detention to prevent, for example, non-violent offending when the purpose of the sentence was to protect the public against violent offending.[19] So, where an offender was detained post-tariff, was there a sufficient causal connection with the original reason for the conviction?

The House of Lords adopted a narrow view in determining the issue; Lord Bridge, agreeing with Lord Judge, asserted 'detention beyond the tariff period is justified because the sentencing court decided that the prisoner would continue to be dangerous at the expiry of the punitive element of the sentence; the necessary predictive judgment will have been made'.[20] The quality of those predicted judgments and their continuing validity was apparently not to be questioned. This is regrettable given evidence that some pre-sentence reports do not provide sufficiently accurate reports on the risk of reoffending for courts to be able properly to make judgments on dangerousness in the first instance; and the fear is that in cases of doubt an IPP

---

15 *Weeks v UK* (1987) 10 EHRR 293 at para 42.
16 *Van Droogenbroeck v Belgium* (1982) 4 EHRR 443.
17 *Thynne, Wilson and Gunnell v UK* (1990) 13 EHRR 666 at para 76.
18 *Hussain v UK* (1996) 22 EHRR 1 at para 53.
19 *Stafford v UK* (2002) 35 EHRR 1121.
20 In *James* in the House of Lords at para 50.

could be imposed inappropriately.[21] But, according to the House of Lords judgment, the only possible breach of 5(1) which could occur would be after a very long delay, amounting to years rather than months, either without a review or with the Parole Board being unable to form a view as to the prisoner's dangerousness. As the House of Lords recognised, the rules, the policy and ultimately common humanity would require at least the possibility of challenge under Article 5(1).

The issue of a possible Article 5(4) breach was more complicated. Article 5(4) concerns the right to take proceedings before a court so that the lawfulness of the detention (or the continuing detention) can be decided speedily.[22] The Secretary of State had made concessions on this issue with respect to the applicant *Lee* and had not appealed the finding against him with respect to the applicant *Wells*, so the House of Lords had no alternative but to remit the claims to the Administrative Court for assessment of (nominal) damages. But the issue did not rest there. The concessions made by the Secretary of State only extended as far as what was known as the evidential role of treatment; namely, that the prisoner should be given a fair chance of demonstrating that he has ceased to be dangerous, not that he should have been given the chance of actually ceasing to be dangerous, the substantive role of treatment. However, the Parole Board, as an Intervener in the case, argued that even this concession went too far, since Article 5(4) was concerned with procedure and not substance: hence, even if the material before the Board is insufficient to enable the Board to reach a view of the prisoner's continuing dangerousness, the decision to continue to detain will be lawful as the Board cannot be satisfied that the prisoner is safe to release; providing, that is, that the prisoner's rule 6 dossier is enough to enable the Parole Board to act as a court for the purposes of satisfying Article 5(4). This looks almost Kafkaesque; and is worryingly reminiscent of the position in which those detained subject to the MHA 1983 used to find themselves prior to the case of *H*.[23] In short, if the Secretary of State has not enabled the prisoner to make a meaningful challenge to the lawfulness of detention has Article 5(4) been breached?

---

21 See Lord Goodhart, and Lord Ramsbotham, in moving an unsuccessful amendment to the Coroners and Justice Bill to abolish IPPs: *Hansard* 28 October 2009 Columns 1248–1250.
22 The argument here is reminiscent of that under *X v UK* (1982) 4 EHRR 118; namely that in order for detention to continue to be lawful under a restriction order there needed to be periodic review to establish that the factors justifying such detention persisted.
23 *R(H) v London and North East Region Mental Health Review Tribunal (Secretary of State for Health intervening)* [2002] QB 1.

The relevance of *H* – developments in mental health law

A diversion is required at this point back into the jurisprudence on the detention of mentally disordered offenders in hospital. After the passage of the Human Rights Act 1998, the first declaration of incompatibility under that Act occurred in a case concerning a mentally disordered offender, then detained in Broadmoor. In *H* the Court of Appeal declared the MHA 1983 to be incompatible with Articles 5(1) and 5(4) on the grounds that the relevant section imposed a burden on a patient to show that his detention was no longer justified, rather than requiring the detaining authorities to show that detention was justified. This led to the Department of Health rectifying the defect through resort to a remedial order which amended ss 72(1) and 73(1) of the MHA.[24]

The theoretical importance of this is considerable. Whilst switching the burden in this way onto the detaining authority may seem like a technicality, it highlighted a fundamental difficulty for patients; proving that you no longer suffer from a mental disorder or are no longer dangerous to the requisite degree when you are detained is a bit like trying to prove there were no weapons of mass destruction in Iraq; some people prove remarkably difficult to persuade. Likewise for tribunals, it was always easier to adopt a cautious approach and argue that the patient had not satisfied them that he or she was not suffering. Shifting the burden onto the detaining authority means that they have to prove the existence of something positive; and if they fail so to do, the MHRT is obliged to direct the patient's discharge. Similar arguments could apply to the difficulties prisoners on IPPs face when trying to demonstrate they are not dangerous, when a presumption of dangerousness has been made based partly on the commission of a particular type of offence. Where prisoners have not had the opportunity to demonstrate reductions in dangerousness, either through completion of particular courses in prison, or, and much less likely, on the basis of time out of prison, this can prove an insurmountable hurdle. In practice, the 2001 *Remedial Order* probably had little impact on the numbers of patients discharged; but its symbolic effect in respect of underlining the need for the detaining authority to be able to justify its case is significant. Thus, mentally disordered offenders held subject to the MHA 1983 are detained primarily on health grounds. When these no longer exist, regardless of whether the nature of the original offence would have required a longer period in confinement for the purposes of punishment or deterrence, detention should come to an end. And, whilst its impact in terms of numbers under the MHA 1983 may be limited, its potential, particularly if the reasoning were to be applied to Parole Board cases, would be far reaching.

---

24 *The Mental Health Act 1983 (Remedial) Order* Statutory Instrument 2001/3712; this came into effect approximately 10 months after the declaration of incompatibility.

However, as an issue the relevance of *H* seems not to have been raised in the sequence of cases on IPPs discussed above; indeed, Article 5(4) was not thought to be directed at the operational inadequacies in a prison regime which might make it impossible for a prisoner to address his offending, but rather to his ability to take proceedings to challenge the legality of his detention because the risk represented at the date of sentence had dissipated. In *James, Lee and Wells* the House of Lords determined on the narrow grounds that Article 5(4) did not require more than procedural adherence; if there was a 'court' which determined speedily whether the prisoner was lawfully detained that was sufficient. Whether it will arise in the ECtHR is another matter, since this court has already found against the UK in *Hutchison Reid* under Article 5(4) where the onus was on the patient to prove that the conditions of detention were no longer satisfied.[25]

Thus, the case of *H* would suggest that the burden should lie on the detaining authority to make the case for detention once the tariff period has elapsed. The House of Lords seemingly avoided this point by asserting that the Parole Board's task is to evaluate all the evidence rather than determine whether the prisoner has discharged a burden of proving he is safe to be released; yet it was also acknowledged that the default position was that prisoners *will* remain detained until the Board are satisfied that they are safe to be released, because the sentencing court had already decided that they would remain dangerous post-tariff.[26]

It is possible that the House of Lords may have been somewhat misled since the cases cited related to life sentence prisoners; moreover Lord Judge asserted that 'the same reasoning holds good'.[27] As noted above, in life sentence cases the indefinite sentence was thought potentially appropriate to the nature of the offence committed as a result of a determination by parliament, not as the result of the application of a presumption: indeed, for IPPs the court fixes the tariff period to reflect the seriousness of the offence and then the indefinite period relates to future risk, not past demonstrated risk. That would seem to place the IPP offender on a more similar footing to the restriction order patient, where the burden does lie on the detaining authority to make the case for continued detention. Notably, Lord Judge acknowledged that it will be difficult for a prisoner to establish that he is not dangerous if he is not provided with the courses normally needed to persuade the Parole Board; but, as Lord Judge also noted, that would not prevent him having access to the Board and arguing his case even if the contents of his parole dossier fell short of the ideal.[28] Procedural fairness and substantive fairness

25 *Hutchison Reid v UK* (2003) 37 EHRR 9.
26 Lord Brown in *James, Lee and Wells* above at para 50.
27 See Lord Judge in *James, Lee and Wells* above at para 127.
28 At para 20.

are thus two different things. Is it really the case that the ECHR only requires the former? Indeed, it is not even clear what burden of proof the Parole Board requires when asking itself whether it is 'satisfied that it is no longer necessary for the protection of the public that the prisoner should be confined'.[29]

More on intersections

The second issue concerning the intersection of mentally disordered offenders and IPPs concerns the unclear basis on which the original determination of 'dangerousness' was made. There was originally a presumption in s 229 in favour of dangerousness once an adult offender had committed a previous specified offence, unless the court considered that it would be unreasonable to conclude that there was such a risk. But the evidential basis for the presumption looks questionable, since the list of specified offences included a number that are not manifestly indicative of dangerousness, in that they will not *necessarily* lead to the defined serious harm of 'death or serious personal injury, whether physical or psychological' (s 224(3)).[30] And, whilst the sentencing court was obliged to look at various categories of information under s 229, it was only obliged to take into account the information available to it, which might lead to variable practices with respect to the enthusiasm with which such information is sought out. Whilst the presumptions under s 229 have now been abolished, the initial notion that these were individualised predictions of dangerousness based on some kind of expertise looked thin; and even if such information were available its usefulness as an accurate predictor of dangerousness has been repeatedly shown to be of limited value in individual cases (Szmukler, 2003; Buchanan and Leese, 2001; Royal College of Psychiatrists, 2008; Brown, 1998). It is inevitable therefore that a number of individuals will have been detained (and will continue to be detained) on the basis of erroneous predictions of dangerousness (and even that some individuals will have been detained incorrectly assessed as dangerous at the time). The figures vary on how many false positives need to be detained in order correctly to incarcerate one dangerous offender but Buchanan and Leese (2001), for personality disordered individuals, put the figure at six to one. How conscionable any court would find this to be in the absence of recent and relevant information about an offender's performance on various assessments and courses during a period

---

29 Crime Sentences Act 1997, s 28(6)(b).
30 For example, exposure (s 66 of the Sexual Offences Act 2003); possessing indecent photographs of a child (s 160 of the Criminal Justice Act 1988); putting people in fear of violence (s 4 of the Protection from Harassment Act 1997) affray (s 3 of the Public Order Act 1986); assault occasioning actual bodily harm (s 47 of the Offences against the Person Act 1861).

of imprisonment is unclear. Thus, for the Parole Board to be making decisions to continue to detain and for the courts to justify this as not a breach of the ECHR since the continuing detention is lawfully justified by the original assessment of dangerousness looks wrong-headed, to say the least.

Third, if the original presumption of dangerousness is based on arguably flimsy evidence, it would be possible to argue that the Parole Board could come to a very different view about risk, even without evidence of the successful completion of courses within prison to address problematic behaviour. Hence, in the Court of Appeal it was rightly observed that there is a difference between the role of treatment in changing the offender so that he ceases to be dangerous and the opportunity that undergoing treatment provides for assessing whether the offender is dangerous.[31] The Parole Board can reach a decision about risk without the offender undergoing treatment: without treatment the outcome may appear a foregone conclusion, but is it necessarily so? This is a particularly pertinent question given the potentially flawed basis upon which the original attribution of dangerousness might have been made.

Finally, and as discussed above, it is important to remember that IPP prisoners are not the direct equivalent of life sentenced prisoners. Although both life sentenced prisoners and IPPs have been deemed dangerous, and are both are on forms of indeterminate sentence, their indeterminacy is based on different considerations. For life sentenced prisoners (s 225(2)) parliament has already fixed the maximum sentence of life, but has now left the courts to determine, on the basis of the seriousness of this offence (or this and one or more associated with it), that it is such as to justify life imprisonment. If a life carrying offence is not so serious as to justify a sentence of life imprisonment, then the courts were obliged (but now, after the 2008 amendments, have discretion) to impose an IPP.[32] Thus, parliament determines who is at risk of a life carrying sentence, but leaves the courts to determine who should receive it, on grounds of the seriousness of the particular behaviour; for IPPs parliament determines the risk of indeterminacy, but the courts determine who should receive it on grounds of perceived future dangerousness. Thus, there is a difference in parliament's intentions between IPPs and life sentenced prisoners.

So, some dangerous offenders will get life sentences; some, having committed offences with a maximum of life will get an IPP (because the seriousness of the offence, with or without other offences associated with it, is not thought to justify a life sentence); and some will get an IPP even though the instant offence is not serious per se, but it falls into the relevant schedule under the Act and the offender is thought to pose a significant risk of serious

31 *Walker and James* above at para 66.
32 This was the IPP by default option: s 225(3).

(future) harm. Can it be right to treat all three categories in the same way as the House of Lords has seemingly done? And if there is supposed to be a difference, how is it supposed to manifest itself beyond the difference in sentence labelling? In categories 2 and 3 the indeterminacy depends on future risk: for category 1 partly future risk, but also partly to do with nature of current offence(s), as opposed merely to their category.

If this argument is valid then the differential impact of IPPs on those with mental health problems will be significant. Not only are they arguably more likely to receive such orders,[33] and then more likely to have their disorders made worse by the pains of indeterminacy, but the protections they would have received had they been given a mental health disposal do not seem to be matched in the prison system. It cannot be an inviting prospect to stay in prison indefinitely; and arguably to have to stay longer than would be necessary were the Secretary of State to provide the necessary rehabilitative courses. Notably, a higher proportion of IPP women than men have been transferred from prison to forensic psychiatric services.

There are, of course, differences between the way in which a decision is made by the Parole Board and by the MHRT, but they are not now as marked as they have been in past years. This is partly because of the increased 'legalisation' of the Parole Board and partly because the nature of imprisonment, especially for those on indeterminate sentences, has become more actively interventionist at a rehabilitative level, even if not therapeutic per se. In both settings clinicians will make representations; at the MHRT as witnesses and, on the Parole Board, as members of the Board. The Parole Board will also have access to more actuarial data than the MHRT, especially with regard to risk prediction. But in essence they are making very similar decisions, based on risk: in one of the risk of re-offending, and in the other, of the risk of relapse. Both probably require some evidence of remorse, although in the MHRT this is more readily described as the need for 'insight'. Increasingly, as more personality disordered patients become subject to the amended provisions of the MHA 1983, both bodies will be looking not just for evidence of stability or recovery in an illness, but also of personality 'change', or at the least an awareness by the offender-patient of the problematic aspects of their own thinking, behaviour and personal life-styles.

It is important to stress that the House of Lords judgment in *James, Lee and Wells* is a narrow technical one. The court stressed again and again that the lawfulness of the decisions related to there being a causal link between the objectives of the sentencing court and the prisoner remaining in custody.

---

33 Whilst an offender's various inadequacies may mitigate culpability, they may also reinforce the conclusion that this is a dangerous offender for the purposes of the IPP (*R v Johnson* [2007] 1 Cr App R (S) 674).

It may be that in due course the courts are asked to think again about whether the purpose of an IPP is indeed partly rehabilitative, with a view to reducing the offender's dangerousness. If so, then the link between the Parole Board's assessment of dangerousness and the availability of treatment would be pertinent. And indeed, all this rather begs the question as to what the MHRT is doing when it reviews the cases of restricted patients. The Home Office have asserted that the restriction order replaces punishment with therapeutic compulsion. So why is it necessary to demonstrate that the patient is still disordered to the requisite degree if the link with dangerousness is present which made the restriction order appropriate in the first place? Are dangerousness and illness not similar in import? If, as Laws LJ put it in the Court of Appeal in *Walker* (albeit criticised in the House of Lords), the state is to claim to have a rational, humane and efficient prison regime, it cannot maintain a 'neutral' stance on whether or not the prisoner ceases to present a danger: the existence of measures to allow an IPP prisoner to progress is inherent in the justification for detention. This is a highly critical observation since it links the indeterminacy of the deprivation of liberty to the State's obligation to have an interest in the reduction of the behaviour that justifies the indeterminacy. And the argument is arguably as effective whether it applies to interventions for dangerousness or treatment for mental disorder.

There are those, of course, who would argue that these offenders, who have committed some of the most heinous offences and who pose some of the most serious risks of reoffending, should simply be detained and that, in this context, all of the above discussion is simply hair-splitting. Whilst it is possible for there to be a legitimate argument about how one converts the seriousness of past offending into the requisite punitive response, the problem for those advocating an additional incapacitative strategy is that the evidence to support the effectiveness of such strategies is weak. Unless one plans to detain such offenders for life, with all of the problems that poses for those who have to do the actual detaining, and for the increasing numbers who would need to be detained, questions about the validity of risk predictions cannot be avoided. And if it seems inconceivable that detention for any but the rarest cases should proceed on this basis, then all of the arguments above apply about the problems of maintaining fairness between offenders and maintaining a healthy and therapeutic environment for those detained on indeterminate sentences. In the context of such vulnerable initial assessments of dangerousness, the strategy begins to look much less defensible. And finally, of course, if such strategies apply disproportionately to those who offend in the context of mental disorder, then they will be discriminatory in their impact.

Chapter 13

Medical treatment

Offenders, patients and their capacity

One of the most problematic issues faced by those dealing with, and legislating for, mentally disordered offenders concerns the circumstances in which compulsory treatment for mental disorder can be imposed on mentally disordered offenders. The starting point is that medical treatment per se requires the consent of the person to whom it is given; where that person cannot give consent, perhaps because they were unconscious or suffering from dementia, treatment was given under the common law doctrine of necessity, provided that treatment was in the patient's best interests. The treatment of those lacking decision-making capacity, for whatever reason, is now subject to the Mental Capacity Act 2005, which has broadly codified the previous common law position.

For those suffering from mental disorder treatment could, and still can, be imposed for mental disorder without consent if the person is detained as a patient subject to the MHA 1983. But that treatment has to take place in hospital. Even the introduction of community treatment orders by the MHA 2007 still necessitates that patients who do not consent to treatment, for example in the form of depot injections,[1] must be returned to a hospital or clinic for the administration of that treatment. However, it is not possible to impose treatment against the capacitous wishes of a detained prisoner:[2] hence the need for legal provisions that allow the transfer of prisoners to hospital for treatment (and for their return to prison on the completion, successful or otherwise, of that treatment). As Baroness Hale (2007) has pointed out, for patients, detention is a means to an end; for prisoners, detention can be an end in itself, albeit that there may be opportunities for rehabilitation. So even if the standards of care were comparable between the two institutional settings, itself a contentious matter, the nature of the care that can be

---

1 A depot injection, an injection often into the buttock, releases its active agent consistently over a considerable period of time. It increases medication compliance but is not immediately reversible.

2 See chapter 9 for an explanation of the technical term 'capacitous'.

provided and the ambience in which it occurs will differ between hospitals and prisons (see Birmingham et al, 2006). And the ECHR here provides only very limited protection; not only does the doctrine of medical necessity set the threshold very high before a breach of Article 3 can be established, but even where conditions fall below what would be ethically acceptable in, for example, the psychiatric wing of a prison, breach will still not necessarily be established.[3]

Whilst this is the formal legal position, it is complicated by the reality that treatment for mental disorder varies according to the nature of the disorder. Hence, those suffering from personality disorder, where the treatment is unlikely to be by medication but rather involve some form of behavioural management, the patient's voluntary participation is a pre-requisite. How that participation is achieved, with varying degrees of persuasion, inducement, pressure and sometimes even frank coercion, will not necessarily cross the legal threshold for what constitutes compulsory treatment, even if its ethical basis is dubious. And this remain true both for the administration of more conventional psychiatric treatments such as medication and for the various forms of behavioural treatments (Szmukler and Appelbaum, 2008).

Having crudely drawn these lines of engagement it should be obvious that offender-patients pose peculiar legal difficulties with respect to the imposition of medical treatment for mental disorder. It has been a matter of some contention as to the extent to which it should be possible to impose compulsory treatment on capacitous patients, either because there is a significant risk to their own health or safety, or to the safety of others; or similarly impose treatment with respect to those detained under s 37 of the MHA 1983 following documented offending (Szmukler et al, 2010). A s 37 order normally requires there to have been a conviction for an offence punishable with imprisonment. It is imposed at the point of sentence where an offender is suffering from a mental disorder which makes it appropriate for him or her to be detained in a hospital for medical treatment and the court is satisfied that a hospital order is the most appropriate method of disposing of the case; the offender can be sent to hospital rather than sentenced to a term of imprisonment. In these circumstances, the patient is diverted irrevocably to hospital for decisions to be made thereafter about their subsequent care and treatment by doctors.

Hospital or prison: the importance of the place of detention?

Thus the route to compulsory treatment should not make a difference to the treatment imposed, insofar as compulsory treatment can only be given to those detained subject to the MHA 1983. This in turn makes the decision

3 As occurred in the case of *Aerts v Belgium* (2000) 29 EHRR.

about the transfer of prisoner-patients, those sentenced to terms of imprisonment whose mental health subsequently deteriorates, critical. Two contrasting cases from the High Court will illustrate this; the first person was held in prison, and the second in hospital. Both were convicted murderers.

W was serving a life sentence for murder and a concurrent sentence of 8 years for aiding and abetting suicide.[4] He was transferred to Broadmoor Special Hospital a year and a half after conviction but was found not to be amenable to treatment and sent back to prison six months later. His psychopathic disorder was deemed to require treatment, but he had been found too difficult to manage at Broadmoor. Once back in prison he variously self-harmed, seemingly in order to secure a return to Broadmoor; he also refused treatment for a serious self-inflicted leg wound which he attempted to turn septic by forcing various objects into the wound. He said he would rather die than live in prison. Psychiatric assessment found him not to be suffering from a mental illness, but from psychopathic disorder characterised by extreme paranoid thinking and an inability to accept responsibility for his own actions. He was held to have capacity to refuse treatment for his leg wound, even if that would lead to his death. Butler-Sloss, the President of the High Court, heard W's application for a declaration that he had capacity to refuse medical treatment; the Court determined that he did have capacity, having heard the views of three psychiatrists. In referring to the judgment in Re T[5] that 'The patient's right of choice exists whether the reasons for making that choice are rational, irrational, unknown or even non-existent' Butler-Sloss noted that that could include 'for manipulative reasons'. We do not know what happened thereafter to W, but the implications of the judgment were that if he continued capacitously to refuse treatment in prison, the prison authorities would not be responsible for his death. It was also evident that the High Court's declaration would be sufficiently detailed to assist the prison authorities in respect of what they should do should W take positive measures to bring about his own death by, for example, attempting to hang himself.

The details of this case are relevant because they make such a stark contrast with how the case of *Brady* was resolved. For the moment it is important just to stress that W was a man who was clearly mentally disordered, but was held to have the requisite capacity to make decisions to refuse treatment in a prison setting, even if those decisions were influenced by his disorder and his manifest manipulativeness. And even if these decisions could result in his death.

Ian Brady, Britain's longest serving prisoner, was convicted alongside Myra Hindley of the notorious 'Moors Murders' in 1966. He was described

---

4 *Re W (Adult: Refusal of Medical Treatment)* [2002] EWHC 901.
5 *Re T (After refusal of treatment)* [1993] Fam 95.

by the trial judge as 'wicked beyond belief'; the Secretary of State in due course fixed a full-life tariff. Some 20 years after his imprisonment he was transferred to Ashworth Special Hospital, as he was deemed to be suffering from mental illness; he has been there ever since. In 1999 a MHRT concluded that he was also suffering from psychopathic disorder. In September 1999, following a move to another ward which he resisted, he suffered a suspected crack fracture of the radius (a bone in his arm). Brady then began a hunger strike, something he had done previously as a tactic in disputes with the authorities. At the time of writing, over a decade later, his hunger strike has not ended and he is fed through a nasal tube. His application for judicial review sought to challenge this force feeding under s 63 of the MHA 1983.[6]

At court his mental illness was held not to have been active during the relevant period, but, as the court observed, there was no doubt that he suffered from a 'psychopathic or personality disorder'. This was described by Professor Maden as a 'severe paranoid personality disorder' which could colour his decision-making but 'could not be regarded as the determining factor of all decisions by that individual'. The Responsible Medical Officer, Dr Collins, took another view and believed that the decision to refuse food was caused by the personality disorder, as did Dr Rix, who observed that Brady thrived on battles with the hospital and, because of the intensity of this involvement, did not give proper regard to the risks entailed. The judge concluded that the hunger strike was a manifestation of his personality disorder. In his application for judicial review Brady stated that he wished to die. Mr Justice Kay concluded that if Brady were merely protesting then s 63 applied; if he wished to die the situation was regarded as more complicated, but in any event the Judge preferred the view that the hunger strike was as a form of protest and not as part of a settled intention to die.

The court went on to consider whether Brady had the capacity to consent to or refuse treatment. It was not strictly necessary to determine this since s 63 does not require the consent of the patient. However, the issues were nonetheless explored. And the court determined that indeed Brady did not have capacity and the doctors would be required to treat him in his own best interests, were s 63 not already satisfied. Dr Collins notably observed that Brady's ability to weigh information, part of the test for determining whether someone had capacity with respect to a particular decision:

> ... was impaired by the emotions and perceptions he had at the time ...
> These emotions and perceptions were related to his personality disorder'. Indeed, as he said in evidence 'His spectacles are blinkered ...

---

6 MHA 1983, s 63 is the general authority for treating detained patients without their consent; *R v Collins and Ashworth Hospital ex parte Brady* [2000] Lloyd's Rep Med 355.

Although he weighs facts, his set of scales are not calibrated properly in a whole range of things, especially related to Ashworth.

(*R v Collins and Ashworth Hospital ex parte Brady* at para 59)

Thus it was possible for a man of well above average intelligence to lack capacity with respect to the issue of food refusal and force feeding.

Two issues arise as a result of the comparison of these cases. First, although the cases were similar in many respects, very different decisions were reached. Prisoners and patients, albeit both manipulative and personality disordered, could be held in diametrically opposed ways either to have or to lack capacity to make decisions with respect to the integrity of their own bodies, decisions which might lead to death. The impact of personality disorder on capacitous decision-making was manifestly complex, an issue that will be returned to in later chapters, but equally manifestly subject to eye of the assessor. Second, the court's preparedness to engage with the issues of capacity in a civil context was evident, where it is apparent that the same offenders' capacities, or lack of them, at their criminal trials were seemingly of little bearing when it came to establishing culpability for murder. Whilst not wholly unheard of, reducing a conviction of murder to one of manslaughter on grounds of diminished responsibility (or a verdict of not guilty by reason of insanity) on the grounds of personality disorder is rare. It is similarly rare for personality disorder to form the basis of unfitness to plead.

The final twist arises out of a comparison with the cases on suicide discussed earlier. There, the state's positive obligations under Article 2, the right to life provisions, acknowledge the special position of vulnerability of both patients and prisoners who are subject to detention where there is a heightened risk of suicide. The state's interest in preserving life, preventing suicide, maintaining the integrity of the medical profession and protecting innocent third parties against the individual right of self determination, pose difficult dilemmas for those with responsibility for detaining prisoners and patients. But these dilemmas are acute in the cases of those suffering from personality disorder where that disorder is associated with a desire to test the limits of the law.

Whilst a number of aspects of detention have been successfully challenged and adverted to above, there has been less success in establishing breach of the ECHR where issues have been raised about the appropriateness of the medical treatment offered to or imposed on patients. Failure to offer the appropriate treatment, or holding disordered offenders in conditions inappropriate with respect to their vulnerabilities, arises more prominently with respect to conditions in prison. Imposing treatment against the capacitous wishes of offender-patients is an issue that arises in hospital settings. In brief, medical necessity seems to have given what might be perceived as carte blanche to clinicians to do as they consider appropriate, provided they act broadly within the bounds of what would be supported by other clinicians. Initially, the domestic courts showed some interest in becoming involved with the issue of the compulsory treatment of capacitous patients (see generally Bartlett and Sandland, 2007). However, a line of relevant cases seems to have ended with the judicial conclusion that medical necessity (the test of whether treatment constitutes of breach of Article 3 so as to amount to torture, inhumane or degrading treatment or punishment under *Herczegfalvy*[7]) is 'a value judgment as to the future – a forecast – to be made by a court in reliance on medical evidence according to a standard of persuasion'.[8] And the standard of persuasion is that the medical necessity has been convincingly shown. The court observed in *Haddock*, perhaps revealing its historic reluctance to get involved with the detail of medical decision-making, that:

> To require of psychiatrists a state of mind of precision and sureness in matters of diagnosis akin to that required of a jury in a criminal case, even in this fraught context of forcible treatment potentially violating detained patients' human rights, is not sensible or feasible.
>
> (*Haddock* [2006] at para 41)

Herczegfalvy is thus a case which both highlights the peculiar vulnerability and powerlessness of those kept within conditions of detention, implying that they need special protection with reference to Article 2, but then gives clinicians broad authority to treat patients on the grounds of medical necessity; yet anything which is a medical necessity is unlikely to be a breach of Article 3 since it is very unlikely, indeed almost impossible, for it to be regarded as inhumane or degrading. Arguably correctly, the threshold for a breach of Article 3 is set high, since it is an absolute right and if the Article is engaged there are no grounds for excusing or justifying the breach. But *Herczegfalvy* does underline how limited a protection the ECHR affords those with mental disorder; and that it will remain so all the time the extent and limits of medical necessity remain unexplored. For offenders with capacity transferred to a hospital this remains an acute problem in the unusual circumstances where they do not consent to treatment.

Hospital or community?

The place of detention can make a critical difference to the lens through which individuals are perceived with regard to the impact their mental disorder might have on their capacity or culpability; but this issue is cast in

---

7 *Herczegfalvy v Austria* (1993) 15 EHRR 437 (ECHR).
8 *R(on the application of B) v Haddock (Responsible Medical Officer)* [2006] EWCA Civ 961 at para 42.

another light when considering the boundary between hospital and the community, since compulsory treatment can be imposed only in hospital, and not in the community. Even after the amendments to the MHA 1983, which introduced community treatment orders, patients on such orders in the community who refuse treatment will still have to be returned to hospital or a clinic if that treatment is to be imposed by force: in the community, the threat of recall may be sufficient to achieve compliance from most patients, but even this extreme coercion does not actually amount to compulsion per se. Hence, where a patient-offender is makes a difference. So decisions about release and recall also form boundary points where tensions arise.

This is perhaps most comically illustrated by the case of *MM*.[9] The patient, who suffered from paranoid schizophrenia and had been convicted of an offence of unlawful wounding, was repeatedly discharged from hospital by the MHRT only to be recalled by the Secretary of State: indeed between December 2005 and September 2006 there were three discharges and three recalls alone. This example of ping-pong between the two bodies arose as a result of changes in the patient's use of illicit drugs: in the context of his mental disorder this was perceived by the Secretary of State as an index of his potential risk and deterioration; yet once recalled to hospital the illicit drug taking ceased and he was regarded by the MHRT as no longer detainable. It is interesting that MM's drug taking would not, in a prisoner on licence, necessarily lead to recall; but rather, if a response were made at all, to a penal one appropriate to law-breaking activity. As a psychiatric patient, in MM drug-taking was responded to as a precursor of something much more worrying. In essence the patient-context coloured the response made. One argument would be that MM was never detainable prior to an actual deterioration in his mental state, since mere breach of his conditional discharge, which the drug-taking could constitute, does not itself constitute grounds for recall. But, as an index of a potential for deterioration, drug-taking became the conduit for recall. And that just led to paralysis in the process (Pezzani, 2007). Ultimately, the court supported the precautionary view of the Secretary of State, supporting again the notion that when in doubt, it is better in these cases of 'mental disorder and risk' to detain.

Whether such multiple recalls are a legitimate use of executive power goes way beyond the discussion here, but the use of such executive power has been dealt with extensively by Boyd-Caine (2010). Yet the place of detention is one area where the ECtHR has had a clear impact. For those with a mental disorder who have 'committed' a criminal offence, but where a conviction has not been returned, perhaps by reason of unfitness to plead

9 *MM v Secretary of State for the Home Department* [2007] EWCA Civ 687.

or having been found not guilty by reason of insanity, only a hospital will suffice; for these people prison is not a lawful place of detention.[10]

Treatment and detention

One aspect of the experience of detention of those suffering from mental disorder that marks it out from mere penal containment is the administration of medication. It goes without saying that treatment should be given for health-based reasons, but its impact can be coincidentally to make detention effectively more likely for the person experiencing it, particularly whether that medication has an overwhelming 'numbing' effect. This has been recognised as a potential factor in the cases of those not formally detained (in establishing whether or not the conditions under which they live constitute detention).[11] It has also been established that those subject to legal detention cannot thereafter be subject to more detention, in that, once you have been deprived of your liberty, through a court's penal intervention or through therapeutic committal to hospital, you cannot be further 'detained' by the administration of medication as there is no residual liberty to infringe. Yet this would seem to underestimate the impact of such medication. If medication affects your ability or inclination to mount a challenge to your detention, it may in turn prolong that detention through a failure of the system to recognise that you are no longer appropriately detained. The mere availability of legal review, and of lawyers, does not ensure that those procedures will be used. And automatic referral under the system in England and Wales only applies after relatively prolonged periods where the individual has failed to initiate a review.

Further support for this view that what constitutes detention is not just the physical conditions in which someone finds themselves, but the interaction between the person and their circumstances, is supported by the case of *JE v DE*.[12] Here there was combination of physical disabilities, impaired sight, impaired mobility and general frailty, together with some cognitive impairments, and the absence of contact with the 'outside' in the form of competent family members who could provide an alternative residence; the court held that the individual was detained. Substituting for the lack of physical mobility a level of medication that significantly impaired the individual's motivation – affecting the freedom to leave – may well be sufficient to constitute detention.

10 See *Aerts v Belgium* (2000) 29 EHRR 50.
11 *HL v UK* [2004] ECHR 471.
12 *JE v DE (1) Surrey County Council (2) EW (3)* [2006] EWHC 3459 (Fam).

Chapter 14

Individual and personal consequences

The case of smoking

Smoking is permitted in a prisoner's cell; it is not permitted in hospital. The former is justified on the basis that this is the prisoner's home, and not a public place, with the consequence that prisoners now choose between smoking and non-smoking cells. In hospitals smoking is not permitted; for the purposes of s 2 of the Health Act 2006, which came into force on 1 July 2007, hospitals are both public places, in the sense that they are open to the public, and they are places of work. Secure hospitals arguably fall between the two, being neither obviously open to the public, but nor are they discounted as places of work or residence. Yet as a result of the Health Act 2006, and the regulations made under it, detained offender-patients are in an anomalous position. Such patients can rightly argue that they will spend as long, and sometimes longer, than their non-disordered offending counterparts in conditions of detention where those conditions constitute, for all effective purposes, their homes. Indeed, some offender-patients will be prisoners transferred under the MHA 1983 from prison accommodation, where they can smoke, to hospitals where they cannot. So should offender-patients be held under comparable conditions to prisoners, or under similar regimes to those in hospitals where conditions of detention do not pertain; that is, where smoking is not permitted but patients can take themselves to areas that are not enclosed or substantially enclosed?[1]

Residential accommodation (including prisons, care homes and hospices, where residents are in the final stages of a progressive disease[2]) is exempt from the provisions of the Health Act 2006. Originally mental health units, where patients were held for more than six months, were also to be exempt as these could be defined as places of residence. This did not mean that

---

1 Many hospitals had banned smoking inside before the implementation of the legislation, leading to the bizarre experience of walking through crowds of patients smoking in various states of undress at the doors of hospitals; an experience which produced the refrain 'the saddest thing I ever saw' in a song by the Editors ('Smokers outside the hospital doors').
2 See Regulation 5 of *The Smoke–free (Exemptions and Vehicles) Regulations 2007* (SI 2007/765).

smoking was permitted per se, merely that the provision of a designated room for smoking would not breach the requirements of the Act to be 'smoke-free' premises. But the exemption for mental health units was temporary,[3] and after July 2008 these premises were no longer subject to the exemptions; patients who wanted to smoke would have to go outdoors.

For patients detained in secure hospitals the problem cannot necessarily readily be solved in this way. Allowing patients to be escorted to smoke would still subject staff to passive smoking, and, regrettably, could also expose detained offender-patients to the unwelcome attentions of members of the public, separated from them, but separated in some circumstances only by a permeable fence (see Mental Health Act Commission, 2008:para 2.65). Should such patients be, in effect, forced to give up smoking during the period of their detention?

This has been a hotly contested issue, both in respect of the public health questions and in respect of issues of personal autonomy and the right to protection of one's private life. The Mental Health Act Commission took the position that loss of liberty should not necessarily entail loss of the ability to choose to smoke. In contrast, some Trusts took the view that the ban on smoking was no greater invasion of Article 8 rights than the ban on alcohol. These matters came quickly to a head when Nottinghamshire Healthcare NHS Trust, which manages Rampton Special Hospital, took the decision to introduce a policy banning smoking even in the hospital's grounds, except in very limited circumstances relating to patients in an acute psychiatric state or with a terminal illness. Thus, the Regulations banned smoking indoors in Rampton, and the Trust's additional policy all but banned it in the hospital grounds.

G and others, detained at Rampton, argued that the ban was an infringement of the right to respect for private and family life: if patients were not free to go elsewhere and the hospital was effectively their home, then to ban them from smoking, where this did not interfere with the rights of others, was a disproportionate interference and constituted a lack of respect for the individual's moral integrity.[4] Accordingly they argued Article 8(1) required the provision of designated rooms, to permit those who wished to smoke to do so.

In the High Court reliance was placed on Baroness Hale's comments in *R (Countryside Alliance) v Attorney General* to the effect that Article 8 was the right most capable of being expanded.[5] Article 8 included both notions around the inviolability of the home (a space where people could communicate privately with one another) and that of a personal and psychological

---

3 See Regulation 10.
4 *R (on the application of G) v Nottinghamshire Healthcare NHS Trust and related cases* [2008] EWHC 1096 (Admin).
5 *R (Countryside Alliance) v Attorney General* [2007] UKHL 52 at para 115–6.

space in which people could develop their own sense of self. Nonetheless, as Baroness Hale observed, Article 8 still fell 'some way short of protecting everything they might want to do even in that private space'. There was, moreover, a difference between the scope of rights conferred by the ECHR, and the freedoms protected by the common law.

The High Court in *G and others* decided that parliament was entitled to approve the regulations that had had the effect of banning smoking in mental health units; and that preventing a person from smoking did not constitute such an interference as to breach Article 8. Although mental health was associated with moral integrity, and respect for mental stability could engage Article 8, the restriction on smoking was nonetheless lawful. The importance of the legislative objective, the measures implemented to achieve this and the means used to impair the right were no more than was necessary to achieve the objective, even taking account of the statement of ECtHR that 'the position of inferiority and powerlessness which is typical of patients confined in psychiatric hospitals calls for increased vigilance in reviewing whether the Convention has been complied with'.[6]

Aspects of the judgment are worth quoting at length:

> In considering what respect for personal autonomy and home life requires in a particular case, regard must be had to the circumstances in which a person is living. A distinction is to be drawn, when considering the engagement of article 8, between a private home in which a person freely resides, with his family if he has one, and an institution. Moreover, distinctions are possible between an institution such as a care home and an institution in which a person is detained. Within institutions in which persons are detained, distinction is possible between a prison in which healthy people live in their own cells and detention of mental patients in high security conditions. Rampton is operated as a hospital under Section 4 of the National Health Act 2006. We do not intend to explore these distinctions in detail but make the general point that the privacy and freedom of action to which a person is entitled, for the purposes of article 8, will in our view vary with the nature of the accommodation in which that person is living and the circumstances in which he is living there. Whether article 8 is engaged in relation to a particular activity will depend on those factors as well as the activity in question, and all the circumstances in which it is sought to practise it. Distinctions as to what is required in different accommodation may be justified.
>
> (Lord Justice Pill, para 102)

---

6 *Herczegfalvy v Austria* (1993) 15 EHRR 437 para 82.

The judgment continued:

> We are not persuaded that the requirement to respect private life and home in article 8 imposes a general obligation on those responsible for the care of detained people to make arrangements enabling them to smoke. Whether it is put in terms of moral integrity, identity or personal autonomy, no general right for mental patients to smoke, or general obligation to permit smoking, arises.
>
> (Lord Justice Pill, para 103)

The reasoning looks a little questionable, with its seeming intention to duck the most difficult issue: hence 'We do not intend to explore these distinctions in detail ...' What is the relevance of the notion that prisoners are 'healthy' whilst those in mental health units are not? What is the relevant distinction from a care home, since people can be detained there as well (Mental Capacity Act 2005 as amended)? Why is there a different policy for prisoners, other than that parliament has legislated it so on policy grounds and after general public consultation? The Court's reasoning seems underdeveloped about the purposes of prisons and hospitals and confused about the nature of detained populations.

In the Court of Appeal

The matter did not rest there. On appeal the Court was split, with the majority holding that Article 8 was not engaged by the issue of a ban on smoking and hence the appeals failed.[7] Even if it had been engaged the Court of Appeal was persuaded that the Trust and the Secretary of State had justified their actions. If there was discrimination within the meaning of Article 14 on the 'Prohibition of Discrimination' in the differences in treatment between mental health units and prisons, care homes and hospices, these were also justified on objective and reasonable grounds. Although the Court accepted that patients could stay in Rampton for many years, it was still a public institution where patients did not have the freedom to do as they pleased; patients could not freely choose what they ate or drank, and smoking was analogous to this. Indeed, the Court concluded that smoking was not so integral to a person's identity as to merit the protection of Article 8. And even if Article 8 was engaged, it was reasonable for the Trust to ban it, given the substantial health benefit. In deciding against the patients on

---

7 On appeal there was a variation in the applicants *R (N) v The Secretary of State for Health and R (E) v Nottinghamshire Healthcare NHS Trust* [2009] EWCA Civ 795. The applicants indicated their intention to seek leave to appeal to the Supreme Court, if legal aid were granted.

their principal grounds of appeal, the Court also denied them permission to appeal on the grounds of a breach of the common law principle of equality, namely the differential practices for patients compared with prisoners and those in care homes, concluding that these different practices were not irrational.

The minority decision came from Keene LJ, a proclaimed non-smoker. He asserted that smoking engaged Article 8 since 'for many people it forms an important part of their personal lives and possesses a value which reaches a level which qualifies for protection under Article 8 as part of their personal autonomy' (para 100). He found against the Secretary of State with reference to regulation 10 of the Exemption Regulations, concluding that the ban was disproportionate to the aim it sought to realise, since the public health objective of protecting people from second-hand smoke could be achieved by lesser measures. Indeed, a total ban had not been pursued in Scotland or Wales where designated smoking rooms were provided. He further concluded that the distinction between prisoners and patients was *prima facie* discriminatory; Regulation 10 was thus a breach both of Article 8 and of Article 14. However, Keene LJ did find in favour of the Trust with respect to their actions since he argued that, given the regulations, if patients were to smoke this would have to be done in the hospital grounds and this would be too costly with respect to the necessary staff supervision and to the vulnerabilities of Rampton's mentally ill patients.

As a minority judgment his reasoning may yet form the basis for a further appeal. Perhaps what is most notable about it is that he concluded (at para 110) that it seemed 'indisputable that a mental illness or other mental disability falls within the scope of the term "personal characteristic"' under Article 14. This is an important, albeit obiter (or incidental) conclusion, in the sense that, as a minority judgment, it has no bearing for the doctrine of precedent. The majority opinion in the Court of Appeal did not allow themselves to be drawn into this discussion, even though they did cite two cases from 2008 in the House of Lords where just such a broader approach to the question had been developing.[8] Indeed, Lord Hope in *Pretty* in 2001[9] had already said as much.

In any event, could the discrimination between prisoners and patients be justified given that their situations could be seen, as the appellants contended, as otherwise similar? The majority answered this question in the affirmative and put forward no fewer than seven reasons to justify why Article 14 would not have been breached had Article 8 been engaged at all. And it is, of course, for those wishing to justify the different treatment to establish that it was both in pursuit of a legitimate aim and proportionate to

---

8 At para 57.
9 *R (Pretty) v DPP and Secretary of State for the Home Department* [2001] UKHL 61.

it. At numbers six and seven were an acknowledgement that there was evidence that applying the smoke-free legislation to prisons would, in the short term, have created the risk of disorder and assaults, and that attaining smoke-free prisons was simply unrealistic in the short term. And at number five, having noted the differences between patients in the care of the NHS and those in prison, the assertion that 'The only respect in which they may be comparable is that in both institutions persons are detained by compulsion of law'. The Court emphasised the health care of the patient as being the prime focus of mental health facilities, albeit that security issues were pertinent. Is it possible that the Court of Appeal had primarily in mind the comparison between civil patients and offenders, rather than forensic patients and offenders? In practice, for the latter groups that are so many similarities and areas of overlap. Of course, and the Court acknowledged this, to have provided an exemption for mental health units would have created discriminatory practices between those in such units and other NHS patients; though the reality of its impact would have been tempered by the fact that NHS patients are free to leave to smoke if they so wish. This leaves hanging the question of whether visible prisoner disorder is a more compelling factor than hidden patient distress?

The discussion underlines the complexity of the intersection between treatment, detention, personal autonomy, and personal and public health. But the implications are clear: mentally disordered offenders are patients in hospital and prisoners in prison. That they may be in hospital because of their deviant behaviour or in prison because of attributions about their future conduct, or have shifted between the two according to the bed space available and the acuteness of their disorders, makes no difference for the purposes of smoking. Prisoners can, patients cannot. In turn this must mean that prisoners in the Dangerous and Severe Personality Disorder (DSPD) Units in prisons can smoke; and those in the Special Hospital DSPD units cannot, even though the latter are largely made up of transferred prisoners.

As with much legislation, attempting to ascertain its effects in reality is quite another matter. Harris (2008) reported almost exclusively positive effects of the ban, yet the Mental Health Foundation (2009) survey noted that the ban was not being enforced, or fully enforced, in 85 per cent of the 109 psychiatric units which responded; this inevitably leads to the problem of covert smoking and/or to staff feeling it necessary to turn a blind eye to such activities. Both of these raise important issues of management. And where the population is detained in conditions of maximum security, as in the Special Hospitals, such undesirable and unintended consequences are likely to continue.

Chapter 15

Impossible paradoxes

It is, of course, a real conundrum as to whether mentally disordered offenders should be dealt with primarily in terms of their disorder, or in terms of their offending behaviour. Hybrid orders, like the hospital and limitation direction, permit both treatment and punishment, but bring with them their own difficulties (Eastman and Peay, 1998). This intermingling of objectives is also reflected in Article 5(1) of the ECHR where mentally disordered offenders are subject both to 5(1)(a) the lawful detention of a person after conviction by a competent court *and* detention on the basis of their 5(1)(e) unsoundness of mind. Only those found not guilty by reason of insanity or those found unfit to plead, and who therefore are not convicted, are exempted from penal detention. Here, Article 5(1)(e), combined with the influence of the *Winterwerp* criteria, means that if they are to be detained at all, it must be in a therapeutic environment.

Whilst questions have been raised above about the relative benefits to an offender's mental health of being treated in hospital, as opposed to being treated on a voluntary basis in prison, there are also issues about the relative disbenefits of being held in either prison or hospital with respect to the individual's health.[1] Clearly, medication, and in particular anti-psychotic medication, has side effects, some of which can be peculiarly problematic to particular individuals; moreover, if that medication is to be administered by force, other risks can arise.[2] Here it seems that neither Article 2 nor Article 3 provide any great protection where clinical interventions are deemed a medical necessity and are in keeping with current medical practice.[3] But

---

1 See *R (on the application of Cooper) v Parole Board* [2007] EWHC 1292 (Admin) which concerned a recalled prisoner, whose fragile mental state was deteriorating, attributed in part by to his detention, where there had been a delay of some 59 days in the Parole Board hearing his case.
2 See *R (Wilkinson) v RMO Broadmoor Hospital* [2001] EWCA Civ 1545, where the patient had a pre-existing heart condition.
3 *Grare v France* [1992] 15 EHRR CD 100.

there is also evidence that those with mental health problems receive less care for their physical disorders than those without (Sartorious, 2007). Moreover, the length of detention, extended in large measure by the move towards indeterminacy in the prison system and the more frequent use of restriction orders as opposed to hospital orders in the hospital system, brings its own problems with institutionalisation and the deprivation of normal relationships with family. And the stigma and pains of deprivation of liberty extend also to those families (see Jamison and Grounds, 2002).

These issues of stigma are probably more acute for those held in the hospital rather than the prison system, or at least are perceived to be so by offenders. However much work is done to redress this issue, those held at Special Hospitals like Broadmoor will never be free of the effects of the assumptions and presumptions made by others, even after discharge. It is undoubtedly the case that to have the label of 'mentally disordered offender' brings with it not only the stigma of mental disorder, and that of being an offender, but arguably also an additional fear that preys on our most primeval of emotions; that these are people where the sum of their parts crystallises into something potentially much more terrible, embodying an uncontrolled, uncontrollable and irrational force. Where victimisation of the mentally disordered, rather than perpetration of further offences by them, is as much a problem, then such portrayals are deeply unhelpful. However, the stereotype and the fear on which it feeds are hard to redress. There is, of course, a painful and profound irony in the fact that Jack Nicholson has starred in two films capturing the extremes of this spectrum; namely, *One Flew over the Cuckoo's Nest* and *The Shining*. But what is true is that our treatment of mentally disordered offenders perhaps reflects the latter end of this spectrum since we do seem prepared to adopt alternative and arguably discriminatory approaches to offenders with mental health disorders.

For example, although the MHA 1983 permits the treatment of detained capacitous patients for mental disorder against their will, such treatment appears less hard to justify (in both legal and moral terms) where those patients pose a risk of harm to others. Indeed, even the Richardson Committee (1999:70–71), with its key emphasis on the need for non-discrimination in the treatment of mental disorder, would have permitted the compulsory treatment of capacitous patients where there was a *substantial risk of serious harm ... to the safety of other persons* and that there were *positive clinical measures ... likely to prevent a deterioration or secure an improvement in the patient's mental condition*. This exception to an approach that could otherwise have been consistent with one that respected a patient's autonomy (albeit for issues of treatment, if not for questions of assessment or detention) would have had, inevitably, the greatest impact on mentally disordered offenders, who had already proven themselves to have posed a risk to others. Of course, much of the treatment available for mentally disordered offenders, such as cognitive behavioural therapy, entails not only the cooperation of the patient, but also motivated cooperation on their part, making the notion of compulsion somewhat more ambiguous; indeed, the coercion of continued detention is as likely to be effective as any more obviously forcible treatment.

Detaining a mentally disordered offender in a therapeutic environment, that is, under clinical supervision, is currently justifiable in human rights terms even though there may be no treatment for them, provided that the offender has been convicted of 'a crime'. Again, there is seemingly no require-ment of a prediction of future harm, or even future harm of a particular degree. Under the MHA 1983 there had to be a therapeutic benefit before someone could be detained with psychopathic disorder; but the ECtHR was, in *Hutchison Reid v UK*,[4] content for the confinement of someone suffering from a mental disorder of the requisite degree to be justified (or, at least, not constitute a breach of Article 5) in order to control and supervise them, and to prevent them causing harm to themselves or others, even where there may be no treatment for their underlying disorder. Similarly, in *Johnson v UK*,[5] the ECtHR rejected an argument that unconditional release should follow immediately where there was no persisting mental illness:

> Such a rigid approach to the interpretation of that condition would place an unacceptable degree of constraint on the responsible authority's exercise of judgment to determine ... whether the interests of the patient *and the community* ... would in fact be best served by this course of action.
>
> (*Johnson v UK* 1999, emphasis added)

Thus, detention can be prolonged with discharge being delayed, provided it is not unreasonably delayed. The tolerance embodied in the term 'unreason-ably' can be judged by the fact that Johnson was held for well over three years on the basis that no suitable hostel place had been found to permit his discharge.

So a cautious policy which combines a therapeutic backstop to a penal approach will permit what might be described as double discrimination: offender-patients who go to hospital on the basis of their mental health needs may end up staying much longer in hospital than would ever have been merited by a proportionate sentence for their offending behaviour: and if they 'recover' from their mental disorder, they may end up staying in hos-pital on the basis of predictions made about their likely future offending, meaning that they may stay longer than the original therapeutic detention would have justified. Some might argue that this is not a problem since such

4 *Hutchison Reid v UK* (2003) 37 EHRR 9.
5 *Johnson v UK* (1999) 27 EHRR 296.

people can be dealt with differently on the basis that they are not only mentally disordered, but also offenders. Perhaps that is right, and it feels seductively justifiable in an era when there has been a marked shift to indeterminate sentencing based on risk for mentally ordered offenders. But, there is no doubt that it goes against notions of proportionality and justice; and that, from the offender-patient's perspective, it may store up unnecessary resentment and miss the ideal moment for discharge (if there is one).

The amendments to the MHA 1983 arguably make the situation worse. The extension of the definition of mental disorder so as to include personality disorder, whilst abolishing the separate category of psychopathic disorder, means that the hospital and limitation direction (the order that allows a court to impose a sentence of imprisonment on an offender-patient, but sends the offender first to hospital for a period of treatment) will become available to all mentally disordered offenders, as it is in Scotland. Burman et al (2000) note that the order had not been widely used in its first two years of operation in Scotland; they argue that this is because it could entail psychiatrists having to recommend what was in part a custodial sentence, since the order is attached to a prison sentence, thereby creating ethical problems for psychiatrists. But it remains a potentially very attractive option to the courts. For the hybrid order has always felt like having your cake and eating it; its extension to England and Wales in this format may bring something of a revolution in the sentencing of mentally disordered offenders. Indeed, one might argue that insufficiently careful thought has been given generally to the consequences of changing the definitions as they apply to mentally disordered offenders: for, if the sub-definitions had acted as a restraint on admission, it is entirely possible that the delicate (if wholly unsatisfactory) balance of distribution of offenders between prison and hospital may be extremely perturbed by these definitional changes.[6]

Whilst this discussion has proceeded as if treatment is something always to be regarded negatively, in practice that is not the case. Indeed, most of the problems those with mental disorder report are not related to fending off unwanted treatment but rather in getting access to services and treatment that might benefit them. And in this context, the earlier discussion of the narrow basis for the House of Lords judgment on indeterminate sentences for public protection reveals how problematic obtaining relevant treatment can be, at least in the prison context. Indeed, the ECHR's general focus on procedure and not substance is not helpful. As Baroness Hale (2007:26) has argued, the ECHR is better at protecting people with mental disorder 'against unwanted or unnecessary treatment and care than supplying them with what they want or need, even within available resources'. In coming to

---

6 The Sainsbury Centre for Mental Health reports that the hybrid order has been used only 34 times since its introduction in 1999 (Personal communication, 9 November 2009).

this conclusion, Baroness Hale probably had in mind those non-offenders with mental disorder or disability who were subject to the MHA 1983 or the Mental Capacity Act 2005. Yet, where the delivery of appropriate and effective treatment must precede any possibility of release from detention for mentally disordered offenders, the ECHR's focus on freedom does not immediately assist. For using the Convention to secure proper treatment for those who need it, is, as Baroness Hale observes, another matter. Where mentally disordered offenders find themselves within the psychiatric system, then they at least head the queue for the treatment that is available; and arguably within those parts of the psychiatric system where such offenders are detained, the treatment available is Rolls Royce in its nature even if it proceeds at the pace of a Trabant. But, the same cannot be said of those who languish in prison.

Mentally disordered offenders also 'suffer' from the emphasis within the ECHR jurisprudence on vulnerable people; and mentally disordered offenders are not classically seen as vulnerable. If anything, they are stereotyped – including by me – as more litigious. So here lurks another paradox; mentally disordered offenders in court may well find themselves being rejected for psychiatric care on the grounds that they are insufficiently vulnerable and more than sufficiently worrying in terms of potential re-offending for a hospital placement. If mental health is the poor relation of medicine, mentally disordered offenders are the Cinderellas of poor relations, for this is the area that perhaps suffers most from neglect and, when it is not being neglected, demonisation.

For mentally disordered offenders who are subject to a court order, there can be no dispute about the fact of their detention. But the effectiveness of the remedies to challenge that detention is questionable. The continuing exclusive responsibility of the Secretary of State (now at the Ministry of Justice) for the granting of leave or the transfer of patients subject to restriction orders could be regarded as an impediment to an effective court review; without information on the responsiveness of patients to lesser conditions of security it can readily be understood how a tribunal finds itself in the position of being satisfied that detention is necessary in respect of the instant case with which they are faced, albeit that they may have reservations about the appropriateness of that place of detention. If a cautionary stance properly represents the decision-making of most tribunals, then the absence of appropriate and relevant information to rebut necessary caution will undermine any effective prospect of discharge.

Another area where there may be a considerable gulf between those matters about which we protest and those that are quietly tolerated, concerns the effectiveness of our mental condition defences. It has already been established that far too many offenders with serious mental disorders are to be found within the prison system when they should more appropriately be located within the hospital system. For a proportion of these, their mental disorders could have developed, or significantly deteriorated, after conviction; but in itself this would constitute a criticism of the effectiveness of the system of transfer from prison to hospital, or of decisions at sentence. But for many of them their presence within the prison system reflects the lamentable state of our mental condition defences. Although the procedures for dealing with those found not guilty by reason of insanity or unfit to plead were tightened to make them compatible with our Human Rights obligations the substance of the tests to be applied has not. Thus, we work with the M'Naghten rules from 1843 and the Pritchard test from 1836; both are so narrowly drawn that they focus on cognitive capacities, excluding volitional and mood disorders as a legitimate basis for exculpation or resulting in some offenders being tried when they are manifestly under a disability. The Law Commission are currently reviewing both areas in substance, but the questions remain about the political viability of redrawing our mental condition defences, with all of the costs that would be entailed to the health care system, were the tests to be appropriately broadened.

In short, these paradoxes look unlikely to be resolved quickly, if at all. The ECHR is a relatively weak instrument where mentally disordered offenders get caught within so many of its exceptional categories; and whilst the Article 14 prohibition on discrimination may create some leverage, it needs another Article to be engaged before it can bite; and even then differences in treatment can be justified provided they are proportionate and serve a legitimate aim. The future protection from harm looks sufficiently malleable thus to serve most purposes. Arbitrary forms of coercion and the possibility of reciprocal rights to community treatment, where coercion is entailed, may prove more fruitful than any initiative for those detained in institutions, where the prior justification for deprivation of liberty casts a very long shadow.

Chapter 16

Treatment, mental disorder, crime, responsibility and punishment

The final chapters of the book take some specific examples of problematic areas to illustrate the lack of compatibility between the various concepts linking mental disorder and crime. First, there is the issue of unfitness to plead, which attempts to filter away those from the criminal justice system who cannot fairly be tried according to criminal justice precepts. Second, the problem that DSPD highlights for those who would wish to medicalise all forms of deviance for therapeutic precepts and endeavours. And third, the narrow ambit of our mental condition defences and curious rules on automatism which lead in part to a number of absurdities in the criminal law; one example would be 'sleepwalking defences' where the criminal law's requirement for *mens rea* to be satisfied before a criminal conviction can be returned in non-strict liability cases has resulted in such offenders being classified under the insanity provisions. None of these have a happy outcome but each illustrates the tensions at borderlines where problem situations are squeezed into inappropriate or artificial categories.

If it were the case that mental disorder caused crime, or indeed that crime caused mental disorder, the logical consequences of these associations, although problematic, would at least be clear: treat the mental disorder, absolve perpetrators of criminal responsibility, and recognise the health consequences of punitive interventions. But the earlier part of this book endeavoured to illustrate that such easy associations cannot be justified in the vast majority of cases. Hence, the issue of what consequences should rightly follow is much more complicated. Mental disorder and offending behaviour can exist within the same individual without there being any pertinent interaction between the two; indeed, it may even be possible (as evidence emerging from the MacArthur studies on mental health courts, and of probation services, appear to indicate) to offer services designed to assist those with mental health problems that are associated with reductions in their subsequent criminal justice involvement, without there being any noticeable reduction in their psychiatric symptomatology.[1] Or there

---

1 See www.macarthur.virginia.edu/ and the work of Steadman and colleagues; and of Skeem and colleagues.

may be partial overlap between mental disorder and offending behaviour with some limited correlations; and in some circumstances the link between the two may be irresistible. But such explanatory associations, albeit limited, are not the end of the story, since questions also arise, for example, about how the integrity of one domain – the criminal justice process – can be sustained in the context of offenders with serious mental health problems. Is it possible to have a fair trial when a perpetrator has a disabling mental illness? Is it right to punish someone who has been held culpable of the offence, but whose mental disorder makes conventional punishment an anathema? And the range of disorders and offences make the presentation of overlap peculiarly problematic. Should those with learning disability who have seriously offended be detained in a health or penal setting? Should those with serious mental disorder who have offended repeatedly in a particularly brutal fashion be confined in a psychiatric hospital or a prison?

And it is important to recall that these are not issues that relate only to a small number of offenders. As Lord Bradley's Report (2009:98) notes, eight per cent of the general population scores within the learning disabled or borderline group and, when one looks at the concentration of those with learning difficulties within custodial populations, he asserts that '20–30 per cent of offenders have learning difficulties or learning disabilities that interfere with their ability to cope within the criminal justice system'. Quite what the implications of this are for the fairness and justice of their convictions in the preceding stages of assessing culpability are not clear; but they are unlikely to have been favourable.

As matters currently stand, most perpetrators are convicted without these issues relating to their cognitive capacities being properly explored: indeed, most perpetrators, for whatever reason, plead guilty, making any thorough examination of their mental state at the time of the offence or at the time of trial unlikely. And the fact of conviction, with all that it entails about culpability, allows greater flexibility about the place of detention; in short, penal disposal is not unlawful, as it would be for those not held criminally culpable. Indeed, conventional punishment can only follow a criminal conviction. For those who are not convicted, arising as a result of a finding of not guilty by reason of insanity or for persons who are found unfit to plead, or where the Magistrates invoke their power to impose a hospital order where they are satisfied that 'the accused did the act or made the omission charged' (s 37(3) MHA 1983) without convicting them, only a health disposal will be justified; and even that may not be permitted where the grounds for admission are not met. In those cases, community disposal becomes the only option.

With the amendments to the MHA 1983, and the broad definition of mental disorder it promotes, it is possible that Magistrates' Courts could find themselves invoking their s 37(3) powers more frequently. Before the amendments, this option only applied to accused persons suffering from mental illness or severe mental impairment; now it applies to all those suffering from mental disorder, that is, including those with personality disorder. This potential expansion in eligibility does not apply to either unfitness to plead or a finding of not guilty by reason of insanity as both are common law tests and both are so narrowly drawn that few defendants fall into them. However, with the current review of these two areas by the Law Commission this may change. It is right that it should since, as was detailed in the earlier chapters, the incidence of mental disorder and learning disability in prison (Singleton et al, 1998) would indicate that neither unfitness nor insanity are currently fit for purpose (Loughnan, 2011). But if either or both tests were broadened, the disposal options, in the sense of excluding punitive or criminal justice 'rehabilitative' options like the community order, would be accordingly more limited. There are also questions that can be asked that go beyond the conventional 'is this person fit to plead or be amenable to deterrence or rehabilitation?' to embrace 'is this person fit to plead guilty and are they fit to be punished?'

That mentally disordered offenders straddle awkwardly the arrangements for dealing with both offenders and those with mental health problems has been long known: that it leads to problems with the medicalisation of offending, the criminalisation of deviance and the undermining of both the values of the mental health and criminal justice system is equally well established. The pollution of the acceptability of punishment by including within its ambit those mentally disordered offenders of dubious culpability, and the similar pollution of the purity of medical imperatives, of beneficence and the avoidance of harm, are both problematic, albeit in different ways. Forensic psychiatrists, falling as they do on these borderlines, have grappled with the ethical dilemmas that arise from their tangential involvement with punishment and also with the assessment of the likelihood of future offending. These issues entail real dilemmas, for example, in respect to their clinical responsibilities in such areas as patient confidentiality. Yet it is only relatively recently that more strenuous efforts have been made to think about effective solutions to these problems.

Two initiatives are worth mentioning, since they tackle the problems from slightly different angles. First, the issue of pre-trial diversion. In this country, whilst issues relating to the offender's mental state have primarily been dealt with after conviction at the point of disposal, and the legal provisions for complete diversion away from the criminal justice process at this point are in many respects admirable, there has been considerable anxiety about the need to avoid even this degree of involvement with the criminal justice process. Hence the development of assorted diversion schemes, both before and at court, which shift alleged offenders into the health system at a variety of points in a relatively informal manner. These have been recently reviewed by Lennox et al (2009) and by the Sainsbury Centre (2009); they have also been promoted by Lord Bradley's Report (2009). The savings in costs, both human and financial, that such schemes can deliver make their relative neglect curious. Second, the mental health courts initiatives developing in other jurisdictions, mainly North America and Australia. Mental Health Courts also come in a variety of guises (Redlich et al, 2006) and they are not without their critics (Seltzer, 2005); indeed, the therapeutic jurisprudence movement generally has had a mixed reception (Eastman and Peay, 1999). But as one initiative to address what appears to be the common problem in a number of jurisdictions posed by mentally disordered offenders they are worth exploring; and indeed, may be at the forefront of a movement for special jurisdiction courts generally.

Chapter 17

Fitness to plead

The problems posed to legal systems by persons accused of criminal offences who, at the point of their trial, are in no fit mental state to participate in that trial, manifest themselves in a number of ways across a number of jurisdictions (Poythress et al, 2002; Dawson, 2008). Similarly, the statutory provisions vary in their relative friendliness to the accused, the nature of the disorders they embrace and the aspects of the trial process they cover.[1] In England and Wales the relevant statute is the Criminal Procedure (Insanity) Act 1964 and a finding of 'unfitness to plead' is still governed by the *Pritchard* test dating back to 1836.[2] The *Pritchard* test requires the court to satisfy itself that the accused is of sufficient intellect to instruct his legal representatives, to plead to the indictment, to challenge jurors, and to comprehend the details of the evidence; in short, fitness to plead is a test of whether an accused can comprehend the course of proceedings so as to make a proper defence. At the time of *Pritchard* the science of psychiatry was, as the Law Commission recognise, 'in its infancy', and the criteria are now widely regarded as outmoded and outdated.[3] Moreover, the test benefits from none of the advances in modern psychiatric thinking which might better discriminate between accused persons who can and should be exposed to a criminal trial and those vulnerable mentally disordered persons who manifestly should not.

Since fitness to plead is potentially one of the gatekeeping points for ensuring that those who have mental disorder who may also have offended are properly allocated between health and penal disposals, or neither, its effective and fair operation is critical. This has been considered elsewhere (Rogers et al, 2008). Would a broader test of 'unfitness to plead' result in a

---

1 See, for example, s 2 of the Criminal Code for Canada; s 4 of the New Zealand Criminal Procedure (Mentally Impaired Persons) Act 2003; and, on Jersey, Mackay (2004).

2 *R v Pritchard* (1836) 7 C & P 303.

3 See: www.lawcom.gov.uk/insanity.htm The Pritchard test is also in conflict with the test of capacity in the Mental Capacity Act 2005 and with the new definition of mental disorder in the MHA 1983, as amended by the MHA 2007.

fairer disposal of those who have committed the *actus reus* of an offence, but who do not have the necessary mental capacity at the point of trial to determine whether they met the necessary *mens rea* criteria, and accordingly be in a position even to be at risk of being held culpable of a criminal offence? Is subsequent civil commitment in this context an example of rights-based legalism working, or of a health-based system governed by paternalism (Peay, 2010a)? The answer to this question is almost impossible to glean, given that the bulk of offenders plead guilty without trial, and that so little is currently known about their mental state when they do so. Indeed are some offenders convicted, following a guilty plea, of offences for which they could not be held liable in a full trial process if a test more in keeping with current understandings of the nature of mental responsibility were devised?

That the current test is unsatisfactory is one problem, but even if there were a more satisfactory test, a number of dilemmas would nonetheless face those using it, including clinicians, lawyers and accused persons, together with those who have to make a judgment about unfitness, currently a judge, and the decision as to whether or not the unfit person 'did the act or made the omission charged' in a trial of the facts. Currently, the various outcomes of a determination of fitness include full trial followed by acquittal or conviction and conventional punishment, or by a determination that the accused performed the *actus reus* of the offence (followed by health disposal), or did not (followed by acquittal).

The focus here is on how these difficult cases with complex and overlapping objectives for all the participants concerned assist our understanding of the relationship between mental health and crime; and why mental disorder in an accused person so unsettles and jeopardises the proper functioning of the criminal justice process. And it is important first to understand the extent of the problem which could, and arguably should, face the courts.

Fitness to plead: the problem of numbers

In all jurisdictions significant numbers of mentally ill and cognitively impaired individuals pass through the criminal justice system. In a proportion of these cases, psychiatrists and psychologists will be asked to advise upon whether the defendants are capable of fairly standing trial. Whilst a number of clinical tests do exist to assist clinicians, and, in turn, lawyers, the approach is largely ad hoc, leading arguably to inconsistent and arbitrary decision making (Mackay, 2007; Akintunde, 2002). And even if clinicians can agree on their findings (James et al, 2001), they may disagree on how these findings relate to the legal test; or they may be asked to speculate many years after about a defendant's condition at the time of an earlier trial. This is discussed further below.

What is evident is that many unfit defendants end up in the penal system following conviction. The numbers revealed by Singleton et al (1998) on learning disability alone in the prison population are worrying. In July 1997 the prison population was 61,944: five per cent of the male sentenced population (then at 46,872), would, according to the authors, have fallen into the lowest category on the Quick Test of intellectual functioning, that is at 25 and below, which is the approximate equivalent of 65 on the IQ scale (Ammons and Ammons, 1962). Thus, there would have been some 2,340 men in the sentenced population with the most serious of learning disabilities. How many of these men came to plead guilty in either the Crown or Magistrates Court is hard to determine, but their mere presence in the prison population should raise concerns. And, in particular, raise concerns about the viability of the test for unfitness to plead; for, in 1997, there were only 50 findings of unfitness to plead (Mackay et al, 2007).[4]

Nor has the situation seemingly changed: other research, based on a systematic review involving some 12,000 prisoners, has estimated that up to 1.5 per cent of prisoners would be diagnosed with intellectual disabilities (Fazel et al, 2008). Even given the preponderance of sentencing by Magistrates in short-term sentences of imprisonment, and their evident failure fully to utilise their powers under the MHA 1983, it is clear that the test of unfitness to plead is failing to filter some of the most intellectually impaired away from the criminal justice process. Moreover, arguments that the disability might have developed after sentence (as can happen with some mental illnesses) are less persuasive with respect to mental impairment.

Both the Prison Reform Trust (2009) and HM Inspectorate of Prisons (2007) have also confirmed worryingly high levels of mental disorder generally in the prison population. And Lord Bradley's review has only served to emphasise the seriousness of the situation with his assertion that 'Custody can exacerbate mental ill health, heighten vulnerability and increase the risk of self-harm and suicide' (Bradley, 2009:Executive Summary para 1). Lord Bradley recommended that 'Immediate consideration should be given to extending to vulnerable defendants the provisions currently available to vulnerable witnesses' (2009:61); in short, those special measures designed to reduce the stresses associated with the court environment and to facilitate effective communication.

Given the general incidence of incapacity in the population, and the levels of mental disability within the prison population, all of the figures would suggest that there is either a failure to detect problems of fitness to plead amongst defendants, or, if it is detected, a failure by the legal system to be able to respond appropriately. Either way, there is a clear problem to be resolved. Getting the balance right is critical since too low a threshold for establishing unfitness will result in many accused persons being diverted

---

4 This was not an exceptional year: there were 329 unfitness findings for the period 1997–2001, an average of less than 66 accused persons per year reported by Mackay et al (2007).

into the health system inappropriately, when they could properly be tried, whilst setting it too high produces the alternative problem of too many unfit accused being tried and, potentially inappropriately punished.

Unfitness and culpability

The figures above suggest that the most common problem with respect to issues of unfitness and culpability will revolve around low level offending by those with learning disability (inevitably, given the frequency of occurrence of this kind of offending and the prevalence of learning disability). This is the kind of offending which rarely attracts detailed legal consideration in the law reports or indeed, much critical examination in court where defendants may plead guilty. The focus here will be on more high profile cases. These cases are both more likely to be reported, and more likely to have attracted psychiatric evidence, which is of particular relevance to the discussion of the defence of diminished responsibility.

A plea of diminished responsibility is only an option in response to a charge of murder (s 2(1) of the Homicide Act 1957). In the absence of a plea being accepted by the court, it is for the jury to decide whether the abnormality of mind was such as to substantially impair the defendant's mental responsibility for the homicide.[5] It is perfectly possible for a defendant to have a serious mental illness at the time of the killing, but still to be held partially responsible for the act, since the jury have to determine, with the benefit of having heard psychiatric evidence, whether the accused understood the physical acts he did and whether he had any power to exercise control over those actions at the time. These are not easy issues to resolve but it is right that the mere presence of serious mental illness does not give carte blanche to excuse criminal responsibility.[6] For complete exclusion of criminal culpability the defendant would have to invoke the M'Naghten Rules and be found not guilty by reason of insanity; this entails the defendant proving on a balance of probabilities that either he did not know the nature and quality of the act he was doing, or, if he did know that, that he did not know that what he was doing was wrong. The test is hard to invoke because of its extremely narrow basis (Mackay et al, 2006 and Mackay, 2009).

Several issues arise. In an adversarial trial system, the model operates best where defendants have, and have the ability to take, legal advice: indeed the system assumes that individuals will act strategically in their own best

---

5 The defence of diminished responsibility under s 2 of the Homicide Act 1957 has been amended in a number of ways by s 52 of the Coroners and Justice Act 2009: notably, the abnormality of mental functioning has now to provide an explanation for the defendant's acts or omissions by causing or being a significant contributory factor to that conduct.
6 See *R v Dawood Khan* [2009] EWCA Crim 1569.

interests. This is sometimes not possible for those with serious mental disorder, even if they may retain sufficient capacity to be determined fit to plead (perhaps not surprising at its current low threshold). These expectations can throw up tragic examples of the criminal justice model serving the interests of those involved extremely poorly: hence, in *Murray*, who killed her five year old daughter, the defendant pled guilty to murder seemingly because she wished to be punished for her crime.[7] Her paranoid schizophrenia was sufficient in the eyes of the clinicians to prevent her from understanding the impact of her disorder on her actions, but it was not sufficient to bring her within a legal test of unfitness; nor, accordingly, to prevent her rejecting advice to enter a plea of diminished responsibility.[8]

In other cases the courts may be less sympathetic on appeal; in *Diamond*, the accused's refusal to countenance psychiatric assessment in the pre-trial period, with a view to tendering a plea of diminished responsibility, could have been based on false premises; he seemingly had an unrealistic expectation of an acquittal and a desire, arising in part from his paranoid beliefs, to 'get one over' on the police.[9] Thus, an accused's (disordered) beliefs about a number of aspects relevant to the decisions to be made may interfere with informed decision-making. Many years later, and following a significant period in treatment, Diamond sought to have his conviction for murder replaced by one of manslaughter by reason of diminished responsibility; but by that stage the court considered it too difficult to establish what the defendant's mental state would have been all those years previously and the conviction was upheld. One might argue that it made very little difference to the defendant, who was being treated in a Special Hospital, and had been so for some years. But there is an important difference in respect of the label attached to the conviction. And, had the defendant been given a hospital order, albeit with restrictions, rather than the mandatory life sentence, there would have been a real difference in the method of release.

Psychiatric evidence and legal certainty

In some cases the appeal process will right these symbolic wrongs. One such case is that of *Erskine*.[10] Erskine, who was known in the popular press as the Stockwell Strangler, posed just such a problem for the Court of Appeal. He had been convicted of seven counts of murder and one of attempted murder;

7 *R v Murray* [2008] EWCA Crim 1792.
8 See also *R v Moyle* [2008] EWCA Crim 3059; *R v Neaven* [2006] EWCA Crim 955; I am indebted to Ronnie Mackay for drawing attention to these cases in his presentation to the Law Commission seminar on unfitness on 19 March 2009.
9 *R v Stewart Michael Diamond* [2008] EWCA Crim 923 at 944.
10 *R v Erskine, R v Williams* [2009] EWCA Crim 1425.

some 20 years later he applied to the Court with a view to quashing the convictions for murder and substituting verdicts of manslaughter by reason of diminished responsibility. This was on the basis of evidence available, but not adduced, at trial; namely, evidence of his severe schizophrenia and psychopathic disorder, all of which arose in the context of borderline mental handicap.

First, the court had to consider whether, under s 23 of the Criminal Appeal Act 1968, it was necessary or expedient in the interests of justice to receive this evidence; in general, it is not possible for defendants to advance a defence on appeal that they did not raise, yet could have raised, at trial. For if this were not the case, there could be no certainty to the jury's decision and no finality for the victim or their family. In the event the court determined that they would permit evidence of the defence to be advanced; the fact that contemporary evidence of his disorder had been available, and there was a reason why the evidence was not presented, was sufficiently persuasive. As the Court of Appeal observed, this evidence:

> ... suggested that as a result of reduced mental acuity, not amounting to unfitness to plead, but part and parcel of his illness, the decision not to advance the defence was irremediably flawed. There was nothing his legal advisers could do about it, and in reality nothing he could do about it himself. The interests of justice require us to admit the fresh evidence.
>
> (R v Erskine [2009] at para 95)

But if Erskine was so disordered at the time, the first logical question to ask is why was the issue of unfitness to plead not raised at the original trial, let alone the failure to advance the plea of diminished responsibility? Indeed, there were serious concerns expressed by three psychiatrists at the time.[11] Dr Hamilton, the then Director of Broadmoor Hospital, noted that his disordered state was such that he would find difficulty in a full professional relationship with his lawyers. Erskine also threatened Dr Hamilton that he would press charges against him if the diagnosis was that he was mentally abnormal. In the event, and because of his fluctuating mental state, Erskine was assessed again shortly before the trial by Dr Bowden and the conclusion was drawn that he was fit: perhaps indicative again of an application of the very low threshold for fitness. But it is notable that the clinicians were also reluctant to address the issue of diminished responsibility because Erskine was maintaining his innocence. The real answer to why diminished responsibility was not advanced lies in the nature of Erskine's defence. Erskine

---

11 Erskine was seen by Drs Hamilton, Bowden and MacKeith, together with a psychological assessment from Dr Gudjonsson: in effect, he had the Rolls Royce service of the time.

claimed he had been a burglar – and hence present at the crime scenes – but that he was not a murderer. The likelihood of this defence succeeding must have raised questions in his legal advisors' minds, but the fact that semen that was not his was found at one of the crime scenes may have given this explanation a scintilla of credibility in the light of his vehement denials of the killings.

But clearly there should have been very real doubts about Erskine's fitness to plead. Courts are understandably very reluctant to re-open this issue, given that legal advice would have been available at the time. And whilst times change, and our understanding, either legal or psychiatric, of what constitutes unfitness can also change, it is evident that the court's tendency is to hold trials 'humanely' for as many defendants as is possible. This is desirable both in principle and in pursuit of the defendant's autonomy; notably, defendants are not required, whether disordered or not, to act in their own best interests.[12] And even those who are 'highly abnormal' at the time of trial can be capable of 'following a trial or giving evidence or instructing counsel and so on'.[13] Defendants, as has been observed on another occasion, 'are sentenced for the crimes they have committed and not for psychological failings to which they may be subject'.[14] Yet Erskine's borderline unfitness, combined with contemporary evidence of it, did provide a basis, 20 years on, to allow evidence of his potential diminished responsibility finally to be heard by the court.

In the event, the Court of Appeal readily quashed the convictions having been presented with evidence from two psychiatrists for the defence saying that Erskine would have been considered diminished, and one for the prosecution saying that he would not, at the time, have advised the prosecution to reject a plea of diminished responsibility. The Court imposed a hospital order with restrictions, rather than a sentence of life imprisonment, in recognition of the reality of Erskine's detention: he had after all been detained in a Special Hospital and not a prison for some 20 years following his transfer there within months of his conviction.

However, what is most interesting about the Erskine case is the interaction between unfitness and diminished responsibility; and the conflicting psychiatric analyses presented.

At the time of the original trial Erskine was manifestly disturbed and yet was still held to be capable of giving coherent instructions to counsel. These instructions were a clear denial of the offences, albeit that they were couched in the context of his equally clear assertion that he did not want to be seen as

12 *R v Robertson* (1968) 52 Cr App R 690.
13 *R v Berry* (1970) 66 Cr App R 156.
14 *R v Criminal Cases Review Commission Ex Parte Pearson* [2000] 1 Cr App R 141 at page 164.

'criminally insane' and he did not want to be detained in a psychiatric hospital. To have pursued a defence of diminished responsibility contrary to his instructions would have been unethical for his legal advisors and would have undermined the defence he did pursue. Hence the court's remarks (above) that there was nothing his legal advisors could do about it. It took nearly 10 years in Broadmoor before Erskine acknowledged or was able to express any responsibility for the murders; and no explanation for the offences emerges from the Court's decision, other than an assertion by his Responsible Medical Officer, the doctor with overall responsibility for his case, that his mental illness played 'a very substantial part in the causation of the homicides'.[15] The denial of the offences at the original trial was subsequently attributed by Erskine to his fear that he might be executed, were the law on capital punishment to change.

The psychiatric evidence presented to the Court of Appeal painted a complex picture. Professor Eastman attributed the offences to the influence of his severe anti-social personality disorder on his symptoms of schizophrenia. Eastman noted that the appellant's delusional thinking and his decision to deny responsibility for the killings were related since this was an attempt 'to avoid a consequence which arose in his mind from his psychosis ... if a defendant is deluded about matters directly related to his choice of plea, it might reasonably be argued that he is disabled as regards fitness to plead'.[16] Professor Eastman did not believe him to have lacked capacity to plead to 'diminished responsibility manslaughter' but that:

> his choice as to which way to plead was determined by a belief about the consequences arising from pleading in such a way as to acknowledge the killing, which would place him at risk of deportation and execution. However his belief was false, and arose directly from his psychotic illness. Hence, if he had not been mentally ill in the way that he was he would not have been hampered by a false belief in deciding whether or not to accept that he killed his victims.

He concluded:

> ... the medical evidence which would have been available to the court at the time of the appellant's trial relating to the appellant's delusional beliefs, arising out of illness, were the same delusional beliefs which inherently disable the appellant from being able to plead 'diminished responsibility', or determine that he did not so plead. Finally, there would have been a robust medical basis for the defendant pleading 'diminished responsibility' at his trial.
>
> (*R v Erskine* [2009] at para 120)

---

15 *R v Erskine* at para 115.
16 *R v Erskine* at para 118.

Dr Horne, his Responsible Medical Officer at Broadmoor, expressed this more clearly. Erskine's state of mind at the time was such that he believed that if he admitted the offences he might be deported and executed. Thus:

> There can be no doubt that he believed it to be true. In psychiatric terms it is a delusional belief. Delusions are false beliefs and they are often, although not always, held with great conviction ... the appellant's (belief) that he was not mentally ill appears to have been held with great conviction ... we need to bear this quality of the belief in mind when thinking about whether it was possible for Mr Erskine to plead not guilty to murder but guilty to manslaughter on the grounds of diminished responsibility. In order to do so he would have coped in some way with his belief that he would be at risk of being executed and with the great anxiety that that would have caused him, and he would also have had to cope in some way with his belief that he was not mentally ill. When the idea that he was ill would have seemed to him obviously incorrect and saying that he was ill would have felt to him like lying.

He continued that:

> ... the illness would thus prevent him from pleading guilty to manslaughter, but even if he did manage to get to that point his lack of insight into his mental illness, which again was a product of the illness, would have prevented him from pleading thus on grounds of diminished responsibility by reason of mental disorder.
>
> (*R v Erskine* [2009] at para 121)

Dr Chesterman, a consultant forensic psychiatrist instructed by the Crown, noted the difficulties of determining some 20 years after the killings whether the appellant had been fit to plead. He rejected the explanation from Erskine about his fear of execution and regarded the not guilty plea as tactical, and one supported by his legal counsel. Indeed, any contemporaneous explanation of the defendant's behaviour was preferable to later explanations, which were likely to be much less reliable. Although Dr Chesterman accepted the evidence of schizophrenia at the time he asserted that it was impossible, even now, to understand why the offences occurred. He noted that given the history of:

> ... extremely disturbed behaviour from a very young age, before he could have conceivably developed schizophrenia, the possibility that (he) could have committed the index offences without having developed schizophrenia cannot be excluded.
>
> (*R v Erskine* [2009] at para 123)

However, he accepted that Erskine's mental illness was of such severity that he could not have advised the Crown to reject a plea of 'diminished responsibility', despite the presence of personality disorder. In his evidence Dr Chesterman expressed himself in this measured way about the appellant's condition at the time of the killing:

> I would say he was seriously ill and whilst that may not have been the overwhelming cause of his behaviour, that he was sufficiently ill for [manslaughter on the grounds of diminished responsibility] not to have been an unjust outcome.
>
> (*R v Erskine* [2009] at para 124)

However, the Crown maintained its position with respect to tactical pleading arguing that this, rather than mental disorder as the defendant contended at the appeal, accounted for the failure to enter a plea to diminished responsibility.[17] The Court seemingly disagreed and quashed the convictions.

Of course, all this in turn raises the question of whether it is likely that a defendant can have sufficient capacity to enter a plea, but insufficient capacity to enter a plea of diminished responsibility. Logically, this is possible since the former requires an understanding of the trial process and an ability to instruct counsel, whereas the latter requires an ability to acknowledge at least partial responsibility in the context of a mental impairment; the latter may make considerably more demands on a defendant. If matters are so acute at trial then unfitness applies; if so acute at the point of offending then potentially a verdict of not guilty by reason of insanity can result (although this has a narrow ambit and in any event will not include diagnoses such as personality disorder, which do not affect capacity and cognition in quite the same way that schizophrenia is likely to do). But what happens to defendants who cannot acknowledge guilt because of the impact of their mental disorder on their thinking processes? A plea of diminished responsibility cannot be tendered against their will, so they will most likely be convicted of the full offence because their disorder not only prevents them tendering the appropriate plea, but makes highly unlikely any successful defence to the charge per se (that is, a straight denial of 'it wasn't me, I wasn't there' etc).

Dr Chesterman's observations on tactical decision-making by defendants and their counsel are astute; and without any contemporaneous explanation of the defendant's motivations for the killings it is hard to accept that explanations given so many years later should be persuasive. But it is manifestly right that such a disturbed presentation, documented at the time, where anxieties were raised about the defendant's fitness, should be sufficient to

17 Para 125 of the judgment appears to have the words 'failure to enter a' missing.

accept now that the decision not to advance the psychiatric evidence at the time was potentially flawed. Would a better outcome have been to have raised unfitness, and delayed the decision on the more complex issue of responsibility until such time as the defendant could properly engage with it and properly consider the issue of a plea in that context on those grounds?

Asking ordered defendants fully to consider the consequences of their engagement with the criminal justice process and with the complex range of decisions that need to be made (early plea, plea to what, different sentence outcomes, etc) is sufficiently challenging. The further element of mental disorder, which may not only corrupt what defendants think they have done and why, but also adds in a disturbed assessment of what may happen to them (to say nothing of the uncertainty associated with psychiatric disposals) raises the stakes further. Added to that may be a consideration whereby all of these matters are not fully disclosed or discussed in a context where the defendant does not wish to be seen as criminally insane or sent to a psychiatric hospital. In total there is a potent brew for disrupting the fairness of the criminal justice process; a process which is based on equal engagement by teams similarly armed for the prosecution and defence. One example of this, which would be almost hilarious but for the consequences for the defendant, can be seen in the case of *Butler*, where the trial's Recorder became so frustrated with the defendant's behaviour that he himself erred by finding the defendant in contempt of court and sentencing him forthwith to two years imprisonment.[18] That the Recorder failed to recognise that this unrepresented defendant was suffering from paranoid schizophrenia is understandable, albeit very regrettable. But the case does illustrate again the arguable inability of mentally disordered defendants to behave in the strategic manner which a smooth and fair operation of the trial process presupposes. So where mental disorder may not explain the crime, it can interrupt, interfere with and fundamentally disturb the processes of determining whether the defendant has committed the offence, and if so, what properly should be done thereafter.

The *Erskine* case, and the discussion on fitness to plead, reveals a number of interesting features. First, the absence of any explanation for the offending, either at the time or afterwards, beyond some bald assertions that it was attributable to the defendant's mental state, is curious. Perhaps some crimes, and Erskine's should fall amongst these, are so ineffably terrible that whatever explanation might be proffered it would be regarded as inadequate. Second, psychiatric issues that are difficult to resolve at the time, become more problematic as a basis for reaching confident conclusions with the passage of time. Third, and following on from this, dealing with the issue of unfitness at the time would have been far preferable to using it subsequently

---

18 *R v Butler (Paul)* [2005] EWCA Crim 2708.

as a hook on which to hang the introduction of evidence that had been available all along. Fourth, psychiatrists are better at arriving at bald conclusions as to whether a defendant is suffering from a mental disorder (albeit there can be disagreement about what the precise form or forms of that might be[19]) than they are at agreeing on what the proper inferences are to be drawn from these diagnoses (see Peay, 2003). Fifth, the courts appear remarkably grateful to receive psychiatric testimony which can then absolve them from what look like unjustifiable decisions taken in a prior legal context. But the main conclusion has to be, as asserted at the start of this chapter, that unfitness to plead is too important a decision for those who have a mental disorder and who have offended to allow it to be sustained on its present unsatisfactory basis. Just outcomes long after the event are not a substitute for good and timely decisions, albeit that they may require practitioners to be robust about their own reservations about a defendant's fitness to participate in trial proceedings.

19 Although disagreements about the existence of disorder per se can be seen in the reported cases: see, for one telling example, *R v Martin (Anthony)* [2003] QB 1.

Chapter 18

Dangerous and severe personality disorder

DSPD constitutes a fascinating area for mental health and crime. In many respects it represents the opposite end of the spectrum of disorder and offending with which we have been dealing, and yet it poses dilemmas of similar difficulty. Here is a category (if it is a category) of offenders for whom offending presents as the most troubling and marked aspect of their behaviour; their disorder, if it indeed exists as an identifiable entity, is one of personality rather than some disruption or disturbance in cognitive or functional processes. So, whilst the offending may be readily apparent, the underlying disorder is contentious. Without an agreed diagnosis, treatment of the disorder becomes highly problematic. Indeed, what is it that one is trying to treat, above and beyond the offending behaviour? Or is one trying to *manage* the behaviour? If many, if not most, of these patients retain capacity, and the treatment being offered is largely one that entails their willing and enthusiastic participation (hence, motivating offenders to participate becomes critical) why is compulsion necessary? Indeed, wouldn't the need for compulsion be the one factor most likely to predict an unsuccessful outcome? But if this is the case why have such efforts and financial resources gone into developing treatment programmes under compulsion for these offender-patients?

A brief and all too crude diversion into history is necessary at this point. The early chapters of this book have established, if anything, that the relationship between offending and mental disorder is at its strongest when the categories of relevant mental disorder focus on either various forms of personality disorder or on offences involving drug and alcohol abuse. Much of the strength of these associations comes from definitional overlap between what constitutes a mental disorder and what constitutes a crime. Hence, the legal definition of psychopathic disorder under the MHA 1983 (unamended) was 'a persistent disorder or disability of mind (whether or not including significant impairment of intelligence) which results in abnormally aggressive or seriously irresponsible conduct on the part of the person concerned' (s 1(2)). It was a manifest tautology. Few patients were sectioned as suffering from psychopathic disorder even where they had offended, and almost none under the civil sections of the MHA 1983.

There were numerous reasons for this: legal psychopathic disorder did not embrace all patients suffering from clinical personality disorder; potential psychopathic patients had to come within the MHA 1983's treatability criterion, namely that treatment in hospital was 'likely to alleviate or prevent a deterioration in his condition'; clinicians were not enthusiastic about taking patients into scarce beds when those patients were of uncertain treatability; courts were unenthusiastic about sending such offenders to hospital even if clinicians were prepared to take them where serious offences were entailed and there was a concern about premature release where patients did not prove treatable; those offenders convicted of murder had to go to prison in the first instance because of the mandatory life sentence. And numerous counter responses: clinicians would take those personality disordered patients with whom they wanted to have a 'therapeutic go' even if they didn't fall within a strict definition of psychopathic disorder; the treatability criterion was a chimera – legally it proved all but toothless and yet it remained a potentially useful tool for clinicians to reject disruptive offenders whom they didn't want in their service; dual diagnosis proved a useful tool for admitting patients who might not satisfy the treatability criterion; anxieties about premature release were probably similarly exaggerated as it became evident that tribunals were as cautious, and sometimes more cautious, than treating clinicians. The system muddled along.

There was admittedly a brief flurry of activity following the discharge of Noel Ruddle in 1999 from Carstairs State Hospital in Scotland; and there were legislative developments in order to try to solve the perceived problem his case raised (see below). Indeed, the resulting Act in Scotland, the Mental Health (Public Safety and Appeals) Scotland Act 1999, was the first one enacted by the new Scottish Parliament. Yet it was the preceding case of Hutchison Reid (also discussed below) that had effectively put an end to the relevance of the treatability test for those suffering from psychopathic disorder.

Scotland was not alone in its legislative developments. The Crime (Sentences) Act 1997 introduced the hybrid order (Eastman and Peay, 1998) as another initiative to address the tricky problem of those with psychopathic disorder who were of uncertain treatability. But this was an initiative never much used in the limited format in which it was introduced.

And then came the new Labour government in May 1997. This government was not only to embark on a major and chequered programme of reform in mental health legislation but it also embraced the seeming opportunities for legislative development alongside the case of Michael Stone.

The Michael Stone case

Michael Stone was convicted of the murders of Lin and Megan Russell, offences which took place in July 1996, and of the attempted murder of

Josie Russell, the Russell's other daughter. The family dog was also killed. Michael Stone was not arrested until a year after the offences, and was convicted in October 1998. Thereafter, there is a complex history relating to the appeal, a retrial and the findings of an Inquiry after Homicide. The Report of this, completed in November 2000, was not published until September 2006. The history is messy; there was never any forensic evidence; it is suggested that the authorities were alerted to Stone as a potential suspect by one of his clinicians, Dr Philip Sugarman, after Dr Sugarman had seen a *Crimewatch* programme featuring the murders;[1] the key evidence given of confessions made by Stone in custody to other prisoners is, like all such alleged confessions, of dubious value and ultimately constituted the principal reason why the initial convictions were quashed (Wolchover, 2006); and the value of the evidence of two other witnesses who allegedly saw him after the killings has also been questioned. The Court of Appeal ordered a retrial. This took place in 2001. Stone was convicted again and appealed on the basis of the judge's summing up. The appeal was unsuccessful. The case was subsequently referred to the Criminal Cases Review Commission. A number of websites chart the problematic history of this case; one website goes so far as to name another potential suspect who was convicted of other murderous random hammer attacks on women.[2]

Michael Stone continues to profess his innocence. It is not unheard of for defendants in such cases to refuse to admit their guilt; however, mainly these are cases where the forensic evidence is overwhelming but the defendant's disordered mental state makes it impossible for them to acknowledge their part in the offence (see *Diamond* above) and it is only as a result of prolonged treatment that perpetrators are enabled so to do. This, in itself, as discussed above with respect to diminished responsibility, causes problems. But Michael Stone has capacity and has consistently maintained his innocence. That his case should have played such a part in the DSPD initiative is accordingly curious.

It is moreover paradoxical that Michael Stone should be associated at all with the DSPD initiative since it is unclear on the basis of the information that has been published whether he would ever have come within the designated criteria. Certainly he would not have been labelled DSPD at the time since this categorisation only emerged in 1999 as a working definition in a government consultation document:[3] DSPD was used to describe people 'who have an identifiable personality disorder to a severe degree, who pose a high risk to other people because of their serious anti-social behaviour

1 See *The Telegraph*, 5 October 2001.
2 See www.michaelstone.co.uk. See also *R v Michael John Stone* [2001] EWCA Crim 297 and *R v Michael John Stone* [2005] EWCA Crim 105.
3 The term was originally 'dangerous severely personality disordered' (Home Office and Department of Health 1999:12).

resulting from their disorder' (Home Office and Department of Health, 1999:12). Over time this working definition has been refined and now, to fall within the criteria for the DSPD programme, an individual would need to satisfy three related criteria (Home Office and Department of Health, 2001).[4] First, being considered more likely than not to re-offend within five years in a way that would lead to serious physical or psychological harm from which the victim would find it difficult or impossible to recover. Second, to have a severe personality disorder with a score of 30 or above on the revised Psychopathy Checklist (PCL-R: Hare, 1991), or a PCL-R score of 25–29 plus a minimum of one DSM-IV personality diagnosis other than antisocial personality disorder, or have two or more DSM-IV personality disorder diagnoses. Third, there has to be a functional link between the personality disorder and the risk of offending.

Before his conviction it is worth noting that Michael Stone was not only known to mental health services, but had presented with a combination of problems including personality disorder. Sometimes this had been described as a severe antisocial personality disorder. He had also abused illicit and addictive drugs and at various times had complained of symptoms that might be features of mental illness, but were also consistent with the adverse effects of drug misuse and/or aspects of his personality disorder: these are all detailed in the Report of the Independent Inquiry into his case (Francis et al, 2006:4/32). He had a number of convictions for offences of dishonesty, in particular burglary, and had two convictions for wounding and two for robbery. There were also convictions for the possession of fire-arms, including an antique firearm. He had spent a number of periods in prison. His was a history of serious offending, but not of the most seriously assaultive.

His psychiatric history was complex, but he seemed not to be regarded primarily as a violent man and had only had one compulsory admission, from which he was discharged by his Responsible Medical Officer. Agencies had been prepared to treat him repeatedly on a voluntary basis. Indeed, the Inquiry Report notes that in this respect services in Kent were to be commended; this was 'emphatically not a case of a man with a dangerous personality disorder being generally ignored by agencies or left at large without supervision' (Francis et al, 2006:5). This then was not a man who had been rejected by services because he was diagnosed with an untreatable personality disorder.

In the five years preceding the Russell murders he had only been in prison for one period on remand and his major problems during this period related to drug abuse. From the records it is notable that he was seen by a community psychiatric nurse on 4 July 1996 (with his mother) when he made threats, amongst others, to kill his probation officer, whom he believed had breached

4 For extensive materials see the DSPD website: www.dspdprogramme.gov.uk.

confidentiality leading to the break-up of a relationship with his girlfriend. However, when he and his mother left the appointment he was reported to be OK, the session having ended in a more amiable fashion.[5] He was contacted again by telephone on 5 July when he sounded repentant and an appointment was made to see him again on 10 July, when he was observed to be much calmer, and was again requesting in-patient detoxification. There was no recorded contact with services on 9 July 1996, the day of the murders. It is, of course, a little curious that a man who had been involved in two brutal murders and an attempted murder only the day before was able to appear so normal when seen by services within 24 hours of the attacks; and particularly curious for a man like Stone who had a documented record of not being able fully to control himself in the presence of professionals. The normality of his behaviour on the day after the killings is a feature of his chronology which has not attracted the attention it perhaps warrants.

His behaviour on 4 July did not go undocumented and the consultant psychiatrist volunteered an explanation to the Inquiry as to why Stone was not subject to a compulsory admission at this point. To paraphrase this clinician's explanation, to have detained Stone at that point in order to try and change his attitude to drug use was, in effect, to detain him on grounds of personality disorder; and that would be to have detained him indefinitely since, as he did not think Stone was treatable in his unit, he would, in effect, be keeping him until he was old and no longer a risk. In this context, the clinician did not think he could make a recommendation for detention under the MHA 1983 (Francis et al, 2006:215).

The DSPD initiative

All of this preceded the government's initiative on DSPD. Although various governments had grappled with how to deal with offenders with personality disorders who did not fit neatly within the then MHA 1983 and, if they did, caused potential problems with respect to their release from psychiatric services, it apparently took the Stone case to galvanise matters. Jack Straw, the then Home Secretary, noted with seeming incredulity:

> Quite extraordinarily for a medical profession, the psychiatric profession has said that it will take on only patients whom it regards as treatable. If that philosophy applied anywhere else in medicine, no progress would be made in medicine. It is time that the psychiatric profession seriously examined its own practices and tried to modernise them in a way that it has so far failed to do.
>
> (*Hansard* 26 October 2000, column 9)

---

5 Francis et al (2006:213).

The DSPD initiative also has a complex history. The DSPD programme website provides ready access to this; and other publications chart the state of flux in which the programme has been located (Mullen, 1999, 2007).[6] It is sufficient here to note that this was an attempt to deal with what were recognised to be offenders with genuine problems, who experienced significant distress and self-harm, who intermittently inflicted harm on others (as well as the threat they posed of such harm) and for whom suicide constituted a high risk. That personality disorder causes real problems for those who have it is not in doubt; that it causes problems to others is also relatively uncontentious. However, what is unclear concerns what can appropriately be done about this by psychiatric services. Where no effective treatment exists or where the treatment that is available entails the cooperation of the offender, attempting to compel offenders and clinicians into a therapeutic relationship with no obvious end-point, or indeed no obvious way of determining that the end-point has been reached, was always going to be tricky. Nonetheless four DSPD units (two in Special Hospitals, Broadmoor and Rampton, and two in high security prisons, Frankland and Whitemoor) were initially established taking some 274 men; latterly in 2006 one facility, the Primrose Unit, became available for women at HMP Low Newton with 12 beds allocated.

A number of assessments of the programme are now being published. Two of the first (Barrett et al, 2009; Tyrer et al, 2009) are hedged with caveats and have elicited a response from their own funders, the DSPD programme (Ramsay et al, 2009). All of this is unsurprising, given the innovative nature of the programme, the methodological difficulties of undertaking research in the field, the downgrading of the programme to a pilot and numerous other problems that were predicted (small numbers of participants, high staff turnover, decreasing moral etc). However, the findings are worth examining, partly because some of them are counterintuitive and partly because they reinforce the highly problematic nature of providing assessment and treatment to these offender patients.

First, Barrett et al (2009:127) detail the additional expense involved in having offenders in the DSPD assessment programme compared with those in the control prisons and the consistent trend for the DSPD assessment group to show worse outcomes. Whilst they acknowledge that theirs was a short-term evaluation and thus they were not able to measure such long term outcomes as re-offending, they do note that 'We consider violence a good proxy for risk of re-offending, and we have not noted any improvements here' (at 130). Tyrer et al (2009), in a linked article, note in detail the problems of establishing a randomised controlled trial and, because of these problems, were reluctant to draw any clear conclusions beyond those on

6 See above: DSPD currently refers to 'Dangerous People with Severe Personality Disorder'.

increased costs. Indeed, it was evident that only one in three of the referrals to the assessment programme satisfied the requisite criteria; as the authors observed, 'If the wrong people are referred, the assessment will only serve as an expensive screen' (2009:141).

Tyrer et al did, however, note a better quality of life for those in the assessment programme with regard to social relationships, an increase in aggression and worse social functioning in those with less severe personality disorder. They attributed these latter findings in part to frustration and unfulfilled expectations in the participants. Another problematic factor concerned the voluntariness of the sample: the first prisoners recruited into the DSPD programme were volunteers, but after the introduction of the Criminal Justice Act 2003 more coercion was entailed, making the Barrett/Tyrer et al sample a cohort of 'prisoner-volunteers' and 'pressured-prisoners'. This makes any generalisations on the basis of the sample problematic. In any event their results, together with the findings of earlier work, do not generate any great confidence in the likely efficacy of these programmes. Of equal interest, of the 71 randomised subjects taken into assessment only 20 ultimately qualified to go into the treatment programme, with only 10 of those actually being taken into treatment. Yet eight other prisoners who were accepted for the treatment programme did not satisfy the entry criteria. Such inconsistent entry criteria are likely to flaw fundamentally any evaluation of the effectiveness of the treatment programme.

The authors' conclusions (Tyrer et al, 2009:143) are understandably downbeat: as they observe 'to date there is no evidence that any treatment is of proven, or even presumptive, efficacy in those with severe personality disorder (Warren et al, 2003)'. The benefits they see in their negative conclusions are that, if replicated, they might lead to the cessation of such unsuitable assessments.

Tyrer et al (2009:144) also conclude 'Our findings, together with concerns about treatability, raise more fundamental concerns about whether medical management of people with these problems is a justifiable use of resources and ethically appropriate (Moran, 2001).' This is a very important point, since it goes to the heart of medicalising criminality. It is taken up by Ramsay et al (2009), on behalf of the funders of the study, in their riposte to the negative publications. They draw attention to this assertion but then seek to suggest that the authors, in their longer report to the DSPD programme, produced a 'rather different perspective'; they cite a paragraph from the Executive Summary to this longer report (Tyrer et al, 2007:6) in which reference is made to some of the positive remarks related by a small majority of prisoners. I appreciate that this begins to read like splitting hairs but it is redolent of some of the arguments made earlier in this book about the way in which evidence is presented. First, you cannot satisfactorily trade-off evidence of positive feedback against the results of a randomised controlled trial (albeit unsatisfactory and small). Second, this was not the authors' main conclusion even in their Executive Summary. Rather, and on the same page, they assert:

> Taken together, the findings suggest that the assessment programme was too long, generally poor in selecting suitable patients, cost-ineffective, and frustrating for prisoners whose expectations may have been unduly raised by the initial enthusiasm for a new venture.
>
> (Tyrer et al, 2007:6)

It is inevitable, albeit demoralising, that the 'owners' of the DSPD programme want to see it succeed, but to be seen to be denigrating the results of research they have funded in this way is regrettable. Particularly where the DSPD research commissioners (Ramsay, 2009:149) seem to misunderstand the very problem the legislative programme was designed to remedy: thus 'DSPD patients can be held in hospital sites after their sentence has ended, but this has always been an option for mentally disordered offenders'. They are correct in asserting that this was an option if they meant those suffering from psychopathic disorder who were deemed treatable; but wrong to assert that this applied generally to DSPD patients who (a) may not have fallen within the classification of psychopathic disorder and (b) who may not have been treatable. Finally, it is notable that the theme which emerges from the commentary as the basis for promoting the DSPD programme appears to be that prisoners claim benefit from it: they like the opportunity to have psychiatric support and most of these offenders wanted more contact with psychologists. This is entirely consistent with the previous work that has been done on, for example, therapeutic communities (Genders and Player, 1995) and with the survey of prisoners on IPPs (Rutherford, 2008; Sainsbury Centre, 2008). But it does not wholly justify an entire programme for DSPD prisoner-patients under costly compulsion; a cost which, by November 2009, was estimated at £488 million since 2001.[7] Indeed, to allocate such a large sum of public resources to treating such a small cohort of prisoner-patients, when the problems of personality disorder are widespread within the prison population, seems unjustifiable.

That clear-cut findings from the programme have not yet emerged is hardly surprising. It was overambitious to expect such early findings in a context where prisoners have very mixed motives for taking part in treatment, where the treatment itself is delivered in a holistic way and is inevitably somewhat unsystematic, where the criteria for success are hard to measure and the treatment is delivered with an accompanying generous investment of resources, both financial, clinical and political. The real question is whether

---

7 Sainsbury Centre for Mental Health, personal communication. This figure includes capital start-up costs.

such certainty is ever likely to emerge. Treating criminality at an individual level seems almost predestined to fail; and even if one had the courage of one's beliefs that treatment had succeeded, decisions about release invariably lie, for the most serious offenders, out of the hands of those delivering the treatment. The Parole Board, the Mental Health Tribunal and the Secretary of State, all of whom have the power to make such decisions, are variously affected by considerations other than the 'simple' treatment question. Thus release into the community, and ultimate validation, are rarely put to the test at the requisite point. In this light, proponents of such programmes will sometimes argue that there has been a measurable change on subjects' responses to the instruments used to assess them; but this may be to place a spurious reliance on what these measures test.

There is one final, and largely unspoken, problem with all of this. And it concerns discriminatory precautionary practices. Amongst those with anti-social personality disorder we can be confident that a proportion of offenders will reoffend. The problem is identifying which amongst them will so do. And our ability correctly to predict is less than impressive. Indeed, Buchanan and Leese (2001) in a systematic review of the evidence relating to personality disorder concluded that six people would have to be detained to prevent one violent act; a conclusion in keeping with other assessments of our impoverished abilities to predict risk. And to date fewer than 300 offenders are in the DSPD programme at any one time. Compared with the numbers of individuals who are convicted of other dangerous activities, domestic abuse and dangerous driving being perhaps the most obvious and the most common, these numbers are modest. It is also curious that the precautionary approach seemingly does not feature for these much larger groups of dangerous offenders; nor is there any agitation for a defined legislative basis for such an approach, nor for an all embracing therapeutic environment in which to assess their suitability for intervention and thereafter to deliver 'treatment' to them. Why is it that mental disorder, and in particular personality disorder in association with dangerous offending, attracts such attention, whereas ordered offending carried out intentionally or recklessly by those without a clinical diagnosis does not?

Treatability and detainability

To understand why any of this matters it is necessary to make a further short diversion into the issue of the treatability of the conditions of personality disorder, severe personality disorder, dangerous and severe personality disorder and psychopathic disorder, and into their legal classifications. Under the Mental Health Act 1959 there was both an age threshold for psychopathic disorder, so that only those under 21 could be admitted under this classification, and a treatability requirement that the disorder had to require or be 'susceptible to medical treatment' (s 4(4) of the MHA 1959).

Under the MHA 1983 the age limit was abolished (together with the option that the disorder might 'require' treatment) but those suffering from psychopathic disorder could only be detained where they satisfied the treatability criterion (treatment was likely to 'alleviate or prevent a deterioration'). These legal devices were an attempt to avoid the spectre of indefinite detention of those with 'personality disorders' who were non-responsive to medical treatment and who thus posed the problem of the long-term occupation of clinical beds to no effect other than an incapacitative one; and in many cases not even doing that but rather providing reassurance against such potential offending.

Treatability as a device for preventing unjustified detention all but evaporated following the 1998 Scottish case of *Hutchison Reid*, where the House of Lords ultimately held, at its minimum, that an environment that permitted anger management constituted treatment for the purposes of detention.[8] But whilst this decision broadened the understanding of what could constitute treatment, it also clarified that the treatability test applied equally at the point of potential discharge as it did at the point of admission.[9] The decision would inevitably raise difficulties in a small number of cases where treatability might still not be satisfied even in its new broadened guise. And indeed, in 1999, the case of Noel Ruddle crystallised just this difficulty; as Ruddle seemingly did not require even 'anger management' he was not detainable.[10] This led to a swift change in the law by the new Scottish Parliament to prevent the possibility of similarly placed patients being released; the amendments clarified that it was lawful to refuse to discharge detained patients where they posed a risk of serious harm to the public even if medical treatment was not the purpose of the detention. In a subsequent challenge to this, *Anderson, Reid and Doherty* achieved only a clarification by the Privy Council that nothing in Article 5 required a condition to be treatable for detention to be lawful.[11] Indeed the Privy Council cited *Guzardi v Italy*[12] noting that a predominant reason why the ECHR permitted deprivation of liberty under 5(1)(e) 'is not only that they are dangerous for public safety but also that their own interests may necessitate their detention', and further citing the unreported case of *Koniarska v UK*[13] to underline the dual medical and social reasons for the detention of those with psychopathic disorder.

8 *Hutchison Reid v Secretary of State for Scotland and another* (1998) House of Lords, 3 December 1998.
9 See Lord Clyde at paras 73–76.
10 For a detailed history of the case of Noel Ruddle see the Scottish Parliament Information Centre (1999) Research Note 99/33.
11 *Anderson, Reid and Doherty v The Scottish Ministers and the Advocate General for Scotland* (2001) Privy Council 15 October 2001.
12 *Guzardi v Italy* (1980) 3 EHRR 333 at para 98; at para 30 in *Anderson, Reid and Doherty*.
13 *Anderson, Reid and Doherty* at para 63.

Even the spectre of retrospective legislation like the Scottish Act would be permitted under the ECHR where there were compelling 'general interest' grounds. Although the burden was to be satisfied by the Sheriff, and to be satisfied on the grounds of necessity not desirability or convenience, imminent risk of serious harm would be sufficient.

Notably Lord Clyde[14] made reference to the delicate balance to be drawn between the rights and freedoms of individuals of unsound mind and those of the public 'to live free from fear of being assaulted or injured by persons whose mental condition is such as to give rise to a risk of such unsocial conduct', but nothing in the ECHR gave the rights of a detainee priority over those of the citizen to live in 'peace and security'. The Privy Council did not discuss the statistics relating to the numbers of false positives who would need to be detained in order to prevent re-offending: nor did they discuss the need to address the public's heightened and unjustified fear of such offending. It was enough seemingly that a risk of serious harm existed. Such arguments are arguably redolent of the approach which maintains that once one has offended seriously, as all these offenders had, one loses the right to be treated as an equal citizen for the purposes of risk prevention.

Has the situation changed? Having sought legal authority in the ECHR for such preventive detention in a clinical setting, the ECtHR subsequently held Article 5(1) does not require a treatability test to be satisfied for compliance;[15] albeit that the burden of proof should lie on the detaining authority and that review of the case should be on a regular basis without undue delay (Article 5(4)). In this context one might question whether the government's amendments to the MHA 1983 by the MHA 2007 were ever necessary? And one answer might lie not in the initial decision as to whether to admit an offender-patient to hospital, but in the greater flexibility the new provisions allow for the transfer of prisoners on fixed-term sentences who are nearing the end of their sentence into hospital on grounds of personality disorder. This is not a new problem (see Grounds 1991); but it is a problem that may be rearing its head afresh.[16]

The (amended) Mental Health Act 1983

By removing psychopathic disorder as a distinct classification under the MHA 1983 and having a definition of mental disorder which is broad enough to embrace all forms of personality disorder the government has eased the position of clinicians; no longer do clinicians have to work with a legal definition which seemingly excluded those with personality disorder.

14 *Anderson, Reid and Doherty* at para 74.
15 *Hutchison Reid v UK* (2003) 37 EHRR 9.
16 *R (on the application of TF) v Secretary of State for Justice* [2008] EWCA Civ 1457.

Moreover, the predictive treatability test (treatment was likely to alleviate or prevent a deterioration) has been replaced by an aspirational test. Now, treatment has to have the purpose of alleviating or preventing a deterioration in the patient's condition. Although an aspiration is manifestly easier to satisfy than a prediction, the difference is likely to be only marginal in practice. However, appropriate treatment has to be available. This now looks like the critical test which could permit clinicians to reject from services anyone they do not wish to take, or about whom they fear a developing long-term relationship where in practice the patient proves untreatable or treatment resistant.

One niche remains. Breach of domestic law can constitute breach of the Convention. Detaining patients, even with mental disorder, where they do not pose a risk of serious harm to the public, or to themselves, should make it necessary for each decision to be judged individually. And this could introduce problematic statistical arguments. It remains possible that clinicians will arrive at a view that they can no longer argue that the purpose of medical treatment is satisfied, or that appropriate treatment is available. Potentially, this makes the research programme into DSPD hazardous. Ultimately, the government may be hung by its own petard of evidence-based medicine; and funding costly treatment that is not effective, or may even be counterproductive, is hardly likely to satisfy any guidelines from the National Institute for Health and Clinical Evidence.

The solution advocated by some (for example Szmukler, Daw and Dawson, 2010) is to treat such personality disordered offenders as offenders; and offer them voluntary treatment within the health justice system once they have been convicted. But the solution is not to seek clinical justifications for what is so evidently a policy based on risk, even though those with severe personality disorder may be undeniably needy. Needs are unlikely adequately to be satisfied where the evidence for so doing is so slim.

Chapter 19

Culpability and treatment

Chasing dragons?

Making sense of any relationship between mental disorder and crime was, as the earlier chapters of this book demonstrated, extremely tricky. Yet in both the popular and broadsheet press there are regular reports of those who have offended where causal responsibility for their offending or (at the least) explanatory significance is attributed to some aspect of the individual's underlying make-up. This is frequently couched in terms of mental disorder; and not infrequently a specific diagnosis is given, as if the label brings with it some scientific weight (Bentall, 2009; Goldacre, 2009). The pervasiveness of this tendency is illustrated by three cases taken from a ten day period in the summer of 2009:

> Driven to marry again and again by mental disorder Emily Horne, a four time bigamist, who had been married five times and was now living with a sixth potential husband, pleaded guilty to bigamy. Judge Khokhar said that he had intended to jail Horne but decided to suspend the sentence because a psychiatric report said she was responding well to treatment for bipolar and personality disorders. Horne observed 'the thing I'm guilty of most is falling in love.'
>
> (*Timesonline*, 27 July 2009)

> Eric Cruz, who suffered from paranoid schizophrenia, had his plea of guilty of manslaughter by reason of diminished responsibility accepted by Judge Henshell who remarked 'Tragically Eric Cruz suffered from a mental illness, apparently for some time. He heard voices. He had fixed and firm beliefs that voices were commanding him to do various things ... He believed he had a mission to protect children and believed it was necessary for him to take the life of Patrick McGee to protect his own child ... He was driven to that wicked and irrational act by the illness he suffers.'
>
> (*The Guardian*, 27 July 2009)

> Hacker Gary Mckinnon lost his High Court battle to avoid extradition
> ... the 43 year old ... who suffers from Asperger's syndrome, could
> now stand trial in the US charged with hacking into 97 top-secret mili-
> tary computers and causing more than $700,000 damage ... Critics
> have also blasted the High Court ruling as a blow to human rights,
> claiming he should not stand trial because of his disorder ... Polly
> Tommey, the founder of The Autism Trust, stated: 'Mr Mckinnon's
> dreadful situation has arisen due to an apparent lack of understanding
> of autism and the autistic condition by politicians, by social services and
> by the wider government organisation. This is not how our country
> should be acting in supporting vulnerable adults.'
>
> (*Hornsey and Crouch End Journal*, 5 August 2009)

The implication in all of these cases is that the offenders are not fully responsible for what they have done and accordingly should not be dealt with as
other ordered perpetrators would be; the other implication is that treatment
could or might prevent a recurrence of offending. It would be unwise, of
course, to place too great a reliance on the newspaper reports of these cases
in respect of their accuracy, but they are worth noting in that they undoubtedly help to shape public understanding of these issues. In fact, the Gary
Mckinnon case was a judicial review of the Secretary of State's refusal to
change his decision on extradition when faced with fresh evidence that
Mckinnon's Asperger's would deteriorate seriously if he were exposed to
the stress of imprisonment in another culture;[1] the Secretary of State argued
that no explanation had been provided as to the comparative effect of the
proceedings to date on Mckinnon's health, nor why US proceedings should
have an effect of a different magnitude. Mckinnon raised both Article 3 and
Article 8 points. Both were rejected by the Divisional Court, the former as
failing to approach the severity required for an Article 3 breach amounting
to inhumane or degrading treatment, given that the US authorities had
given assurances that the US courts would have regard to his health; and the
latter since extradition was a lawful and proportionate response to his
alleged offending and therefore not a breach of his right to respect for his
private and family life.

So whilst popularly available media reports may link mental disorder and
offending in some causal nexus, the legal system has a more nuanced
response. In any event, all of this may seem specious since, if the earlier
chapters are given credence, there is no reason why those with autism,
Asperger's, bipolar disorder, personality disorder or even schizophrenia are

---

1 *R (on the application of Gary Mckinnon) v Secretary of State for Home Affairs: R (on the
application of Gary Mckinnon) v Director of Public Prosecutions* [2009] EWHC 2021
(Admin).

not capable of resisting their impulses or adhering to the tenets of the criminal law. Of course, there are some circumstances in which they may not be so capable, and some circumstances in which they should not be held fully culpable or indeed culpable at all, but mental disorder is not a blank cheque to excuse or explain offending. And whilst it can cogently be argued that emotional vulnerability or a heightened risk of suicide are factors that ought to have a bearing on the way in which punishment is imposed, or even if it is imposed at all, such concerns relate as much to the nature of the punishment we impose on all offenders as to those individuals deemed mentally disordered.

A more interesting question is how the law responds to those who do not, and arguably could not in the circumstances, adhere to the restraints the law imposes by reason of an underlying mental abnormality. The most extreme illustration of this arises in the context of sleep-walking. In the paradigm case, where an individual engages in an act whist sleepwalking (and which would be an offence if committed when the individual was awake), the law should in principle have little difficulty in acquitting him as having no *mens rea* for the offence, and certainly no conscious control over his actions: in essence the offence is committed during a state of automatism.[2] In practice the law struggles with this, for all the reasons so eloquently set out in a pair of combined articles in the *Criminal Law Review* (Ebrahim et al, 2005; Wilson et al, 2005). The conflict between principle and practice has not been as fully addressed in case law as it should perhaps have been, in part because whilst the phenomenon of sleepwalking is relatively common, carrying out acts that would otherwise constitute criminal offences during periods of sleepwalking is uncommon; successful defences based on sleepwalking are extremely rare. Indeed, in the most recent case of a man suffering from pavor nocturnus, who was acquitted of murdering his wife, the judge directed the jury to acquit the defendant, Brian Thomas, only when the prosecution chose to offer no more evidence. The prosecution had argued that the defendant's automatism created a basis for a verdict of not guilty by reason of insanity, but following expert evidence from a psychiatrist were persuaded that 'no useful purpose would be served by Mr Thomas being detained and treated in a psychiatric hospital' (Morris, 2009).

In much the same way that the argument was made in the earlier part of this book that crime occurs in messy contexts, the states of 'unconscious' activity that are associated with offending are similarly messy. The law initially looks clear, albeit wrongheaded. For example, the defence of automatism requires a total destruction of voluntary control on the defendant's part; impaired or reduced control is not enough. Even driving without

---

2 Both the doctrine of prior fault and issues related to the need for a complete destruction of voluntary control can confuse this principled position.

awareness does not involve total destruction of voluntary control where the ability to steer the vehicle and the capacity to react to stimuli appearing in the road ahead remain.[3] But is sleepwalking a form of non-insane automatism for which one would be entitled to a complete acquittal on the basis that there was no voluntary control? The two exceptional and unreported cases of *Bilton* and *Davies* cited by Mackay and Mitchell (2006) would suggest yes. This conclusion is reached even though, as the authors observe, the verdicts, if based on episodes of sleepwalking, should more properly have been ones of insane automatism following *Burgess* since the cause of the disturbance of the mind (or somnambulism) is an internal factor.[4] Insane automatism leads to a health disposal, in the same way as would a verdict of not guilty by reason of insanity, albeit that that health disposal can only be under compulsion in hospital where the criteria for admission under the MHA 1983 are satisfied. Mackay and Mitchell make the further critical point that sleepwalking, as a form of automatism, is unique since the defect of reason which derives from being asleep actually precedes the episode of sleepwalking, and the associated criminality; in that sense whatever it is that causes the asleep person to arise and behave deviantly could well be an external factor, converting the event from insane to non-insane automatism; this in turn should attract a verdict of not guilty.

If this were not messy enough, the true complexity of this area is illustrated by the case of *Roach*.[5] Roach was convicted of wounding with intent to do grievous bodily harm following an assault with a knife by him on a colleague, consequent to a comparatively trivial incident at work. Several bystanders witnessed the incident and said that the appellant appeared calm afterwards; one said in cross examination that Roach stopped the attack because it appeared he had a sudden realisation of what had happened and dropped the knife. Roach's case was that he had no knowledge or memory of the incident itself, while being aware of events up to moments before, and then almost immediately after, the stabbing.

The psychiatric testimony was in conflict. The prosecution psychiatrist asserted that there was no evidence of a psychotic illness and that Roach's amnesia, even if genuine, did not necessarily prevent him forming the required intention. He did not support a case for automatism and argued that, had that been the case, Roach would have been bewildered after the event and have had no memory of the incident. Rather, his behaviour was consistent with someone who had lost his temper.

Two psychiatrists for the defence disagreed. The first believed that Roach had an anti-social personality disorder. He considered that the sudden

---

3 *Attorney-General's Reference (No. 2 of 1992)* [1993] 97 Cr App R 429.
4 *R v Burgess* [1991] 2 QB 92.
5 *R v Michael Roach* [2001] EWCA Crim 2698.

violent attack with total amnesia for the event, which had not modified over the past month, indicated a diagnosis of automatism. He went on:

> Based on his childhood experiences and his lifelong relationship with his father, his recent conflict with his rather strong-willed partner and finally confrontation with a perceived humiliation from a fellow worker and specially under the mitigation of fatigue, alcohol and prescribed medication, *the most likely diagnosis is obviously an insane automatism of psychogenic type.*
> (Quoted by Potter LJ, in *Roach* [2001], para 12 emphasis added)

Thrown into the equation were the possibilities of frontal lobe damage from a childhood playground accident and temporal lobe epilepsy.

The second psychiatrist also attributed events to a combination of factors. He noted that poor impulse control meant that under certain circumstances the impulse to behave violently could overwhelm the cognitive process which might have controlled it; such irresistible impulses were particularly powerful in the context of those who were relatively inarticulate in areas of powerful feeling. Through his life Roach had had many experiences of humiliation at the hands of others and, on the night of the offence, his weakened cognitive processes were confronted with perceived provocation and humiliation by his incompetent supervisor, the victim. Although there was no evidence of any underlying physical condition, such as epilepsy associated with automatism, there were strong psychological factors in a man already impaired by fatigue, alcohol and prescribed medication at the time of the offence. The second psychiatrist also concluded that the offence fell into the category of 'insane automatism of psychogenic type'. But there was no internal physical factor which solely triggered the incident; powerful non-conscious psychological events appeared to have overwhelmed a man with an underlying personality disorder whose mental state was chemically impaired, lowering the threshold of psychogenic automatism.

This combination of external and internal factors meant a number of verdicts could have been available to the jury; not guilty (intent not made out); not guilty on grounds of non-insane automatism (a complete acquittal); not guilty by reason of insanity (insane automatism – which leads to a health disposal) and guilty as charged. It is perhaps understandable that the judge failed fully to explain these to the jury; this led, amongst other reasons, to the conviction being quashed, albeit reluctantly, by the Court of Appeal. There is a sense when reading the judgment that the Court took the view that the trial jury were not blinded by the psychiatric testimony but rather preferred the strong view of the prosecution expert; however, cumulative irregularities in the way in which the Judge had conducted the trial meant that the verdict of the jury was deemed unsafe.

It is interesting to speculate, had the matters been properly aired before the jury, what verdict might have emerged. There was an array of possible explanatory factors which might have mitigated the defendant's culpability sufficient, in the jury's mind, for a conviction not to be returned; yet, there was also evidence of what looked like an assault which went beyond a momentary lashing out. And, to reiterate, for automatism the law requires a complete destruction of voluntary control over one's actions. There was evidence of a troubled background, an underlying personality deficit, and a lack of conscious control, albeit brought about in part by the voluntary consumption of moderate quantities of alcohol and prescription drugs; namely, an anti-depressant and a mood stabiliser, neither of which would obviously have induced violence to the defendant's knowledge, and both of which are external factors for the 'internal-external' doctrine.[6] Certainly, the defendant was the beneficiary of a defective summing up by the judge and had been subject to some unfair trial procedures: would the jury have adopted a robust approach to the conflicting psychiatric evidence had this not been the case? It is impossible to know how sympathetic juries are to psychiatric opinion; how far, for example, are they persuaded by factors relating to a disadvantaged upbringing or the effects of alcohol or drugs – all of which may be familiar to them? But are they equally familiar with the effects of the interaction of a whole series of factors on a person with a personality disorder? Or does it require frank mental illness or seemingly unconscious behaviour during periods of sleep before a jury is prepared to accept the influence of the mind on behaviour, and in particular on behaviour which the law otherwise condemns? These are intractable questions.

6 A transitory malfuctioning of the mind brought about by drink or drugs is not a disease of the mind, and hence not classified as an 'internal factor' cause of automatism *R v Quick* [1973] QB 910 at 922.

Chapter 20

Conclusions

Paradoxically, neither those mentally disordered offenders with high capacity, namely those with various forms of personality disorder, nor those with very low or even absent capacity, namely those with various states of automatism which get classed as insanity by the law, fully escape the consequences of their actions. Perhaps this is right. And it certainly feels right for those who do not readily acknowledge a causal link between mental disorder and crime, in that the justifications for dealing with those individuals differently are less persuasive. Thus, why should the presence of a mental disorder result in preferential treatment within the criminal justice system when the existence perhaps of an impoverished upbringing or on-going poverty would not be deemed relevant? These are, of course, issues that may go personally to mitigate the severity of punishment, and there are compelling arguments that we need a more consistent approach to the relevance of such personal mitigation; but they should not go to culpability in the absence of an established causal link.

However, for those individuals who believe that there is a causal link between mental disorder and offending, or who believe there might be one in specified circumstances in particular individuals, the failure fully to absolve those lacking in capacity, or the active imposition of compulsory treatment on those who have infringed the criminal law with capacity, seems anomalous. And this perhaps arises from our differential approach to establishing the presence of criminal culpability (which requires a very high threshold of doubt to be crossed with significant protections for the accused to prevent it being crossed unjustifiably) and diagnosing the presence of a disorder (which appears to be done with a less rigorous application of a threshold of doubt). No doubt the latter is variously justified because the receipt of a diagnosis is not generally regarded as bringing with it significant additional negative consequences for the individual, over and above those the disorder itself inevitably entails.

The fact that criminal culpability is assessed at one point in time, and on the basis of a high threshold, will make for an uncomfortable fit with the diagnosis of mental disorder; mental disorder is more obviously long-term in its presentation, albeit that this may vary considerably in severity and form over time. And achieving a better fit between the two might be achieved were a more nuanced approach to diagnosis adopted. That the time has come for just such an approach has been advocated by Professor David Goldberg who has remarked that when the terms of DSM-V are finally agreed it should be recognised that there are gradations within disorders: not all of those experiencing only some of the symptoms, or some of the symptoms but to an insufficient degree, should be given the label of the diagnostic category.[1] And if there are gradations, there may be gradations within the alleged link between mental disorder and crime, making the relationship even more complicated than it is perhaps by some currently understood to be.

Boundaries and borders

One place to start to try to make sense of this would be to think about the multiple boundaries between disorder (the proper domain of mental health professionals), dysfunction (which may be within the domain of mental health professionals where it entails distress); deviance (for peers, parents and professionals generally – a crystallisation of what we deem society) and culpable law-breaking (the domain of the law and the criminal justice system). These boundaries are necessarily fluid, but too much seepage between them is likely to generate ethical problems as to the proper limits of intervention. Being clear, for example, about the borderline between dysfunction and deviance should avoid psychiatrists finding their role converted from that of doctors to those of therapeutic gaolers; and prevent the burden of risk prediction being passed to them. This is an argument which favours professionals retaining expertise within their own domain, and not assuming either that all are equally skilled or that pursuing multiple objectives necessarily aids the attaining of any of those objectives. It is also an argument that should resonate with criminologists familiar with David Garland's (2001) analysis of 'responsibilisation', the notion that responsibility for crime control has been progressively shared between government, and a number non-state actors and organisations, with the blurring of boundaries this necessarily entails between professionals.

Derek Bolton (2008:189), in his admirable book *What is Mental Disorder?*, argues that one approach to the issue of boundaries is to consider the extent to which disorder is defined either by natural dysfunction or by distress and disability. If it is the latter then a medicalised approach makes sense; this would entail first an assessment of the condition, then a diagnosis of it (assuming it crosses the requisite threshold of severity) and finally

1 *Rewriting the Psychiatrists' Bible*, Radio 4, 9 August 2009.

treatment, if treatment is appropriate, available and effective. But none of that will necessarily have any impact on the offending behaviour, although it may make the individual's life, and of those around them, more tolerable. Moreover, the medicalised approach, for all the reasons we promote treatment of disorder generally, has considerable merit. If on the other hand the disorder is defined primarily by natural dysfunction Bolton (2008:170) questions whether treatment is even possible.

Too rigid an approach to what constitutes the boundary between disorder and personal dysfunction or deviance risks ossifying whatever benefits a treatment-oriented approach might bring; this is the Jack Straw problem of arguing that there will never be any therapeutic progress if mental health professionals do not take on what look like difficult or potentially untreatable populations. The result of this reluctance is that clinicians can be stereotyped as uncaring and unnecessarily defensive about what is the proper terrain for their work and at whom the benefits of their work should be directed. The obverse, looking at it from the perspective of an unsuccessful therapeutic intervention, is that clinicians are accused of expanding their remit beyond the proper limits of their expertise with the risk that they end up in the position of gaolers to those who cannot be discharged from therapeutic beds, whilst at the same time draining resources away from, and generally prejudicing the treatment of, those who might be successfully treated. The horns of this dilemma would militate in favour of flexibility between therapeutic and penal institutions if clinicians are to try to treat the untreatable. But at the same time flexibility (and its bedfellow 'no certainty of disposal') may militate against a successful therapeutic intervention (in the sense that some offenders are not motivated or willing and able to engage in therapy until there is no possibility of a return to a penal environment where a conviction might be overturned or a determinate sentence fulfilled). And the solution to this dilemma may be the progressive convergence between mental health and penal disposals with an increasing reliance in the latter on indeterminate sentences. In turn, this comes with costs. First, of inappropriately detaining those – false positives – who are predicted to constitute a significant risk of serious offending, but who would never go on to offend in practice. And second, of greater fragmentation of services, with all of the consequential bureaucratic costs that entails, and with the potential for the prolongation of intervention where multiple objectives (of risk reduction and therapeutic benefit) apply.

None of this is easy.

One of the immediate problems in opening up disorder to embrace dysfunction or even deviance in the context of offending is that of numbers. As has been discussed earlier, prisons are populated with offenders who have various degrees of personality disorder. Indeed, figures have suggested that only one in ten of the prison population is free from disorder, albeit that a generous definition of what constituted disorder was applied by the authors

(Singleton et al, 1998). And if an unknown proportion of these offenders were indeed suffering from a dysfunction that constituted some adaptation to a particularly damaging, noxious or toxic environment, which may be longstanding, and a therapeutic intervention may be available, then what would be the arguments for not embarking down a medicalised route? Why is it that our response to the paedophiles and baby killers, who seem invariably to be the product of abusive and emotionally impoverished backgrounds themselves, is primarily penal not therapeutic? I would argue that the answer lies in their residual capacity for choice. No matter how awful those backgrounds, and truly awful some of them clearly are, we do not assume some hydraulic relationship between background and current behaviour; the former may be a significant factor, but it is not the only factor. And thus some element of punishment, perhaps a very large element, is there to reflect the culpable choices people have made.

But if this is right for those with personality disorder, why is it not also right, albeit to a more mitigated degree, for those with mental illness, where the argument has been made that the capacity to choose persists and not all, or even most, offending by those with mental illness should be seen as determined or driven by the underlying disorder? Court decisions can reflect the complexity of these judgments, sometimes to the extent of rejecting psychiatric recommendations for a hospital order where there is sufficient residual culpability for a prison sentence. And this can occur in the context of disorders as severe and well-documented as schizophrenia; the case of *Khelifi*, where the defendant was convicted of fraudulent activity, perpetrated over a significant period of time, makes this point well.[2] Perhaps the answer lies here not so much with what is just, but whether our common humanity permits such fine gradations of responsibility to be made in contexts where an individual's capacity is more greatly reduced; and that the benefit the individual may gain from punishment, if indeed benefit is to be had from punishment at all, is more uncertain. Thus, to punish the mentally ill demeans both those who punish and those who are punished, without any certain benefit to either group. Diminished capacity erodes both the justification for punishment and its likely efficacy. Should treatment be the default option?

Such an approach would imply that the majority of offenders would be held culpable for their offences (as currently happens), that there are limited mental condition defences for those whose offending is causally linked to their disorder, or for those who lacked the capacity to choose to offend, and that issues of disposal are determined by either the absence of culpability or an overriding need for treatment at the point of disposal. But once a decision has been made to enter the therapeutic route there should be no going back to a penal environment. And, of course, should an offender's mental

2 *R v Khelifi* [2006] EWCA Crim 770.

health problems develop after sentence, facilities should be available for appropriate treatment, either by way of transfer or, with consent, within the prison estate. And, critically, that within the prison estate that the conditions of confinement should not themselves be damaging to an offender's mental (or physical) health. Setting aside an evaluation of the nature of imprisonment, since within the prison estate there are real variations in the quality of the environment provided, the disposal options set out above broadly capture the position that applied until 1997 (when the hybrid order was introduced).

Moving from culpability and disorder to need?

Another way of considering these issues is not to start either from established criminality nor from where clinicians define and diagnose disorder, since these have both been shown to be moveable (and largely expansionary) activities (see, for example, Horwitz and Wakefield, 2007; Spitzer and Wakefield, 1999). As discussed earlier, three per cent of Americans are now thought to suffer from generalised anxiety disorder, which first appeared in the 1985 publication DSM IIIR but has become one of the most common diagnoses made (Rygh and Sanderson, 2004). And even if psychiatrists agreed definitively on what can constitute a recognised disorder that would not necessarily stop the politically inspired generation of new variants which go on to attract funding, as has DSPD. Moreover, since having a disorder recognised does not necessarily mean that treatment will be made available, where efficacy or cost is a determining criterion (see, for example the NICE guidelines restricting the prescription of Aricept before those with Alzheimer's have reached the moderate stage of the disease, or NICE's refusal to fund Nexavar for liver cancer), the diagnostic advantages to patients may be limited. Although it is notable that a disorder linked to risk to others (as with DSPD or, arguably, most recently swine flu) will seemingly attract almost unlimited resources. Or, as John Monahan argued in the John Gunn Lecture, the asserted linkage between mental disorder and dangerousness has always had the capacity to attract resources and has the potential to retain them even in times of the greatest financial restraint.[3]

Perhaps then a better place to start is from where and of about what people complain in terms of symptoms (see Bentall, 2009:182). This has the advantage of focusing clinical efforts on the person who is to be treated by addressing the matters that trouble them. In a non-criminal clinical context this has considerable merits. But where the double stigma that is associated with mental disorder and offending remains prevalent, it is unlikely that offenders will perceive the advantages of revealing any problematic mental

3 Institute of Psychiatry, Denmark Hill, London, 28 October 2009.

health state: indeed, the incentives for so doing are scarce. Moreover, such an approach also neglects the less immediate issue of harm to others from the 'complained about behaviour' of others. This, in turn, leads down the route of compulsory treatment for mental disorder where that mental disorder has been identified in the context of offending behaviour. Capacitous offending in the context of mental disorder remains a key challenge.

What gets complained about, as an index of distress by either the individual or those around them or subject to their behaviour, is partly a product of our norms, values and expectations. And, as Bolton observes, the scientific questionability of this is pertinent. Undoubtedly, having a diagnosis helps to identify what treatment might be appropriate, but it would be overly optimistic to conclude that these have the validity or reliability of some other clinical diagnoses. It is not just that starting from the position of 'individual – complained of – distress' looks subjective, but that it also casts into a falsely scientific light the clinicians' determinations of their own diagnostic categories, making these appear perhaps more robust than arguably they are. Or as Bentall, albeit controversially, asserts:

> ... most psychiatric diagnoses are about as scientifically meaningful as star signs, a diagnostic system which is similarly employed to describe people and predict what will happen to them, and which enjoys a wide following despite compelling evidence that it is useless.
>
> (Bentall, 2009:110)

So is it easier to be right about what is just in the field of mentally disordered offenders as determined by a retrospective lens, than it is to determine what is effective through the prospective lens of therapeutic intervention? Probably yes.

Capacity or culpability as a filtering mechanism?

In the same way that there are gradations across the spectrum from disorder to offending behaviour, so there is a series of disjunctive and to some extent overlapping concepts to characterise the proper response to these presented categories, colloquially madness and badness; these might perhaps better be characterised as disordered states and disorderly behaviours. Capacity, or a lack of it, is the test for intervening against someone's wishes medically, socially, legally and as a criterion for determining whether someone ought to be at risk of being judged by the criminal justice system. But capacity is a concept that has shown itself to be remarkably malleable, filtering out very few from the criminal justice system, some from the mental health sector, albeit that such judgments are rarely necessary when someone is subject to a section under the MHA 1983, and a surprising number when considering issues relating to pregnant women, children, those with personality disorders and those suffering from anorexia. It is a concept that can be used without much consistency and arguably unjustifiably, either to deny or allow people their autonomous choices, as was discussed earlier with reference to *Brady* and *W*.

Culpability is the test for determining whether one is at risk of punishment; it is not so much a malleable concept as one that comes in a variety of guises. One very crude equation would posit its presence where the prosecution has proved beyond a reasonable doubt that the accused committed the offence by doing the requisite act (*actus reus*) or, much more rarely, failing to do something they were required to do, with the requisite mental or fault state (*mens rea*) and in the absence of any appropriate defences for their actions. This is too crude even to cover such variants as strict liability offences, which require no *mens rea* with respect to at least one element of the *actus reus*. And *mens rea* also manifests itself in a number of ways: there are a variety of offences in the negligence bracket which variously place burdens on the defendant with respect to due diligence or on the prosecution to establish an objective standard of reasonable behaviour; then there are offences which require recklessness and those which require a specific intention to be made out by the prosecution; and then for murder charges there are the limited 'defences' of provocation and diminished responsibility.[4] And this has not even begun to detail the various overarching issues of mistake, duress, necessity etc. The criminal law's facility for slicing and dicing mental states is considerable. Already the possible permutations across capacity and culpability, and assorted criminal offences and mental states, look daunting. And then what needs to be added to the mix are the issues relating to disposal under the MHA 1983 (presence of disorder of the requisite severity, appropriateness and availability of treatment, need for treatment in terms of health and safety etc) and conventional sentencing options which take account of issues of mitigation. Undoubtedly, the relationship between the criminal justice process and the mental health world is amongst the most complex with which either has to grapple.

The legal response to such complexity is invariably, despite the promulgation of extremely helpful guidelines for sentencing purposes from the Sentencing Guidelines Council, that 'each case should be treated on its own merits'. And we have not even tried to address the way in which these various factors should or do have an impact on the different stages of the

4 Both provocation and diminished responsibility will be affected by the *Coroners and Justice Act 2009* (ss 52–56). The Act abolishes the common law defence of provocation and replaces it by a partial defence to murder based on loss of control; and provides a definition of diminished responsibility requiring an abnormality of mental functioning arising from a recognised medical condition *and* that the abnormality has to provide an explanation for the defendant's involvement in the killing. This will be the case where it is at least a significant contributory factor in causing the defendant to carry out the conduct.

criminal justice process from initial arrest, through prosecution, to sentence, disposal and release; nor on their innovative and sometimes inappropriate use by the different agencies dealing with mentally disordered offenders (see, for one example, Docking et al, 2007). Nor does it consider the implications arising from the pilot developments of mental health courts in this country, albeit that they look less like the North American version of specialist courts and more like conventional courts properly informed and prepared to deal with mental health issues. An analysis of these matters of process is covered elsewhere (see, for example, Littlechild and Fearns, 2005; Stone, 2003; and, briefly, in Peay, 2007) but the consequences, both personal, social and financial, of unsettling or intervening in any one of the links in this rusty chain are legion (see, for example, the Bradley Report 2009 and the Criminal Justice Joint Inspection 2009).

Multiplying objectives and muddying the terrain?

To this already complex mix has now been added a further order of difficulty. It always was the case that issues of risk and dangerousness, which permeated both sentencing and compulsory mental health care, arose with respect to both the safety of the individual in terms of self-harm, passively or actively, and to the safety of others. Discretionary life sentences within the penal estate and restriction orders within the therapeutic regime had a number of parallel elements, reflecting the dilemmas dangerous offender-patients posed. However, with the advent of IPPs, the DSPD regime and the extension of hybrid orders to all categories of disordered offender, these dilemmas have been multiplied and risk toppling the existing edifice by applying concepts of risk and of therapeutic intervention on an unrivalled and unjustified scale. The figures given earlier of the massive growth in the IPP population and the extraordinary cost entailed in running the DSPD programme are evidence of this. Added to these 'top-end' interventions, the advent of the Criminal Justice Act 2003, with its multiplicity of sentencing purposes and its explicit promotion of an offender's reform and rehabilitation (s 142(1)(c)), is likely to make further demands on services to address the needs of disordered offenders. Perhaps this is right, but it comes at the cost of abandoning a cleanliness of intervention based on a proportionate measure of intervention grounded in an offender's culpable activity. Multiple forms of therapeutic intervention in an offender-patient's life can produce chaos rather than orderly recovery.

These developments, of course, merely highlight the problem of knowing when to stop interventions, either ideally because they have been successful or because such efforts can no longer be justified. How can one know if that point has been reached? If a disorder is defined by the presence of a complaint, then the absence of complaint may mean the disorder has ameliorated, or that the person no longer chooses to complain about it. If it is defined by the harm caused, then one could adopt measures that are proportionate to the objective measure of the harm. But if it is defined by the risk of harm then that sense that one can never be too careful becomes dangerously all pervasive. The contours and boundaries of such interventions are, have always been, and are likely to remain too difficult justly to delineate.

References

Akintunde, A., 'The MacArthur Competence Assessment Tool – Fitness to Plead: A Preliminary Evaluation of a Research Instrument for Assessing Fitness to Plead in England and Wales', *Journal of the American Academy of Psychiatry and the Law* (2002) 30:476–82.

Alper, J., 'Genes, Free Will and Criminal Responsibility', *Society, Science and Medicine* (1998) 46:1599–1611.

American Psychiatric Association *Diagnostic and Statistical Manual of Mental Disorders* (4th edn) (DSM-IV). Washington, DC: APA 1994.

American Psychiatric Association *Diagnostic and Statistical Manual of Mental Disorders* (4th edn) Text Revision (DSM-IV-TR). Washington, DC: APA 2000.

American Cancer Society *Cancer Facts and Figures 2007*. Atlanta: American Cancer Society 2007.

Ammons, R. and Ammons, C., 'The Quick Test (QT): Provisional Manual'. *Psychological Reports* 11: 111–161 Monograph Supplement I-VII 1962:50.

Amos, T., Frost, J., Lewis, G., Walker, J., Payne, S., Lart, R., Rogers, P., Lester, H. and Wall, M. *Forensic Evidence 2006: systematic review of reviews in forensic mental health*, Final report to the National Forensic Mental Health Research and Development Programme (2006).

Amos, T., Walker, J., Gordon, H., Peay, J. and Gunn, J. 'Eighty Percent of Crime: Theft, motoring and criminal damage (including arson)' in Gunn J. and Taylor P., ed., *Forensic Psychiatry: Clinical, Legal and Ethical Issues* 2nd edn. London: Hodder (forthcoming) 2010.

Angermeyer, M., 'Schizophrenia and Violence' *Acta Psychiatr Scand Suppl* (2000) 407:63–67.

Appelbaum, P., Robbins, P. and Monahan, J., 'Violence and delusions: Data from the MacArthur violence risk assessment study'. *American Journal of Psychiatry* (2000) 157:566–572.

Appignanesi, L., *Mad, Bad and Sad: A History of Women and the Mind Doctors from 1800 to the Present*. London: Virago Press 2008.

Appleby, L., Shaw, J., Sherratt, J. and Amos, T., *Safety First: Five Year Report of the National Confidential Inquiry into Suicide and Homicide by People with Mental Illness*. London: Department of Health 2001.

Appleby, L., Shaw, J., Kapur, N., Windfuhr, K., Ashton, A., Swinson, N. and While D., *Avoidable deaths: five year report of the national confidential inquiry into suicide and homicide by people with mental illness*. Manchester: University of Manchester 2006.

Arboleda-Florez, J., Holley, H. and Crisanti, A., *Mental illness and violence: proof or stereotype*, Ottawa, Canada: Minister of Supply and Services 1996.

Arboleda-Florez, J., Holley, H. and Crisanti, A., 'Understanding causal paths between mental illness and violence', *Social Psychiatry and Psychiatric Epidemiology* (1998) 33:S38–S46.

Arrigo, B., 'Transcarceration: A Constitutive Ethnography of Mentally Ill "Offenders" ' *The Prison Journal* (2001) 81:162–186.

Arseneault, L., Caspi, A., Moffitt, T., Taylor, P. and Silva, P., Mental disorders and violence in a total birth cohort. Results from the Dunedin study' *Archives of General Psychiatry* (2000) 57:979–986.

Ashworth, A., *Sentencing and Criminal Justice*, 4th edn, Cambridge: Cambridge University Press 2005.

Badger, D., Nursten, J., Williams, P., Woodward, M., *Systematic Review of the International Literature on the Epidemiology of Mentally Disordered Offenders* Centre for Reviews and Dissemination, CRD Report 15 1999.

Barrett, B., Byford, S., Sievewright, H., Cooper, S., Duggan, C. and Tyrer, P., 'The assessment of dangerous and severe personality disorder: service use, cost, and consequences' *The Journal of Forensic Psychiatry and Psychology* (2009) 20(1):120–131.

Bartlett, P. and Sandland, R. *Mental Health Law: Policy and Practice* 3rd edition Oxford: Oxford University Press 2007.

Bartlett, P., Lewis, O. and Thorold, O., *Mental Disability and the European Convention on Human Rights*. Leiden: Martinus Nijhof 2006.

BBC News (2002) 'Brain tumour "caused paedophilia" ' 21 October 2002.

Bean, P., *Madness and Crime*, Cullompton, Devon: Willan Publishing 2008.

Bentall, R., *Madness Explained: Psychosis and Human Nature*, London: Allen Lane 2003.

Bentall, R., *Doctoring the Mind: Why Psychiatric Treatments Fail*. London: Allen Lane 2009.

Bickle, A., 'The dangerous offender provisions of the Criminal Justice Act 2003 and their implications for psychiatric evidence in sentencing violent and sexual offenders' *The Journal of Forensic Psychiatry and Psychology* (2008) 19:603–619.

Birmingham, L. Wilson, S. and Adshead, G., 'Prison medicine: ethics and equivalence' *British Journal of Psychiatry* (2006) 188:4–6.

Bisson, J., 'The army psychiatrist: second-hand trauma of war' *The Guardian* 7 November 2009.

Blackburn, R., 'On moral judgements and personality disorders: The myth of the psychopathic personality revisited' *British Journal of Psychiatry* (1988) 153: 505–512.

Blackburn, R. and Coid, J., 'Psychopathy and the dimensions of personality disorder in violent offenders' *Personality and Individual Differences* (1998) 25:129–145.

Bleuler, E., *Textbook of Psychiatry* (AA Brill Trans). New York: Macmillan 1924.

Bluglass, R., 'Shoplifting' in Bluglass R. and Bowden P., eds., *Principles and Practice of Forensic Psychiatry*. Edinburgh: Churchill Livingston 1990.

Blumenthal, S. and Lavender, A., *Violence and Mental Disorder: a critical aid to the assessment and management of risk*. London: Zito Trust 2000.

Board, B. and Fritzon, K., 'Disordered personalities at work' *Psychology, Crime and Law* (2005) 11:17–32.

Bolton, D., *What is Mental Disorder? An Essay in Philosophy, Science and Values.* Oxford: Oxford University Press 2008.

Bourdon, K., Rae, D., Locke, B., Narrow, W. and Regier, D., 'Estimating the prevalence of mental disorders in US adults from the epidemiologic catchment area survey', Public Health Rep (1992) 107(6):663–8.

Bowen, P., *Blackstone's Guide to the Mental Health Act* Revised edn. Oxford: Oxford University Press 2008.

Boyd-Caine, T., *In the public interest? The role of executive discretion in the release of restricted patients*, PhD thesis submitted to the London School of Economics, University of London 2008.

Boyd-Caine, T., *Protecting the Public? Executive Discretion in the Release of Mentally Disordered Offenders.* Cullompton, Devon: Willan Publishing 2010.

Bradley Lord Keith *Lord Bradley's review of people with mental health problems or learning disabilities in the criminal justice system.* London: Department of Health, COI 2009.

Brennan, P., Mednick, S. and Hodgins, S., 'Major mental disorders and criminal violence in a Danish birth cohort', *Arch Gen Psychiatry* (2000) 57:494–500.

Brookbanks, W., 'Sexual Predators, Extended Supervision, and Preventive Social Control: Risk Management under the Spotlight' *Journal of Mental Health Law* (2007) 97–106.

Brown, M., 'Serious Violence and the Dilemmas of Sentencing: a Comparison of Three Incapacitation Policies' *Criminal Law Review* (1998) 710–722.

Buchanan, A. and Leese, M., 'Detention of people with dangerous severe personality disorder: a systematic review' *Lancet* (2001) 358:1955–1959.

Buchanan, A. and Virgo, G., 'Duress and Mental Abnormality' *Criminal Law Review* (1999) 517–531.

Buchanan, A., Reed, A., Wessely, S., Garety, P., Taylor, P., Grubin, D. and Dunn, G., 'Acting on delusions II: the phenomenological correlates of acting on delusions' *British Journal of Psychiatry* (1993) 163:77–81.

Bull, R. and Green, J., 'The relationship between physical appearance and criminality' *Medicine, Science and the Law* (1980) 20:79–83.

Carvel, J., 'Patients in mental crisis not getting help promised' *The Guardian* 7 December 2007.

Checkley, H., *The Mask of Sanity* 5th edn, St Louis: Mosby 1976.

Cheng, A., 'Case definition and culture: are all people the same?' *British Journal of Psychiatry* (2003) 179:1–3.

Cheung, P., Schweitzer, I., Crowley, K., and Tuckwell, V., 'Violence in schizophrenia: role of hallucinations and delusions' *Schizophrenia Research* (1997) 26:181–90.

Choi, C., 'Brain tumour causes uncontrollable paedophilia' *New Scientist* 21 October 2002 available at www.newscientist.com (2002).

Coleman, K., Hurd, C. and Povey, D., 'Violent Crime Overview, Homicide and Gun Crime', 2nd edition. Supplementary volume to Crime in England and Wales 2004/2005' *Home Office Statistical Bulletin* 02/06. London: Home Office 2006.

Coleman, K., Jansson, K., Kaiza, P. and Reed, E., 'Homicides, Firearms Offences and Intimate Violence 2005–6', *Home Office Statistical Bulletin* 25 January 02/07 Table 1.06 (2007).

Collins, R., *Violence: a micro-sociological theory*. Woodstock: Princeton University Press 2008.

Colombo, A., *Violent Victimisation: Understanding why people with schizophrenia often feel 's'cared in the community*, Paper presented to the British Society of Criminology Conference, London School of Economics, September 2007.

Connell, R., *Gender and Power: Society, the Person and Sexual Politics*. Stanford CA: Stanford University Press 1987.

Connelly, C., Burman, M. and Connelly, K., *Mentally Disordered Offenders and the Use of Hospital Directions and Interim Hospital Orders, Main Findings 56/2000* The Scottish Executive Central Research Unit 2000.

Cooke, D., Michie, C., Hart, S. and Clark, D., 'Reconstructing psychopathy: clarifying the significance of antisocial and socially deviant behaviour in the diagnosis of psychopathic personality disorder', *Journal of Personality Disorders* (2004) 18:337–57.

Cooper, J., *Blair's Laws: New Labour's Obsession with Creating New Criminal Offences*. Oxford: Oxford University Press 2008.

Corbett, K. and Westwood, T., 'Dangerous and severe personality disorder: A psychiatric manifestation of the risk society' *Critical Public Health* (2005) 15(2):121–133.

Cornish, D., and Clarke, R., eds., *The Reasoning Criminal: Rational Choice Perspective on Offending*. New York: Springer-Verlag 1986.

Corston, J., *The Corston Report: A Report by Baroness Jean Corston of a Review of Women with Particular Vulnerabilities in the Criminal Justice System*. London: Home Office 2007.

Coulter, J., *Approaches to Insanity: A Philosophical and Sociological Study*. Chichester: John Wiley and Sons 1973.

Criminal Justice Joint Inspection *A review to ascertain the circumstances in which Anthony Leon Peart, also known as Anthony Leon Joseph, came to be at liberty on 29 July 2005*, Criminal Justice Joint Inspection Report http://inspectorates.justice. gov.uk (2008).

Criminal Justice Joint Inspection *A joint inspection on work prior to sentence with offenders with mental disorders*. HMI Probation, HMI Court Administration, HMI Constabulary and HM Crown Prosecution Service Inspectorate http:// inspectorates.justice.gov.uk (2009).

Crow, I., *The Treatment and Rehabilitation of Offenders*. London: Sage Publications 2001.

Dawson, J., 'Capacity to stand trial: old and new law in New Zealand' *Psychiatry, Psychology and Law* (2008) 15:251–260.

Day, K., 'Crime and Mental Retardation: A Review', in Howells, K. and Hollin, C., eds., *Clinical Approaches to the Mentally Disordered Offender*. Chichester: John Wiley and Sons 1993.

Dennett, D., *Brainstorms*, Montgomery, VT: Bradford Books 1967.

Denno, D., 'Considering lead poisoning as a criminal defense', *Fordham Urban Law Journal* (1993) 20:377–400.

Department of Health *Smoking Kills – A White Paper on Tobacco*. London: HMSO 1998.

Department of Health *Inpatients formally detained in hospitals under the Mental Health Act 1983 and other legislation, NHS Trusts, care trusts and primary care trusts and independent hospitals 2003–4*. London: NHS Health and Social Care Information Centre 2008.

Department of Health *Code of Practice: Mental Health Act 1983*. London: The Stationery Office 2008.

Department of Health *Improving Health, Supporting Justice. The National Delivery Plan of the Health and Criminal Justice Programme Board*. London: COI, Department of Health 2009.

Docking, M., Grace, K. and Bucke, T., 'Police Custody as a "Place of Safety": examining the use of section 136 of the Mental Health Act 1983', *Independent Police Complaints Commission*, Research and Statistics Series: Paper 11 2007 .

Doll, R. and Peto, R., *The Causes of Cancer*. New York NY: Oxford Press 1981.

D'Orban, P., 'Child stealing: a typology of female offenders', *British Journal of Criminology* (1976) 16:275–81.

D'Orban, P., 'Kidnapping, abduction and child stealing' in Bluglass, R. and Bowden, P., eds., *Principles and Practice of Forensic Psychiatry*. Edinburgh: Churchill Livingston 1990.

Durcan, G., *From the Inside: Experiences of Prison Mental Health Care*. London: Sainsbury Centre for Health Care 2008.

Durkheim, E., *The Division of Labour in Society*. New York: Free Press 1964.

Eastman, N., 'Can there be a true partnership between clinicians and the Home Office?' *Advances in Psychiatric Treatment* (2006) 12:459–461.

Eastman, N., and Campbell, C., 'Neuroscience and legal determination of criminal responsibility' *Nature Reviews Neuroscience* (2006) 7:311–318.

Eastman, N., and Peay, J., 'Sentencing Psychopaths: Is the Hospital and Limitation Direction an Ill-Considered Hybrid?' *Criminal Law Review* (1998) 93–108.

Eastman, N., and Peay, J., 'Law without Enforcement: Theory and Practice' in N. Eastman and J. Peay., eds., *Law without Enforcement: Integrating Mental Health and Justice*. Oxford: Hart Publishing 1999.

Ebrahim, I., Fenwick, P., Wilson, W., Marks, R. and Peacock, K. 'Violence, Sleepwalking and the Criminal Law: (1) The Medical Aspects' *Criminal Law Review* (2005) 601–613.

Eysenck, H., 'Personality and Crime: Where Do We Stand?' *Psychology Crime and Law*, (1996) 2:143–52.

Eysenck, H., *Crime and Personality* 3rd edn. London: Routledge & Kegan Paul 1997.

Farrington, D., 'The Twelfth Jack Tizard Memorial Lecture: The Development of Offending and Antisocial Behaviour from Childhood: Key Findings from the Cambridge Study in Delinquent Development', *Journal of Child Psychology and Psychiatry* (1995) 36:929–64.

Fazel, S. and Danesh, J., 'Serious mental disorder in 23,000 prisoners. A systematic review of 62 surveys', *Lancet* (2002) 359:545–550.

Fazel, S. and Grann, M ., 'The population impact of severe mental illness on violent crime'. *American Journal of Psychiatry* (2006) 163:1397–1403.

Fazel, S., Xenitidis, K. and Powell, B., 'The prevalence of intellectual disabilities among 12000 prisoners – A systematic review' *International Journal of Law and Psychiatry* (2008) 31:369–373.

Fennell, P., *Mental Health: The New Law*. Bristol: Jordan Publishing 2007.

Fleisher, M., *Beggars and thieves: lives of urban street criminals*. Wisconsin: University of Wisconsin Press 1995.

Francis, R., Higgins, J. and Cassam, E., *Report of the independent inquiry into the care and treatment of Michael Stone* 2006. South East Coast Strategic Health Authority, Kent County Council and Kent Probation Area (Final Report presented to the Authority in November 2000 available at www.kent.gov.uk/publications/council-and-democracy/michael-stone.htm).

Garland, D., *The Culture of Control: Crime and Social Order in Contemporary Society*. Chicago: University of Chicago Press 2001.

Geddes, J. and Kendell, R., 'Schizophrenic subjects with no history of admission to psychiatric hospital'. *Psychological Medicine* (1995) 25:859–868.

Genders, E. and Player, E., *Grendon: A Study of a Therapeutic Prison*. Oxford: Clarendon Press 1995.

Gigerenzer, G., *Reckoning with Risk: Learning to Live with Uncertainty*. London: Penguin Press 2002.

Glendinning, L., 'Children too young to charge suspected of 3,000 crimes' *The Guardian* 3 September 2007.

Goldacre, B., 'Bad science: some numbers in abortion debate just can't be relied on', *The Guardian* 27 October 2007.

Goldacre, B., *Bad Science*. London: HarperCollins 2009.

Goshen, C., *Documentary History of Psychiatry*. London: Vision Press 1967.

Gostin, L. and Gable, L., The Human Rights of Persons with Mental Disabilities: A Global Perspective on the Application of Human Rights Principles to Mental Health *Maryland Law Review* (2004) 63:20–121.

Gottfredson, M. and Hirschi, T., *A General Theory of Crime*. Stanford, California: Stanford University Press 1990.

Gould, M., 'You can teach a man to kill but not to see dying', *The Guardian* 10 October.

Grounds, A., 'The transfer of sentenced prisoners to hospital 1960–1983' *British Journal of Criminology* (1991) 31:54–71.

Grounds, A., 'Psychological Consequences of Wrongful Conviction and Imprisonment' *Canadian Journal of Criminology and Criminal Justice* (2004) 46:165–182.

Grounds, A., 'Understanding the effects of wrongful imprisonment' in M. Tonry, eds., *Crime and Justice: A Review of Research, Volume 32*. Chicago: University of Chicago Press 2005.

Haffner, H. and Bocker, W., *Crimes of Violence by Mentally Abnormal Offenders. A Psychiatric and Epidemiological Study in the Federal German Republic*. Cambridge: Cambridge University Press 1982.

Hagan, J., *The Disreputable Pleasures*. Toronto: McGraw-Hill Ryerson 1977.

Hagan, J., Simpson, J. and Gillis, A., 'The Sexual Stratification of Social Control: A Gender-Based Perspective on Crime and Delinquency', *British Journal of Sociology* (1979) 30:25–38.

Hale, B., 'Justice and equality in mental health law: The European experience', *International Journal of Law and Psychiatry* (2007) 30:18–28.

Harper, W., *Statistics* 6th edn. London: Pitman 1991.

Harris, M., 'Introduction of a Smoke-Free Regime'. Paper presented at the 8th Annual International Association of Forensic Mental Health Services Conference, Vienna, July 2008.

Harry, B., 'Violence and official diagnostic nomenclature', *Bull Am Acad Psychiatry Law* (1985) 13:385–388.

Hartvig, P. and Kjelsberg, E., 'Penrose's Law revisited: The relationship between mental institution beds, prison population and crime rate' *Nordic Journal of Psychiatry* (2009) 63:51–56.

Hayward, K., *City Limits: Crime, Consumerism and the Urban Experience*. London: Glasshouse Press 2004.

Healthcare Commission *National Audit of Violence. Final report – working age adults 2006/7*, Royal College of Psychiatrists' Centre for Quality Improvement 2008.

Hemphill, J. and Hare, R., 'Psychopathy and recidivism: a review' *Legal and Criminological Psychology* (1998) 3:139–170.

Hiday, V., 'Putting community risk in perspective: A look at correlations, causes and controls', *International Journal of Law and Psychiatry* (2006) 29:316–331.

Hirschi, T., *The Causes of Delinquency*, Berkeley, California: University of California Press 1969.

Hodgins, S., eds., *Mental Disorder and Crime*. London: Sage Publications 1993.

Hodgins, S., 'The aetiology and development of offending among persons with major mental disorders,' in Hodgins S., ed., *Violence among the mentally ill*. Dordrecht: Kluwer 2000.

Hodgins, S., 'Offenders with Major Mental Disorders' in Hollin C., ed., *The Essential Handbook of Offender Assessment and Treatment*, Chichester: John Wiley and Sons 2004.

Hodgins, S., Cote, G. and Toupin, J., 'Major mental disorders and crime: An etiological hypothesis' in Cooke, D., Forthe, A. and Hare, R., eds., *Psychopathy: Theory, research and implications for society*. Dordrecht: Kluwer 1998.

Hodgins, S., Mednick, S., Brennan, P., Schulsinger, F. and Engberg, M,. 'Mental disorder and crime: Evidence from a Danish birth cohort', *Arch Gen Psychiatry* (1996) 53:489–96.

HM Inspectorate of Prisons, *The mental health of prisoners. A thematic review of the care and support of prisoners with mental health needs*. London: HM Inspectorate of Prisons 2007.

Hollin, C., 'Criminological Psychology' in Maguire, M., Morgan, R. and Reiner, R., eds., *The Oxford Handbook of Criminology* 4th edn. Oxford: Oxford University Press 2007.

Home Office, *Criminal careers of those born between 1953 and 1973*, Home Office Statistical Bulletin 14/95 1995.

Home Office and Department of Health, *Managing Dangerous People with Severe Personality Disorder: Proposals for Policy Development*. London: HMSO 1999.

Home Office and Department of Health, *DSPD Programme: Dangerous people with severe personality disorder initiative: Progress report*. London: Home Office 2001.

Honig, A., Romme, M., Ensink, B., Escher, S., Pennings, M. and DeVries, M., 'Auditory hallucinations: A comparison between patients and non-patients' *Journal of Nervous and Mental Disease* (1998) 186:646–51.

Horwitz, A. and Wakefield, J., *The Loss of Sadness: How psychiatry transformed normal sorrow into depressive disorder*. New York: Oxford University Press 2007.

Hotopf, M., Hull, L., Fear, N ., Browne, T., Horn, O., Iversen, A., Jones, M., Murphy, D., Bland, D., Earnshaw, M., Greenberg, N., Hughes, J., Tate, A., Dandeker, C., Rona, R. and Wessely, S., 'The Health of UK military personnel who deployed to the 2003 Iraq war: a cohort study' *The Lancet* (2007) 367 (9524):1731–1741.

Howard, R., 'How is personality disorder linked to dangerousness? A putative role for early-onset alcohol abuse', *Medical Hypotheses* (2006) 67:702–708.

Howells, K., Krishnan, G. and Daffern, M., Challenges in the treatment of dangerous and severe personality disorder *Advances in Psychiatric Treatment* (2007) 13:325–332.

Hunter, R. and Macalpine, I., *Three Hundred Years of Psychiatry 1535–1860*, London: Oxford University Press 1963.

Iversen, A., Morris, R., Greenberg, N. and Wessely, S., 'Bridging the Gulf: "Gulf War Syndrome" – what we know and what we don't' *Advances in Clinical Neuroscience and Rehabilitation* (2007) 7(3):6–7.

Iversen, K., Høyer, G. and Sexton, H., 'Coercion and patient satisfaction on psychiatric acute wards' *International Journal of Law and Psychiatry* (2007) 30(6):504–511.

James, D., Duffield, G., Blizard, R. and Hamilton, L., 'Fitness to plead. A prospective study of the inter-relationships between expert opinion, legal criteria and specific symptomatology' *Psychological Medicine* (2001) 31:139–50.

James, D., Farnham, F., Moorey, H., Lloyd, H., Blizard, R. and Barnes, T., *Outcome of psychiatric admission through the courts*. Home Office: RDS Occasional Paper no 79 (2002).

James, O., *Juvenile Justice in a Winner-Loser Culture: Socio-Economic and Familial Origins of the Rise of Violence Against the Person*. Stanmore: Free Association Books Ltd 1995.

Jamieson, R. and Grounds, A., *No sense of an ending: The effects of long-term imprisonment amongst Republican prisoners and their families*. Co Monaghan: SEESYU Press Limited 2002.

Joint Committee on Human Rights, *A Bill of Rights for the UK?* Twenty-ninth Report of Session 2007–08, House of Lords HL 165-1, House of Commons HC 150-1, London: The Stationery Office 2008.

Jones, S., *Nature, Nurture or Neither? The view from the genes* Royal Institution of Great Britain Lecture, 29 January 2010.

Jørgensen, K. and Gøtzsche, P., 'Overdiagnosis in publicly organised mammography screening programmes: systematic review of incidence trends' *British Medical Journal* (2009) 339:b2587.

Karli, P., *Animal and Human Aggression*. Oxford: Oxford University Press 1991.

Kemshall, H., *Understanding Risk in Criminal Justice*. Maidenhead: Open University Press 2003.

Kendell, R., 'The distinction between mental and physical illness' *British Journal of Psychiatry* (2001) 178:490–493.

Kjellin, L., Høyer, G., Engberg, M., Kaltiala-Heino, R. and Sigurdjonsdottir, M., Legal Status and Patients' Perceptions of being Coerced at Admission to Psychiatric Care in the Four Nordic Countries. Paper presented at the XXVI International Congress on Law and Mental Health, Montreal 2001.

Kolko, D., 'Firesetters' in Hollin C., ed., *The Essential Handbook of Offender Assessment and Treatment*. Chichester: John Wiley and Sons Ltd 2004.

Kolko, D., and Kazdin, A., *Two year follow-up of child firesetters: Late starting and recidivism*. Poster presented at the Annual Meeting of the Association for the Advancement of Behaviour Therapy, Washington, DC 1995.

Kraemer, H., Kazdin, A., Offord, D., Kessler, R., Jensen, P and Kupfer, D., 'Coming to terms with the terms of risk', *Archives of General Psychiatry* (1997) 54:337–343.

Kratzer, L. and Hodgins, S., 'Adult outcomes of child conduct problems: a cohort study' *Journal of Abnormal Child Psychology* (1997) 25:65–81.

Lacey, N., *The Prisoners' Dilemma. Political Economy and Punishment in Contemporary Democracies*. Cambridge: Cambridge University Press 2008.

Large, M., Smith, G., Swinson, N., Shaw, J. and Nielssen, O., 'Homicide due to mental disorder in England and Wales over 50 years' *British Journal of Psychiatry* (2008) 193:130–133.

Law Commission *Murder, Manslaughter and Infanticide*, Report: Law Commission No 304 (2006).

Lemert, E., 'Paranoia and the Dynamics of Exclusion', *Sociometry* (1962) 25:2–20.

Lennox, C., Senior, J. and Shaw, J., *Offender Health: Scoping Review and Research Priorities within the UK*. Report for Offender Health at the Department of Health, University of Manchester: Offender Health Research Network available at www.ohrn.nhs.uk (2009).

Lindqvist, P. and Allebeck, P., 'Schizophrenia and crime. A longitudinal follow-up of 644 schizophrenics in Stockholm' *British Journal of Psychiatry* (1990a) 157: 345–350.

Lindqvist, P. and Allebeck, P., 'Schizophrenia and assaultive behaviour: the role of drug and alcohol abuse' *Acta Psychiatrica Scandinavica* (1990b) 82:191–195.

Link, B., Andrews, H., Cullen, F., 'The violent and illegal behaviour of mental patients reconsidered', *American Sociological Review* (1992) 57:275–92.

Link, B., and Stueve, A., 'Psychotic symptoms and the violent/illegal behaviour of mental patients compared to community controls' in Monahan, J. and Steadman, H., eds., *Violence and Mental Disorder: Developments in Risk Assessment*. Chicago, Illinois: University of Chicago Press 1994.

Littlechild, B. and Fearns, D., eds., *Mental disorder and criminal justice. Policy, provision and practice*. Lyme Regis: Russell House Publishing Ltd 2005.

Lockyer, K. *Service Review – Indeterminate Sentenced Prisoners* ISP Review Group. London: Ministry of Justice, National Offender Management Service 2007.

Long, C. and Midgley, M., 'On the closeness of the concepts of the criminal and the mentally ill in the nineteenth century: yesterday's opinions reflected today' *Journal of Forensic Psychiatry* (1992) 3:63–78.

Loughnan, A., *'Manifest Madness': Non-Responsibility in Criminal Law*. Oxford University Press 2011 (forthcoming).

Loughnan, A., 'Manifest Madness': Towards A New Understanding of the Insanity Defence', *Modern Law Review* (2007) 70(3):379–401.

Lowman, J., Menzies, R. and Palys, T., *Transcarceration: Essays in the Sociology of Social Control*. Aldershot: Gower 1987.

McAlinden, A., 'Indeterminate Sentences for the Severely Personality Disordered' *Criminal Law Review* (2001) 108–123.

MacDonald, J., Haviland, A. and Morral, A., 'Assessing the relationship between violent and nonviolent criminal activity among serious adolescent offenders' *Journal of Research in Crime and Delinquency* (2009) 46:553–580.

Mackay, R., 'On being insane in Jersey. Part Three – the Case of *Attorney-General v O'Driscoll*' (2004) *Criminal Law Review* 291–296.

Mackay, R., 'The Provocation Plea in Operation: An Empirical Study' in Law Commission *Murder, Manslaughter and Infanticide* – Report Law Com No 304 Appendix A, 2006.

Mackay, R., 'AAPL Practice Guideline for the Forensic Evaluation of Competence to Stand Trial: An English Legal Perspective', *Journal of the American Academy of Psychiatry and the Law* (2007) 35:501–504.

Mackay, R., 'Righting the Wrong? Some Observations on the Second Limb of the M'Naghten Rules' (2009) *Criminal Law Review* 80–89.

Mackay, R., and Mitchell, B. 'Sleepwalking, Automatism and Insanity' *Criminal Law Review* (2006) 901–905.

Mackay, R., Mitchell, B. and Howe, L., 'Yet More Facts about the Insanity Defence' *Criminal Law Review* (2006) 399–411.

Mackay, R., Mitchell, B. and Howe, L., 'A continued upturn in unfitness to plead – more disability in relation to the trial under the 1991 Act' *Criminal Law Review* (2007) 530–545.

McMurran, M., 'Offenders with Personality Disorders', in Hollin, C., ed., *The Essential Handbook of Offender Assessment and Treatment.* Chichester: John Wiley and Sons Ltd 2004.

Maden, A., 'Violence, mental disorder and public protection', *Psychiatry* (2004) 3(11):1–4.

Maden, A., *Treating Violence: a guide to risk management in mental health.* Oxford: Oxford University Press 2007.

Maden, A., 'Violence, mental disorder and public protection', *Psychiatry* (2007) 6(10):399–403.

Maguire, M., 'Crime Data and Statistics' in Maguire M., Morgan R. and Reiner R., eds., *The Oxford Handbook of Criminology* 4th edn. Oxford: Oxford University Press 2007.

Maguire, M., Morgan, R. and Reiner, R., eds., *The Oxford Handbook of Criminology* 4th edn. Oxford: Oxford University Press 2007.

Marshall, P., *A reconviction study of HMP Grendon Therapeutic Community.* London: HMSO 1997.

Matthews, E., 'Mental and Physical Illness – An Unsustainable Separation?', in Eastman, N. and Peay, J., eds., *Law Without Enforcement: Integrating Mental Health and Justice.* Oxford: Hart Publishing 1999.

Meltzer, H., Gill, B. Petticrew, M. and Hinds, K., *OPCS Surveys of Psychiatric Morbidity in Great Britain, Report 1: the prevalence of psychiatric morbidity among adults living in private households.* London: Office of Populations Censuses and Surveys 1995.

Mental Health Act Commission, *Risk, Rights, Recovery: Twelfth Biennial Report 2005–2007.* London: The Stationery Office 2008.

Mental Health Foundation, *Death of the smoking den: The initial impact of no smoking legislation in psychiatric units in England in 2008,* Mental Health Foundation, 22 June 2009.

Mendelson, G., ' "Compensation neurosis" revisited: outcome studies of the effects of litigation' *J Psychosom Res* (1995) 39(6):695–706.

Mendelson, G., 'The concept of nomogenic disorders with special reference to "functional somatic syndromes".' Paper presented at the 30th International Congress on Law and Mental Health, Padua, June 25–30 2007.

Merton, R., 'Opportunity Structure: The Emergence, Diffusion and Differentiation of a Sociological Concept, 1930s–1950s' in Adler F. and Laufer W., eds., *The Legacy of Anomie Theory*. New Brunswick: Transaction 1995.

Millie, A., Tombs, J. and Hough, M., 'Borderline Sentencing: a comparison of sentencers' decision making in England and Wales, and Scotland' *Criminology and Criminal Justice* (2007) 7:243–267.

Mind, *Another assault* available at www.mind.org.uk/anotherassault (2007).

Ministry of Justice, *Lord Bradley's report on people with mental health problems or learning disabilities in the Criminal Justice System: the Government's response*. Ministry of Justice 30 April 2009.

Ministry of Justice, *Prison Population and Accommodation Briefing 2nd October 2009*. London: National Offender Management Service Population Strategy 2009a.

Ministry of Justice, *Statistics of Mentally Disordered Offenders 2007 England and Wales*. London: Ministry of Justice Statistics Bulletin 5 February 2009b.

Mischon, J., *Independent Inquiry into the Care and Treatment of Peter Bryan*. A report for NHS London available at www.london.nhs.uk (2009).

Moley, S., Taylor, P., Kaiza, P. and Higgins, N., *Crime in England and Wales Quarterly Update to June 2007* Home Office Statistical Bulletin 16/07. London: Home Office 2007.

Monahan, J., 'Mental disorder and violence: another look', in Hodgins S., ed., *Mental Disorder and Crime*. Newbury Park, CA: Sage Publications 1993.

Monahan, J., 'Clinical and Actuarial Predictions of Violence. II Scientific Status' in Faigman, D., Kaye, D., Saks, M., Sanders, J. and Cheng, E., eds., *Modern Scientific Evidence: The Law and Science of Expert Testimony*. St Paul, MN: West Publishing Company 2007.

Monahan, J., Lidz, C., Hoge, S., Mulvey, E., Eisenberg, M., Roth, L., Gardner, W. and Bennett, N., 'Coercion in the Provision of Mental Health Services: The MacArthur Studies' in Morissey, J. and Monahan, J., eds., *Research in Community and Mental Health Vol 10 Coercion in Mental Health Services – International Perspectives*. Stamford, Connecticut: JAI Press 1999.

Monahan, J. and Steadman, H., 'Crime and mental disorder: an epidemiological approach', in Tonry, M. and Morris, N., eds., *Crime and Justice: An Annual Review of Research, Volume 4*. Chicago: University of Chicago Press 1993.

Monahan, J., Steadman, H., Silver, E., Appelbaum, P., Robbins, P., Mulvey, E., Roth, L., Grisso, T. and Banks, S., *Rethinking risk assessment: The MacArthur study of mental disorder and violence*. New York: Oxford University Press 2006.

Moran, P., 'Dangerous severe personality disorder: Bad tidings from the UK' *International Journal of Social Psychiatry* (2001) 48:6–10.

Morey, L., Waugh, M. and Blashfield, R., 'MMPI Scales for DSM-III personality disorders: their derivation and correlates', *Journal of Personality Assessment* (1985) 49:245–251.

Morris, S., 'Devoted husband who strangled wife in his sleep walks free from court' *The Guardian* 20 November 2009.

Muir, W., *Police: Streetcorner Politicians*. Chicago: University of Chicago Press 1977.

Mullen, P., 'Dangerous people with severe personality disorder. British proposals for managing them are glaringly wrong and unethical' *British Medical Journal* (1999) 319:1146–1147.

Mullen, P., 'Schizophrenia and violence: from correlations to preventive strategies' *Advances in Psychiatric Treatment* (2006) 12: 239–248.

Mullen, P., 'Dangerous and severe personality disorder and in need of treatment' *British Journal of Psychiatry* (2007)190, (supplement 49):S3–S7.

Mulvey, E., 'Assessing the evidence of a link between mental illness and violence', *Hospital and Community Psychiatry* (1994) 45:663–668.

National Association of Probation Officers *Armed Forces in Custody* available at www.napo.org.uk (2009).

National Confidential Inquiry into Suicide and Homicide by People with Mental Illness *Independent Homicide Investigations*. Manchester: University of Manchester 2008.

National Confidential Inquiry into Suicide and Homicide by People with Mental Illness *Annual Report: England and Wales*. Manchester: University of Manchester 2009.

Needleman, H., Reiss, J., Tobin, M., Biesecker, G. and Greenhouse, J., 'Bone lead levels and delinquent behaviour' *Journal of the American Medical Association* (1996) 275: 363–369.

Nelkin, D. and Tancredi, L., *Dangerous Diagnostics: The Social Power of Biological Information*, 2nd edn. Chicago: University of Chicago Press 1994.

Newburn, T., *Criminology*, Cullompton. Devon: Willan Publishing 2007.

Nicholas, S. Kershaw, C. and Walker, A., *Crime in England and Wales*, Home Office Statistical Bulletin 2006/07 11/07. London: Home Office 2007.

Parker, G. and Barrett, E., 'Personality and personality disorder: Current issues and directions' *Psychological Medicine* (2000) 30:1–9.

Pearson, G., 'Madness and Moral Panics' in Eastman, N. and Peay, J., eds., *Law Without Enforcement: Integrating Mental Health and Justice*. Oxford: Hart Publishing 1999.

Peay, J., *Inquiries after Homicide*. London: Duckworth 1996.

Peay, J., *Decisions and Dilemmas: Working with Mental Health Law*. Oxford: Hart Publishing 2003.

Peay, J., 'Mentally Disordered Offenders, Mental Health and Crime' in Maguire, M., Morgan, R. and Reiner, R., eds., *The Oxford Handbook of Criminology* 4th Edition Oxford: Oxford University Press 2007.

Peay, J., 'Civil admission following a finding of unfitness to plead' in McSherry, B. and Weller, P., eds., *Rethinking Rights-Based Mental Health Laws*. Oxford: Hart Publishing 2010a.

Peay, J., 'Suicide and Homicide in Psychiatric Hospitals: Caring for Victims?' in Newburn, T., Downes, D. and Hobbs, R., eds., *Festschrift in Honour of Paul Rock*. Oxford: Clarendon Press 2010b.

Peirce, G., 'Obituary of Jim MacKeith: Forensic Psychiatrist who changed the attitude of the courts to confession evidence' *The Guardian* 13 August 2007.

Perlin, M. and Szeli, E., 'Mental Health Law and Human Rights: Evolution and Contemporary Challenges' New York Law School, Legal Studies Research Paper No. 07/08–28; available at SSRN: http://ssrn.com/abstract=1132428in (2008).

Pescosolido, B., Monahan, J., Link, B., Stueve, A., and Kikuzawa, S., 'The public's view of the competence, dangerousness and need for legal coercion of persons with mental health problems' *American Journal of Public Health* (1999) 89:1339–45.

Peters, E., Joseph, S., Garety, P., 'Measurement of delusional ideation in the normal population: introducing the PDI (Peters et al. Delusions Inventory)' *Schizophrenia Bulletin* (1999) 25(3):553–576.

Pezzani, R., 'The Re-call of Conditionally Discharged Patients – the breadth of the Secretary of State's discretion' *Journal of Mental Health Law* (2007) 219–223.

Philan, J. and Link, B., 'The growing belief that people with mental illnesses are violent; the role of the dangerousness criterion for civil commitment' *Soc Psychiatry Psychiatric Epidemiology* (1998) 33:S7–12.

Philo, G., ed., *Media and Mental Distress*. London: Longman 1996.

Platt, A, and Diamond, B., 'The origins and development of the 'wild beast' concept of mental illness and its relationship to theories of criminal responsibility' *Journal of the History of the Behavioural Sciences* (1965) 355–72.

Poythress, N., Bonnie, R., Monahan, J., Otto, R. and Hoge, S., *Adjudicative Competence: The MacArthur Studies*, New York: Kluwer Academic/Plenum Publishers 2002.

Presdee, M., *Cultural Criminology and the Carnival of Crime*. London: Routledge 2000.

Prison Reform Trust *Too Little, Too Late: An independent review of unmet mental health need in prison*. London: Prison Reform Trust 2009.

Prior, P., 'Mentally disordered offenders and the European Court of Human Rights', *International Journal of Law and Psychiatry* (2007) 30(6):546–557.

Raine, A., *The Psychopathology of Crime: Criminal Behavior as a Clinical Disorder*. California: University of Southern California Academic Press 1993.

Ramsay, M., Saradjian, J., Murphy, N. and Freestone, M., 'Commentary on the article by Peter Tyrer and others about the assessment phase of the Dangerous and Severe Personality Disorder Programme' *Journal of Forensic Psychiatry and Psychology* (2009) 20(1):147–150.

Redlich, A., Steadman, H., Monahan, J., Clark Robbins, P. and Petrila, J., 'Patterns of Practice in Mental Health Courts: A National Survey' *Law and Human Behavior* (2006) 30:347–362.

Reiner, R., *Law and Order: An Honest Citizen's Guide to Crime and Control*. Cambridge: Polity Press 2007.

Rennie, C., Senior, J. and Shaw, J., 'The future is offender health: evidencing mainstream health services throughout the offender pathway' *Criminal Behaviour and Mental Health* (2009) 19:1–8.

Rhee, S. and Waldman, I. 'Genetic and environmental influences on antisocial behaviour: a meta analysis of twin and adoption studies' *Psychological Bulletin* (2002) 128:490–529.

Rice, M., Harris, G. and Cormier, C., 'Evaluation of a maximum security therapeutic community for psychopaths and other mentally disordered offenders' *Law and Human Behavior* (1992) 16:399–412.

Richardson, G., *Review of the Mental Health Act 1983. Report of the Expert Committee*. Presented to the Parliamentary Under Secretary of State for Health 15 July 1999, published November 1999.

Richardson, G., 'Coercion and human rights: A European perspective' *Journal of Mental Health* (2008) 17:245–254.

Robbins, P., Monahan, J. and Silver, E., 'Mental Disorder and Violence: The Moderating Role of Gender', *Law and Human Behavior* (2003) 27:561–571.

Roberts, A., *The Lunacy Commission, A Study of its Origin, Emergence and Character*, an e-book available at http://wwwmdx.ac.uk/WWW/STUDY/01.htm (2004).

Rock, P., 'The Inquiry and Victims' Families' in Peay, J., ed., *Inquiries after Homicide*. London: Duckworth 1996.

Rock, P., *After Homicide: Practical and Political Responses to Bereavement*. Oxford: Clarendon Press 1998.

Rock, P., 'Sociological Theories of Crime' in Maguire, M., Morgan, R. and Reiner, R., eds., *The Oxford Handbook of Criminology* 4th edn. Oxford: Oxford University Press 2007.

Rogers, T., Blackwood, N., Farnham, F., Pickup, G. and Watts, M., 'Fitness to plead and competence to stand trial: a systematic review of the construct and its application' *Journal of Forensic Psychiatry and Psychology* 576–596.

Royal College of Psychiatrists *Rethinking risk to others in mental health services. Final Report of a scoping group*. College Report 150 available at www.rcppsych.ac.uk (2008).

Rutherford, M., 'Imprisonment for Public Protection: an example of "reverse diversion"' *The Journal of Forensic Psychiatry and Psychology* (2009) 20(S1):S46–S55.

Rutherford, M., 'Imprisonment for Public Protection: Genesis and Mental Health Implications' *Mental Health Review Journal* (2008) 13(2):47–55.

Rygh, J. and Sanderson, W., *Treating Generalized Anxiety Disorder: Evidence-Based Strategies, Tools, and Techniques*. New York: Guilford Press 2004.

Sainsbury Centre for Mental Health *In the dark: The mental health implications of imprisonment for public protection*. London: Sainsbury Centre 2008.

Sainsbury Centre for Mental Health *Diversion: A better way for criminal justice and mental health*. London: Sainsbury Centre 2009.

Sampson, R., Raudenbush, S. and Earls, F., 'Neighborhoods and Violent Crime: A Multilevel Study of Collective Efficacy' *Science* (1997) 277:918–924.

Sartorius, N. 'Physical illness in people with mental disorders' *World Psychiatry* (2007) 6(1):3–4.

Scull, A., *Museums of Madness: the Social Organisation of Insanity in Nineteenth-Century England*. London: Allen Lane 1979.

Scull, A., *Decarceration: Community Treatment and the Deviant – A Radical View*, 2nd edn, Englewood Cliffs, NJ: Prentice Hall 1984.

Sellars, C., Hollin, C. and Howells, K., 'Mental Illness, Neurological and Organic Disorder, and Criminal Behaviour' in Howells, K. and Hollin, C., eds., *Clinical Approaches to the Mentally Disordered Offender*. Chichester: John Wiley and Sons 1993.

Seltzer, T., 'Mental health courts: A misguided attempt to address the criminal justice system's unfair treatment of people with mental illness' *Psychology, Public Policy and Law* (2005) 11:570–586.

Sentencing Guidelines Council *Dangerous Offenders: Guide for Sentencers and Practitioners*. London: Sentencing Guidelines Council 2008.

Seymour, L., Rutherford, M., Khanom, H. and Samele, C. 'The Community Order and the Mental Health Treatment Requirement' *Journal of Mental Health Law* (2008) 53–65.

Shalev, S., *A sourcebook on solitary confinement*. London: Mannheim Centre for Criminology, London School of Economics and Political Science 2008.

Shaw, J., Hunt, I., Flynn, S., Turnball, P., Kapur, N. and Appleby, L., 'Mental Illness in people who kill strangers: longitudinal study and national clinical survey', *British Medical Journal* (2004) 328:734–737.

Shaw, J., Creed, F., Price, J., Huxley, P. and Tomlinson, B., 'Prevalence and detection of serious psychiatric disorder in defendants attending court' *The Lancet* (1999) 353:1053–1056.

Shaw, J., Hunt, I., Flynn, S., Meehan, J., Robinson, J., Bickley, H., Parsons, R., McCann, K., Burns, J., Amos, T., Kapur, N. and Appleby, L., 'Rates of Mental Disorder in People Convicted of Homicide: National Clinical Survey' *British Journal of Psychiatry* (2006) 188:143–147.

Shift *What's the Story? Reporting mental health and suicide*. A resource for journalists and editors available at www.shift.org.uk/mediahandbook (2008).

Shift *Mind Over Matter 2: Improving Media Reporting of Mental Illness* available at www.shift.org.uk (2007).

Siegal, L., *Criminology* 2nd edn. St Paul, Minnesota: West Publishing 1986.

Silver, E., 'Extending social disorganization theory: A multilevel approach to the study of violence among persons with mental illnesses' *Criminology* (2000) 38:1043–1074.

Silver, E., 'Mental disorder and violent victimisation: The mediating role of involvement in conflicted social relationships' *Criminology* (2002) 40:191–212.

Silver, E., Understanding the relationship between mental disorder and violence: the need for a criminological perspective' *Law and Human Behavior* (2006) 30:685–706.

Silver, E., Mulvey, E. and Monahan, J., 'Assessing violence risk among discharged psychiatric patients: Towards an ecological approach', *Law and Human Behavior* (1999) 23:237–255.

Singleton, N., Bumpstead, R., O'Brien, M. Lee, A. and Meltzer, H., *Psychiatric Morbidity Among Adults living in Private Households, 2000*, Social Survey Division of the Office for National Statistics. London: HMSO 2001.

Singleton, N., Meltzer, H., and Gatward, R., *Psychiatric morbidity among prisoners in England and Wales*, Office for National Statistics. London: The Stationery Office 1998.

Skeem, J., *High risk, not hopeless: Recent research on treating individuals with psychopathy*. Keynote presentation to the annual meeting of the International Association of Forensic Mental Health, Vienna, Austria 2008.

Small, G. and fourteen colleagues, 'PET of Brain Amyloid and Tau in Mild Cognitive Impairment' *New England Journal of Medicine* (2006) 355:2652–2663.

Solomon, E., Eades, C., Garside, R., Rutherford, M., *Ten Years of Criminal Justice under Labour: An Independent Audit*. London: Centre for Crime and Justice Studies 2007.

Sonuga-Barke, E., ' "It's the *environment* stupid!" On epigenetics, programming and plasticity in child mental health' *The Journal of Child Psychology and Psychiatry* (2010) 51:113–115.

Soothill, K., 'Arson' in Bluglass, R. and Bowden, P., eds., *Principles and Practice of Forensic Psychiatry*. Edinburgh: Churchill Livingston 1990.

Spitzer, R. and Wakefield, J., 'DSM-IV diagnostic criterion for clinical significance: does it help solve the false positives problem?' *American Journal of Psychiatry* (1999) 56:1856–1864.

Srinivas, J., Denvir, S. and Humphreys, M., 'The Home Office Mental Health Unit' *Advances in Psychiatric Treatment* (2006) 12:450–458.

Starmer, K., *European Human Rights Law*. London: LAG Education and Service Trust 1999.

Stavert, J., 'Mental health, community care and human rights in Europe: still an incomplete picture?' *Journal of Mental Health Law* (2007) 182–193.

Steadman, H., Mulvey, E., Monahan, J., Robbins, P., Appelbaum, P., Grisso, T., Loren, H., Roth, L. and Silver, E. 'Violence by People Discharged from Acute Inpatient Facilities and by Others in the Same Neighbourhoods', *Archives General Psychiatry* (1998) 55:393–401.

Steadman, H., Osher, F., Clark Robbins, P., Case, B. and Samuels, S., 'Prevalence of serious mental illness among jail inmates' *Psychiatric Services* (2009) 60:761–795.

Stinchcombe, A., 'Institutions of Privacy in the Determination of Police Administrative Practice' *American Journal of Sociology* (1963) 69:150–160.

Stompe, T., Ortwein-Swoboda, G. and Schanda, H. 'Schizophrenia, delusional symptoms and violence: The threat/control-override concept re-examined', *Schizophrenia Bulletin* (2004) 30:31–44.

Stone, N., *A Companion Guide to Mentally Disordered Offenders* 2nd Edition. Crayford: Shaw and Sons Ltd 2003.

Stueve, A. and Link, B., 'Violence and psychiatric disorders: results from an epidemiological study of young adults in Israel' *Psychiatric Quarterly* (1997) 68:327–342.

Swanson, J., Swartz, M., Estroff, S., Borum, R., Wagner, R. and Hiday, V., 'Psychiatric impairment, social contact, and violent behaviour: Evidence from a study of out-patient committed persons with severe mental disorder', *Social Psychiatry and Psychiatric Epidemiology* (1998) 33:86–94.

Swanson, J., Holzer, C., Ganju, V. and Jonjo. R., 'Violence and psychiatric disorder in the community: evidence from the Epidemiologic Catchment Area surveys', *Hospital and Community Psychiatry* (1990) 41:761–770.

Swanson, J., Schwartz, M., Van Doren, R., Elbogen, E., Wagner, R., Rosenheck, R., Stroup, S., McEvoy, J. and Lieberman, J., 'A national study of violent behaviour in persons with schizophrenia', *Archives of General Psychiatry* (2006) 63:490–499.

Szmukler, G. and Appelbaum, P. Treatment pressures, leverage, coercion, and compulsion in mental health care', *Journal of Mental Health* (2008) 17:233–244.

Szmukler, G., Daw, R. and Dawson, J., 'A model law fusing incapacity and mental health legislation', *Journal of Mental Health Law* (2010) 11–22.

Szmukler, G., 'Risk assessment: "numbers" and "values"' *Psychiatric Bulletin* (2003) 27:205–207.

Taylor, P., 'Schizophrenia and Violence' in Gunn, J. and Farrington, D., eds., *Abnormal Offenders, Delinquency and the Criminal Justice System*. Chichester: Wiley 1982.

Taylor, P., Garety, P., Buchanan, A., Reed, A., Wessely, S., Ray, K., Dunn, G. and Grubin, D., 'Delusions and Violence' in Monahan, J. and Steadman, H., eds., *Violence and Mental Disorder: Developments in Risk Assessment*, Chicago: University of Chicago 1994.

Taylor, P. and Gunn, J. 'Violence and Psychosis' *British Medical Journal* (1984) 288:1945–9.

Taylor, P. and Gunn, J., 'Homicides by people with mental illness: myth and reality', *British Journal of Psychiatry* (1999) 174:9–14.

Teasdale, B. *Violence by and against persons with major mental disorders: A total life circumstances approach*. Dissertation research, Pennsylvania State University 2004.

Teasdale, B., Silver, E. and Monahan, J., 'Gender, Threat/Control-Override Delusions and Violence', *Law and Human Behavior* (2006) 30:649–658.

The Telegraph 'Parkinson's drugs "trigger gambling addiction" ' 12 July 2005.

Teplin, L., McClelland, G., Abram, K. and Weiner, D., 'Crime victimization in adults with severe mental illness: comparison with the National Crime Victimization Survey', *Archives of General Psychiatry* (2005) 62:911–921.

Thornicroft, G., *Shunned: discrimination against people with mental illness*. Oxford: Oxford University Press 2006.

Tiihonen, J., Isohanni, M., Rasanen, P., Koiranen, M. and Moring, J., 'Specific major mental disorders and criminality: A 26-year prospective study of the 1966 northern Finland birth cohort' *American Journal of Psychiatry* (1997) 154:840–845.

Tisdall, S. 'Mental stress of troops in Iraq no bar to longer duty, says report', *The Guardian* 21 June 2007.

Tribal *Financial support to the Bradley Review* 4 December 2008 www.tribalgroup. co.uk 2008.

Turner, M. 'Psychiatry and the Human Sciences', *British Journal of Psychiatry* (2003) 182:472–474.

Tyndel, M. and Egit, M. 'The concept of nomogenic disorders' *Med Law* (1988) 7(2):167–76.

Tyrer, P., Barrett, B., Byford, S. and others *Evaluation of the assessment procedure at two pilot sites in the DSPD programme (IMPALOX Study)* Report to DSPD Programme. London: Home Office, Department of Health, Ministry of Justice 2007.

Tyrer, P., Cooper, S., Rutter, D., Sievewright, H., Duggan, C., Maden, A., Barrett, B., Joyce, E., Rao, B., Nur, U., Cicchetti, D., Crawford, M. and Byford, S., 'The assessment of dangerous and severe personality disorder: lessons from a randomised controlled trial linked to qualitative analysis' *The Journal of Forensic Psychiatry and Psychology* (2009) 20(1):132–146.

US Department of Health and Human Services *Reducing the Health Consequences of Smoking: 25 years of Progress*. Rockville MD: US Department of Health and Human Services, Public Health Service Centres for Disease Control and Prevention, Centre for Chronic Disease Prevention and Health Promotion, Office on Smoking and Health 1989.

Vizard, E., Hickey, N. and McCrory, E. 'Developmental trajectories associated with juvenile sexually abusive behaviour and emerging severe personality disorder in childhood: The results of a three year UK study', *British Journal of Psychiatry* (2007) Supplement 190:27–32.

Walker, A., Kershaw, C. and Nicholas, S. *Crime in England and Wales 2005–6*. London: Home Office Research Development Statistics Division 12/06 2006.

Walsh, E., Gilvarry, C., Samele, C., Harvey, K., Manley, C., Tattan, T., Tyrer, P., Creed, F., Murray, R. and Fahy, T., UK700 Group 'Predicting violence in schizophrenia: a prospective study' *Schizophrenia Research* (2004) 67:247–52.

Warren, F., Preedy-Fayers, K., McGauley, K. and others *Review of treatments for severe personality disorder: Home Office online report 03/03*. London: Home Office 2003.

Wessely, S., 'The Epidemiology of Crime, Violence and Schizophrenia', *British Journal of Psychiatry* (1997) Supplement 32:8–11.

Wessely, S., Buchanan, A., Reed, A., Cutting, J., Garety, P. and Taylor, P., 'Acting on Delusions I: Prevalence', *British Journal of Psychiatry* (1993) 163:69–76.

Wessely, S., Castle, D., Douglas, A. and Taylor, P. 'The criminal careers of incident cases of schizophrenia' *Psychological Medicine* (1994) 24:483–502.

Wessely, S. and Taylor, P., 'Madness and crime: criminology or psychiatry?' *Criminal Behaviour and Mental Health* (1991) 1:193–228.

White, R., 'Remedies in a Multi-Level Legal Order: The Strasbourg Court and the UK' in Kilpatrick, C., Novitz, T. and Skidmore, P., ed., *The Future of Remedies in Europe*. Oxford: Hart Publishing 2000.

Wilkins, N., 'Shoplifting in Midlands foodstores', unpublished thesis. University of Birmingham 1971.

Williams, R., 'Pilkington case may be a Lawrence moment for disability hate crime' *The Guardian* 28 September 2009 available at www.guardian.co.uk.

Wilson, W., Ebrahim, I., Fenwick, P. and Marks, R., 'Violence, Sleepwalking and the Criminal Law: (1) The Legal Aspects' *Criminal Law Review* (2005) 614–623.

Wilson, S., 'The principle of equivalence and the future of mental health care in prisons' *British Journal of Psychiatry* (2004) 184:5–7.

Wolchover, D., 'The vexed issue of gaol cell confessions' available at www.david-wolchover.co.uk (Head of Chambers, 7 Bell Yard, Temple Bar, London WC2A 2JR) 2006.

Woodward, M., Williams, P., Nursten, J. and Badger, D., 'The epidemiology of mentally disordered offending: a systematic review of studies, based on the general population, of criminality combined with psychiatric illness', *Journal of Epidemiology and Biostatistics* (1999) 4(2):101–113.

Wootton, D., *Bad Medicine: Doctors Doing Harm since Hippocrates*. Oxford: Oxford University Press 2006.

World Health Organization *International Statistical Classification of Diseases and Related Health Problems*, Geneva: WHO 1992.

Young, J., *The Vertigo of Late Modernity*. London: Sage 2007.

Zito Trust *Memorandum Submitted by the Zito Trust, MH 45* to the House of Commons Public Bill Committee on the Mental Health Bill 2007 (available at www.parliament.uk) 2007.

Index